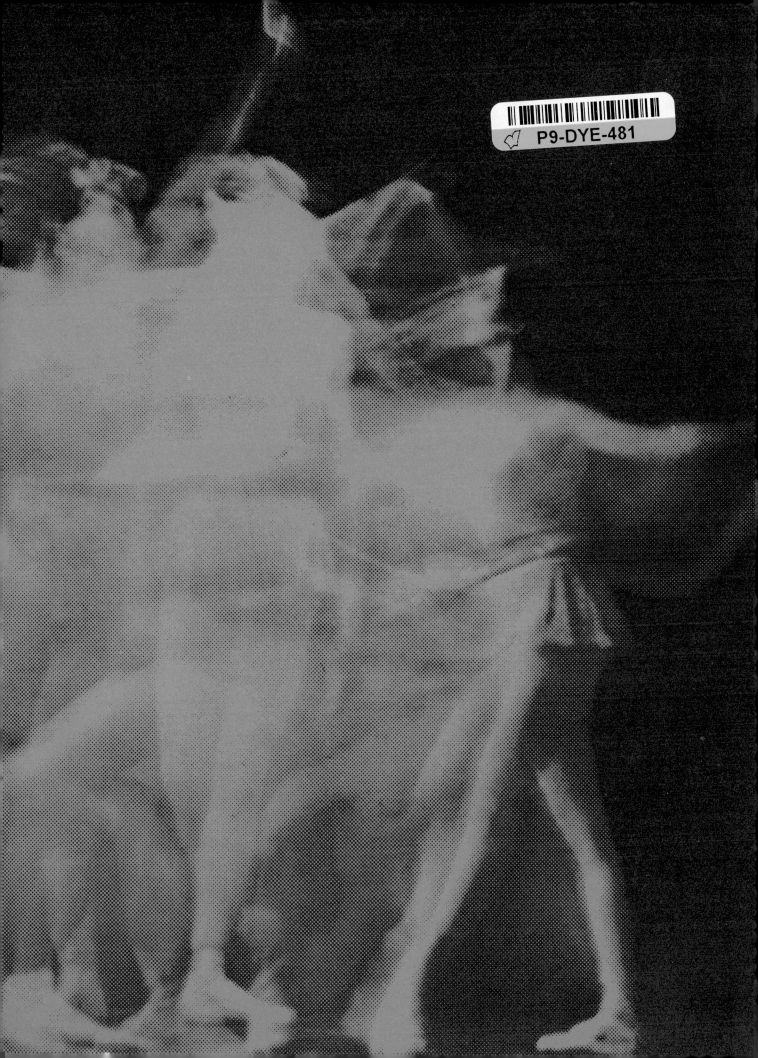

*the Dance*

*A Chanticleer Press Edition*

# *the Dance*

## through the Ages

*Walter Sorell*

*GROSSET & DUNLAP*

*Publishers, New York*

Published, 1967, in New York by Grosset & Dunlap, Inc.
Published simultaneously in Canada


Planned and produced by Chanticleer Press, Zurich - New York


All rights reserved under International
and Pan-American Copyright Conventions
Printed by Conzett & Huber in Zurich, Switzerland


Library of Congress Catalog Card Number: 67-19545


*End papers: City Center Joffrey Ballet. (Herbert Migdoll)*

# Contents

# Foreword

Before man found a means of artistic expression in measured, rhythmic movement, he enjoyed the sensation of stepping, turning, swaying, swinging, stamping and leaping. He has always done so in his folk dances, or in those dances that were fashioned into theatrical forms—simply because there is endless joy in dancing. It is a medium of man's self-assertion, an outlet for surplus energy, a supreme means of expression. This book tries to capture some of the rejoicing innate in the dance.

The story of the development of the dance from its beginnings to the present is a long and fascinating one. It would take several volumes to cover all of its aspects and phases. Light would have to be shed on its development in each country, on its relation to the other arts, on its theories and techniques, and on its many social and cultural ramifications. I have devoted to these subjects as much space as is possible in one volume.

Every attempt at recording the past—as well as the present—involves, however hidden, a personal evaluation. A historian is a critic with hindsight. This hindsight grows out of accumulated knowledge and a set of values that determines an interpretation. This, therefore, is an account of the dance as I have come to understand and love it. It is a result of a career and a concern of many years as a critic of the dance and a teacher of its history.

I wish to acknowledge my indebtedness to Mr. Paul Steiner, publisher of Chanticleer Press, for encouraging me to write this book, to my editors, Mr. Milton Rugoff, for many suggestions, and Miss Dori Watson for her help and understanding.

I am greatly indebted to Mr. George Chaffee for his invaluable counsel and for making available so many items from his unique collection, to Miss Genevieve Oswald, Curator of the Dance Collection at the New York Public Library, and her staff for their assistance in finding pictorial material. Also Miss Barbara Morgan and Miss Martha Swope and Mr. Herbert Migdoll have helped with their selection of photographs and have my sincerest thanks, as does Mr. Geoffrey Clements for photographing Mr. Chaffee's New York collection.

I am most grateful to Miss Anna Greta Stahle, dance critic at the Dagens Nyheter, Stockholm, for her advice; to the Indian dancer Lalli for permission to use her letter, for her interest and for her recreation of the Indian dance photographed especially for this book; to Lucy Venable, president of the Dance Notation Bureau; to Lydia Joel, editor-in-chief of *Dance Magazine,* to the editors of *Ballet Today, Dance Observer, Dance Scope* and *Shakespeare Quarterly* for allowing me to use a few ideas from articles I wrote for their magazines.

Many friends, editors, librarians, dancers and choreographers contributed their share to the realization of this book. My thanks go to all of them, and to my wife for her patience.

*Walter Sorell*

# *1 Primitive Dancing*

It is said that dancing is older than man. We know of early man that he moved in imitation of various animals and tried to reproduce their motions while in attack or flight, while in search for food or in courtship. The Greek Lucian, writing in the second century, thought that dancing was as old as love.

Dancing is certainly as old as man and his desire to express himself, to communicate his joys and sorrows, to celebrate and to mourn with the most immediate instrument at his disposal: his body. His instinctive and organic life, his mental complexi-

*Energy and ecstasy are suggested in figures from the Cyclades. (Andreas Feininger: Brooklyn Museum) Above: Asadata Dafora of Sierra Leone. (Barbara Morgan)*

ties, his spiritual desires demanded communication.

We know from various cave drawings that man danced before he found other means of self-expression. Havelock Ellis considered dancing and building "the two primary and essential arts." It seems obvious that man must have found his own body the best instrument with which to express what moved him and that he must have also sought shelter.

Basically, dance is rhythmic movement, and early man must soon have realized the importance of rhythm. We know he strongly felt himself a part of nature and the animal world and, seeing himself surrounded by rhythm, he could not help being caught up in it and expressing himself rhythmically.

Primitive dances are still performed on South Pacific islands, in Africa, in Central and South

America. Although many tribes have been trapped by the allurements of white man's civilization and have lost interest in and the feeling for their native arts, some of their dancing can still give us a fair knowledge of the dances done several thousand years ago. The Asiatics, however, have best preserved their centuries-old cultures and dances, since with them, as with primitive man, the dance has always been a viable part of their way of living.

What are the criteria of primitive dancing? When we observe the dancers in night clubs and discothèques in Paris or New York, in Rome or Stockholm and compare them with the dancers of primitive cultures, we at first find little difference in the quality of their basic movements. But the motivations of dancing in primitive societies were vitally different. The twentieth-century "primitive" may "play it cool," may move completely detached from his partner in spasmodic jerks and contortions, immersed in earsplitting, amplified drum beats, lost to the world as if hypnotized, and yet his dancing only superficially resembles in ecstatic derivation the dance in primitive cultures.

In primitive man, freedom of movement is complete in itself; even in his moments of fear his dance is never the result of despair or a feeling of futility. It is always serious because it is religious in a self-expressive and communicative sense and it is social because it is an integrated part of his life. To him, dancing is never a superficial act of self-enjoyment; it is spontaneous and never without purpose. It is not done because it "is the thing to do," but because it "is" the thing.

His body works and plays, it speaks and prays. Motion is in him tuned to his whole body. He need not wait for music to come to him from outside, to stimulate him; rhythm is primordial with him, controlled and yet wild. The beat of the drum organizes his rhythm. With primitive man dance is a way of thinking and feeling.

Buffalo Dance *by the Mandan Indians. (Smithsonian Institution) Right: A 1585 painting by John White of a Virginia Indian fertility round dance, with the three most beautiful virgins of the tribe in the center.*

There is no occasion on which he would not dance: birth, death, marriage, war, victory, harvest, hunting, hailing a new chief, healing the sick, exorcising evil spirits; and there are his many incantations for rain, sun, fertility, protection, and forgiveness. It is inconceivable that chieftains, shamans, witch doctors, warriors should not be able to dance. And there is not one member of the tribe who could not join them. But with the exception of communal orgies, men and women do not touch each other when dancing together. They mostly dance separately, each having his own, and different, contribution to make to the various dances of the community. One can safely say that in any primitive society dancing has always been the prerogative of the male, and above all, of the chieftains

*Overleaf: The Senegal Dance Company in a dance around a magic center. (Peter Larsen: Nancy Palmer Agency)*

11

and priests. They are called upon to lead the tribe in wars, to prepare for the hunt, to exorcise evil spirits. We also find the male charged with the more important dances, and only part of the explanation of this is that great physical demands were made on the dancer, his strength and endurance tested to the limit. Man in prehistoric days was close to the animals, feeling kinship with them, even though some were dangerous enemies, and he may have continued the function of the male bird which has the more beautiful feathers and does the dancing.*

With primitive man on the level of primeval tribes dance is synonymous with life in all its major aspects: with love, work, and ritual. But in his mind these three aspects are closely interrelated. For instance, the members of the Mexican Indian tribe

Tarahumara knew only one word for dance and work. Almost everywhere dance and growth, i. e. fertility, were part of one and the same magic. And how inseparable the religious aspect from dancing is could not be better proved than through the natives along the Swan River in Africa who, when first introduced to the sacrament of Communion, called it a dance.

In the mind of primitive man the borderline between the concrete and the symbolic is blurred. This is why in putting on a mask he tries to implant in himself another being, or the spirit and magic of the god image. He sees the supernatural as a living force and needs to identify with it. Since early man had no other means with which to express himself and,

* It is significant that the role of the male is dominant at the beginning of each cultural phase and decreases in importance towards the end of it, with the female dancer taking the spotlight. In our own recent history we have seen how the role of the male dancer was reduced to that of a supernumerary during the climactic days of the Romantic ballet in which stylistic refinement coincided with social decadence.

*A North African cave painting (from a drawing by Battiss) depicts the* Mantis Dance. *Right: Destiné's "Yoruba Bakas" enacts an African legend of the creation of goat-man beings. (Courtesy Jean León Destiné)*

14

above all, to communicate his "within-ness" than through movement, the concept of the dancing god has been in the foreground in many cultures.

No dancer in primitive society is a performing artist in our sense of the word, although in time many tribes began to have their professional dancers, too. For all ceremonies and feasts they were as important as the priests are for our churches. They were held in great esteem, and their tribe cared for them. They had nothing to do but to dance. Small wonder then that their bodies became so developed that they had absolute control over every muscle. They could leap and turn, spin their heads on their necks and thrust their arms and legs into the air with breath-taking speed and precision. They could make the muscles of their thighs quiver or throw

*Left: Discothèque dancers doing the "Swim." Despite great differences in motivation, such dances strikingly resemble primitive dancing. (Jim Healy: Black Star) Above: Rhythmic Neolithic painted figures from the Hoggar Mountains of the Sahara. (Musée de l'Homme, Paris)*

the drums began again to whip the air; at a steady pace every movement of the dancer's body was intensified; his turns became more and more rapid, then frantic until his consciousness disappeared. The evil was challenged, perhaps banned.

The dance in the round is seen time and again, and vestiges of it are still found in the many round dances of our time, from various folk dances to the waltz. But for primitive man the round dance had particular purpose and meaning: to ban spirits or to ingratiate himself with them, to heal and to preserve the tribe from misfortune. Primitive man also favored stamping, a gesture that has become universally accepted. It is, above all, a major feature of the Spanish dance. In general, stamping is a motor expression of exceptional intensity. Primitive man is absorbed by the idea that he makes the earth tremble under his feet. Symbolically, he takes possession of the ground, and we may even say that stamping is an assertion of man's ego.

Primitive man has no technique, no artistry. But he achieves complete, in some ways disciplined, freedom of movement. And if today his dancing seems to us, in its spontaneity, without form and limits in time, we forget that it stems from other sources and is performed for other reasons than any dances of European man. Only unfailing masters of their bodies can dare subject them to such a disorganized range of movements and think nothing of dancing themselves into a frenzy until they collapse.

It may be said that with the loss of its religious motivation, with its gradual separation from worship, dance lost some of its creative urge, meaningfulness and purpose. On the other hand, it has gained refinement, stylistic variation and the stamp of individual originality.

Probably all art loses its deeper justification when divorced from religion. But all dance is a rite and has retained its ritualistic roots even in such stylized forms as the ballet. The dancer in our day may have forgotten his ties with man's early beginnings. But he can never deny them.

any part of their body into a state of convulsive trembling.

They never danced for the mere sake of dancing. Their dancing always had meaning to all members of their tribe. They could fully translate their feelings into movement. They could turn into a snake, wind themselves around the trunk of a tree and, when they felt imbued with the healing power of the invoked god, they encircled the sick and tried to drive the evil spirits from his body. Or several dancers moved in a circle, some of them mumbling incantations. With the growing beat of the drums, the chanting became louder, the movements faster. Then one of them would step into the middle of the circle. First he danced slowly. But the voices and

# 2  *The Rules of Ritual*

Biblical man is not very different from primitive man. His movements are not yet bent on harmonic effects. They stem from a state of joy or sadness, of frenzy or ecstasy. This must have been the kind of convulsive dance referred to in *Exodus* when Moses comes into the camp and sees the people dancing around the golden calf. When Moses "took the calf which they had made, and burnt it in the fire," he turned against the god of gold, against the idol, not against their way of praising it.

With the exception of Salome's dance, there is nowhere in the Bible any mention of solo or figure dancing. But we must imagine that—no matter what the occasion may have been—someone led

*An Etruscan dancer. (Giraudon: Bibliothèque Nationale)*

the dance and, particularly in processions, was imitated by those who joined him. This is not unlike most Oriental dancing in which, instead of a soloist, a leading or principal dancer is followed by the others. Idolatrous and barbarous elements were gradually eliminated, but no dance pattern ever crystallized. Every dance was born of the occasion, and the spontaneity of the people's expression made rules and formulas impossible. But this much is certain: the soft line and rhythmic movement of trunk, head and arms, demonstrating the restraint of inner passion, was invariably interrupted by violent leaps. The stress of all dances seemed to have been on the circular form, the sacred concept, though we also know of "moving lines."

After the crossing of the Red Sea, "Miriam, the prophetess, the sister of Aaron, took a timbrel in her

18

hand; and all the women went out after her with timbrels and with dances." And Judith led a great chorus of women crowned with olive wreaths.

The most outstanding example of a principal dancer being followed and probably greatly imitated by the others was King David. In such a religious procession, organized in honor of Jahwe, as the removal of the Ark, David, dressed in the official robe of the high priest, danced in ecstasy before the Deity. It was a rotary dance rich in gesture, accentuated by violent leaps.

> And David danced before the Lord with all his might; and David was girded with a linen ephod....
> And as the Ark of the Lord came into the city of David, Michal, Saul's daughter, looked through a window, and saw King David leaping and dancing before the Lord; and she despised him in her heart.
> *II Samuel VI: 14–16*

During the dance David must have thrown off his robe and danced with no other covering than a linen ephod.* Michal reproached David probably not so much for having danced as for having "uncovered himself today in the eyes of the handmaids of his servants as one of the vain fellows shamelessly uncovereth himself." But David rejected such reproof, saying that he had not even thought of the people. "It was before the Lord!" he emphasized (*II Samuel VI: 14–21*). His wild dance was the expression of religious joy.

How very much the dance was part of the life of Biblical man is borne out by the many references to dancing in the Old Testament and by such pronouncements as Rabbi Eleazar's:

> Some day the Holy One, blessed be He! will give a dance for the righteous, and He will sit among them in the Garden of Eden, and each one will point his finger at Him, saying as it is written, 'Lo, this is our God; we have waited for Him, and He will save us....

It is a short way from exaltation to ecstasy, from such an abnormal intensification of feelings to the complete yielding of sense perception and control of reason. The revelation of the Biblical prophets were, to a great extent, based on their gift of ecstasy.

The dance, movement and gesture, also play a part in prophecy which must not be underestimated. Today we know that movement precedes speech. Before our tongue and lips can form the word, our arms, hands and face—obeying the commands of our thought-feelings—paint them through the involuntary expression of movement. And every gesture, the symbolic language, reaches our fellow men more quickly than words, the factual language. The exalted and ecstatic voice may awake our spirit, but it is movement that carries us away, that makes us ready to follow the voice. No conception of any divine thought or message is feasible as long as man is held down by the burden of his everyday thoughts. Dancing lends our physical being the feeling of freedom from daily dullness, from earth ties.

## Dancing Before God

The Jewish and early Christian prophets danced in their communion with God. They danced before conveying the word of the Lord to the people, the symbolism of movement being more soul-stirring than words. The prophets had come a long way from the mysticism of primitive man when they strove to rouse their people to their relationship to a higher conception of a deity. And if man is to rise above himself and embrace God, he must be lifted and carried away. Since this movement of flight from reality cannot be performed in its entirety, it is symbolized in ecstatic dance.

The string of dancing prophets continues with Jesus, as described in the Acts of John. The often violent opposition to dancing by the Church Fathers throughout the centuries has made us forget the significant role of the dance in the life of the early Christians. People have almost never ceased to dance, nor could the threat of punishment stifle their impulse to seek freedom from that bodily

---

* This act was repeated by Mohammed, who had joined the pilgrims of Mecca to circle the Kaaba, the shrine, clothed with no more than the *ihram*.

*A manuscript drawing, "Mary and the Hebrew Maidens Dancing," reflects the close association of dance and worship in the early Christian period. (Vatican Library)*

heaviness which is indicative of wordly attachment.

Notwithstanding the opposition of the post-Constantine Church to dancing as pagan, the very idea of dancing had a sacred meaning to the early Christians. The most sublime illustration of sacred dancing in the early Church is quoted by Eusebius, the father of Church history, from a description of the worship of the Therapeuts by Philo:

> After the banquet they keep the sacred all-night festival. And this is how they keep it. They all stand up in a body, and in the middle of the banqueting-place they first form two choroi, one of men and the other of women, and a leader and conductor is chosen for each,

the one whose reputation is greatest for a knowledge of music; they then chant hymns composed in God's honor in many metres and melodies, sometimes singing together, sometimes one choros beating the measure with their hands for the antiphonal chanting of the other, now dancing to the measure and now inspiring it, at times dancing in procession, at times set-dances, and then circle-dances right and left.

We also possess the priceless Gnostic "Hymn of Jesus" from the second-century Acts of John. This wonderful hymn is the earliest Christian ritual of which we know. We can see in it a sacred dance wherein the newborn disciple is united with the Master, the purified human nature with the Divine Presence. No matter what interpretation we give it, it clearly describes the Last Supper, at which Christ takes leave of his disciples. It is the source of the

Catholic Mass, which originally was a dance, a divine pantomime. Jesus gathered his disciples, as John tells us, and, before going out to fulfill His destination, commands them to dance around Him in a circle. In this sacred union he speaks the words: "Whoso danceth not, knoweth not the way of life. Now answer thou to my dancing. Behold thyself in me who speak, and seeing what I do, keep silence about my mysteries...."

To some of us it may be bewildering to think of the early Christians dancing, let alone to imagine Jesus leading a dance. But we must then blame our misconception of the role dancing played as ritual when man tried to come closer to the mystery of the great unknown. Then we find his deities dancing. In Egypt it was Osiris, in Greece Dionysus who, in his more spirited and more wanton way, typified the rejoicing that is dance. And the most perfect type of a dancing god is India's Shiva who danced the world into being and whose dance keeps it in sacred order.

The whole life of the Egyptians has always depended on the annual inundation by the river Nile, and this gave rise to a resurrection legend, in which man's belief in immortality is manifest. Their god Osiris was betrayed and killed by his brother Set who cut the God's body into fourteen parts. But Osiris' sister-wife Isis, who introduced dancing and singing to the people, reassembled the parts and enabled the god's resurrection. When the Nile started to rise each year, the festival for Isis took place, and in midsummer, with the harvest in, Osiris was mourned. The festival was a pageant in which dance and music played a great part and in which Isis's search for the god's body was dramatized. These rites were celebrated in Abydos where Osiris was buried, and lasted eighteen days. It was a dramatic pageant, the first mystery play of which we know, and a forerunner of Greek tragedy.

*The mosaicist who decorated St. Mark's church in Venice with Biblical scenes showed Salome dancing even after receiving the head of St. John the Baptist. (Scala)*

This or similar rituals were always expressed by a dancing group led by a dancer with whom the group could identify, and who was instrumental in whipping up emotional tension. It is very likely that on these occasions several of the dancers wore masks and impressive head adornments. However grave some of these ritual dances were, the resurrection of the god was always greeted with joyous dancing. As in all archaic cultures, joy and dancing were synonymous. With joy the climactic point of all rituals, singing and dancing groups, male and female, were constantly attached to the temples and charged with honoring the god.

The mystery of the stars, the turning of the sun, all celestial phenomena made a deep impression on primitive and archaic man. The imitation of the astral movements has led to all circle dances, and the Egyptian astronomer-priests had their Dance of Stars, a very intricate dance in which the priests, moving from east to west around a sun-altar, made the signs of the Zodiac.

The way from Egypt to ancient Greece is via Crete. The Greeks recognized the great influence of the Cretans in many ways and ascribed the origin of certain dances and dance forms to them. Their mythology describes how Rhea, wife of Cronus, fled to Crete and hid her youngest son, the god Zeus, with the Curetes who danced wildly and noisily around the baby to keep Cronus from hearing him cry since Cronus had the habit of devouring his children. This leaping dance, in which the dancers beat their swords against their shields and shouted with all their might, later became a part of the Curetes' ritual and was preserved by these priests of Zeus through the centuries. Still later, members of the nobility continued this dance.

The Greeks believed the dance came from the gods, and there is no doubt that dancing was originally connected with all kinds of rituals and the revelries in honor of Dionysus, with the Maenads, the women possessed by the god,* dancing in wild frenzy through the woods. We know from Aristophanes' comedy *Thesmophoriazusae* that dancing was a major part of the rites of Demeter and Persephone because, while poking fun at them, he describes circular formations moving at first lightly and quickly, then in measured rhythms invoking the goddesses, then rapidly again, rising into a joyous finale. Also, there were the Orphic and Eleusinian mysteries, with the Eleusinian rites still performed at the end of the fourth century A. D. In these secret rites the initiate was promised a happy afterlife; nocturnal torch dances were one of the main features on these occasions. The importance of the dance in Greek life is best proved by the inclusion of Terpsichore as one of the nine Muses. But the Greeks were realistic people, and Plato conceded that while dancing is a gift of the gods, it is a natural act that man moves his body to express emotions.

The Greco-Roman period was one of general deterioration, and the dance suffered during it. Already in the late second century Athenaeus referred to the dance of his day, as having lost its active and mobile presence and, above all, its orderly beauty. In Rome—with its growing imperialist notions and its loss of the feeling for the more spiritual values of life—we encounter an ambivalent attitude towards dancing. A great deal of dancing went on in Rome, in the northern provinces and in Sicily, but it was mainly left to foreigners. Some of the leading Romans had a priggish-puritanical feeling about dancing, a double standard characteristic of any decadent society.

All of this may have had something to do with the social status of dancers, mimes and actors who no longer held the honored position most of them had enjoyed during Greece's Golden Age. Now mainly Greek slaves, owned by the nobility, or dancers from

*This fresco detail from an Etruscan tomb shows a characteristic* Chain Dance. *(Alinari)*

* In these orgiastic and originally barbarous rites it was thought that the god had actually entered these women and determined their actions. The dance of the Maenads was so intense that bystanders were caught in the sweep of their fury, and many, particularly women, succumbed to this mass hysteria. The word enthusiasm is a weak derivative of *entheos-iasmos*, or *enthousiasmos*, that is, the condition "of having the god within one."

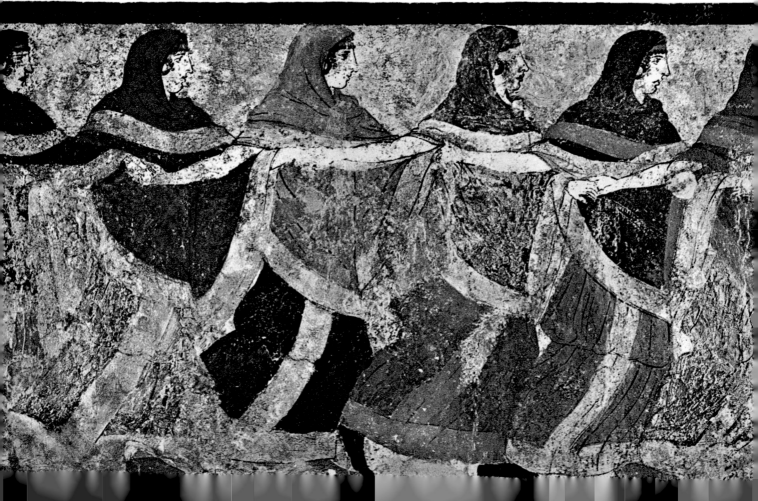

the south of Italy, they were treated like slaves. True, some of them were freed by the emperors because of their artistic accomplishments or the favor they gained with the pleasure-hungry populace. But these were exceptions.

Dance as a ritual, however, was not dead in Rome. On the contrary, a religious intent even permeated what little stage dancing there was. A great many processional dances were performed on several occasions. They were most often simple round dances executed with much solemnity, as in religious purification ceremonies or the feast of Ceres. The holy processions of the Salii, in March and October, were of the greatest importance. The Salii, priests of Mars who was a vegetation god before being a war god, performed a religious dance called Tripudium in the rhythm of a three-step. They sang their own accompaniment, wore an embroidered tunic, a tall conical cap and a sword. Also, the Salii, a priesthood originally of two bodies of twelve members each, were united in historical times with the function of securing the favor of the war god. But they reveal vestiges of a primitive belief in magic when they honored Saturn with high leaps into the air in order to induce the corn to grow.

Dancing priests performing rituals connected with the ancient fertility rites existed everywhere on the peninsula. We can readily see that nothing ever completely disappears and that man has remained a ritualistic creature whose customs never lose their tie with man's original needs and beliefs.

There is also hardly any clear-cut line between the ritual of the temple and the festival of the people. Most rites, even those of the Salii, ended with splendid entertainments or on a note of revelry. The famous feast of Saturnalia, beginning on December 17th, lasted a whole week. In this festival the difference between master and slave was wiped out, both sitting together and serving each other. It was the only time when the bondsmen could say what they pleased. These festivities usually turned into what we would call a carnival, with merrymaking, drunkenness and a great deal of uncontrolled dancing in the streets and at home. The Saturnalia was the descendant of the village revelries in the early days of ancient Greece. One important aspect of the Saturnalia was the exchange of presents, and later, the spirit of Christmas undoubtedly embodied most of what the Saturnalia had meant to the Roman people.

## The Festival of the People

> Return, return O Shulammite;
> Return, return, that we may look upon thee,
> Why will ye look upon the Shulammite,
> As upon the dance of Mahanaim?

These lines from the Song of Solomon paint a word picture of a wedding dance. They seem to refer to a whirling movement, at least to a dance pattern that turns in all four directions, even though it is not clear whether Mahanaim is a place (east of the Jordan), or a dance in which two rows of per-

formers face each other, or an allusion to the angels.

In Biblical days, to celebrate joyous family events such as marriages and births, women improvised choruses and dances. Also, at the annual vintage festival at Shiloh—"a feast of the Lord"—the maidens went out to the vineyards; "and behold, if the daughters of Shiloh come out to dance in dances, then come ye out of the vineyards, and catch you every man his wife of the daughters of Shiloh, and go to the land of Benjamin" *(Judges 21:21)*.

The structure of all these dances seems to emphasize the circle, although we are told of "moving lines" too. In the dedication of the walls of Jerusalem under Ezra and Nehemiah we find references to two "moving choruses of praise," while men of unstained character danced, threw flaming torches in the air and caught them. The Talmud describes the dances of Jewish maidens which were related to the mating dance of primitive people.

On the day preceding the Feast of Tabernacles everyone went to the house of Sho'ebah at the appointed time and carried branches with lemons attached to them for the procession around the altar. Men known for their piety and good works danced carrying lit torches and such great scholars as Hillel deemed it not beneath their dignity to join in before the admiring crowd. The Levites made music to the dance with the lyre and harp, with cymbals and trumpets.

Biblical man danced in his desire to express himself through movement without being aware of any of the aesthetic feelings or rules we encounter in the more advanced archaic cultures. The only mention of dancing in the Bible that has any artistic overtone is found in *Matthew 14:6*. When Herod's birthday was celebrated, Salome, the daughter of Herodias, "danced before him and his guests and pleased Herod."

We may assume that what "pleased" Herod was not a dance limited in scope, unconscious in its approach and repetitious in its movements—the three main characteristics of primitive dancing. From medieval times when dancing was considered by many the devil's dominion we find pictorial images of Salome dancing and turning somersaults (as reproduced on the porch of the Cathedral at Rouen). The concept of the seven-veil-dance was added by a later, far more sophisticated era. At that time, the Mediterranean countries were strongly influenced by the dancers from the East who, already many centuries previously, had introduced figure dancing.

Salome's dance is the only indication that figure dancing was also used by late Biblical man. But the beginning of solo dancing goes back to the Egyptians who, even if they performed in groups, underlined the rhythmic beauty and expressiveness of the in-

25

dividual. Therefore, we can designate ancient Egypt as the birthplace of Western civilized dancing, of a personalized form of the dance.

For the Egyptians as much as for the ancient Greeks dance was synonymous with joy. The upper strata of society would dance only on rare occasions, but the populace, like any other, desired to dance and to make merry in celebrating rites and in festivities. Their dancing was of a rather acrobatic or burlesque nature. There was a sense of the theatrical about whatever the ancient Egyptians did, although they did not know theater in our sense of the word. Even their temple dancers assumed acrobatic positions, and on their reliefs we see women doing a "split" or the "bridge." Some of those pictorial representations show a woman being hurled through the air and caught by two men; or a man standing on one foot seems to be about to begin what we would call a pirouette.

Of course, speaking of the ancient Egyptians we look back over a span of about three thousand years. Funeral dancing, of the utmost importance from the very beginning, or the dancing connected with the Abydos festivals were undoubtedly marked by austerity and a linear sparseness. But with progressing civilization, two major changes took place. More and more the stress shifted to the theatrical and the habit of "importing" foreign dancers. Small wandering troupes would give little shows on public squares of the big cities, such as Memphis or Alexandria. They would dance, mime and execute some acrobatic feats to the clatter of tambourines and castanets. They were in a way professionals. Even for religious services, solo dancers were imported from regions known for their good dancers—chiefly East Africa, the lower parts of the Nile where the popular dwarf dancers were found. About 1500 B.C. when the immigrant bayaderes—the South Indian temple dancers—arrived from the conquered countries in the East, the austere angularity, the strong, somewhat stiff but unrestricted movements, changed into softly flowing lines. These captive Asiatic girls brought a truly feminine style to the Egyptian dance and, as so often happens in history,

26

*Inbal, Israel's most professional folk dance group, is a modern exponent of ancient Hebrew tradition.*
*Left: Scene from the dance suite, "Yemenite Wedding."*
*(Israel Office of Information) Above: A Shepherd Dance from "In the Footsteps of the Flock." (Courtesy Dance Collection, New York Public Library)*

the conquerors were conquered. But whatever changes it may have undergone, the Egyptian dance remained theatrical without being of the theater; it created a dance concept which had great influence on the surrounding countries and islands.

Some Greek writers associated the acrobatic dance, the dance of jugglers and tumblers, with the Cretans. And there can be no doubt that sailors and travelers brought the Egyptian way of dancing to Crete, whose influence on Greece was impressive. The Greeks had a broad conception of dancing: it included Sophocles leading the procession of the naked youth through Athens after the victory at Salamis, a juggling or acrobatic act, and a military drill (especially since dancing was a part of their military training). Homer tells of Meriones, first professional dancer in Crete, who, dancing while he fought, could not be hit by any lance or stone. To the Greeks dancing was a means of achieving health in every part of the body; it was a rhythmic ball game, a funeral or wedding procession, or the gesticulations of a chorus on the stage.

In other words, dancing was gymnastic and mimetic to them. They took their inspiration from the world of nature, but simultaneously they aspired to a stylization that fused organic and ideal beauty into an expressive whole.

Perhaps we believe too easily in the Greeks as a people of great originality. But the Greeks themselves ascribed many of their dances to other nations and cultures—their orgiastic dances to Thrace and also to Phrygia, and their weapon dances to Crete.

Cretan culture was as dance-oriented as the Greek. The Cretans had a harvest dance in which

27

the men of the village marched around with their legs thrust high, carrying objects symbolic of cereals or tools. Surrounded by rows of singing girls, one of the male dancers would move about in a crouching position and strike the soil. Their dance of the first fruits offered to the goddess of vegetation was, in essence, identical with a parallel dance of the ancient Hebrews.

Sappho wrote that "once upon a time the Cretan woman danced in rhythm with her delicate feet around a beautiful altar, treading upon the soft, smooth flowers of the meadow." This refers again to the magic circle of primitive and archaic people. But since the Cretan women wore bolero jackets and flaring skirts, according to some of their representations, these circle dances may have easily turned into *skirt dances*. The people also did a variety of animal dances, and the snake dance in which priestesses carried live snakes in their hands, is of greatest significance if for no other reason than its relation-

ship to the famous Delian dance, the *geranos*. The geranos is derived from the mythological story of the Athenian prince Theseus who, with the help of Ariadne, daughter of the Cretan king, killed the Minotaur. The dance imitates the winding twists and turns in the Cretan labyrinth, and the dancers on Crete may originally have used serpent-like objects, such as a long rope. But maze and snake dances occur among many primitive people, whether in pre-Columbian Mexico, Hindustan or on Crete.

The Pyrrhic dance described in Homer and known from reliefs and vases, was very much alive for many centuries. The literary references speak of a funeral dance intent on infusing life again into the dead by a display of physical activity. Originally, on the island of Crete, it was executed with strong arm movements and a rhythmic noise created by clashing shields and swords intended to scare away evil spirits. The Mycenean Greeks had a very similar dance, which may have been associated with Pyrrhus, son of Achilles, or it may be derived from the Greek word *pyr*, which means fire. The pyrrhic dance never quite died out. It was still done in Roman days, and Apuleius, the author of *The Golden Ass*, described it as a dance performed by girls and boys:

> After having taken their positions, they began with a variety of delicate turns. Now they would turn like a wheel in a circle, then holding each other's hands, they formed a long, oblique row, and then they approached each other by four and four, then separating again and crossing their lines in seeming confusion.

Here is very little left of what had once been a

*Dionysian cult dances were wild and passionate. Left: A maenad with drum and thyrsus dances in honor of Dionysus in a fourth century B.C. Attic vase painting. (Walters Art Gallery, Baltimore) Right, above: A youth pipes as a girl, clad as a maenad in a leopard skin, dances. From a kylix, 510 B.C. (British Museum) Right, below: Dancing satyrs and a maiden. From an Etruscan vase painting, fourth century B.C. (Walters Art Gallery, Baltimore)*

*A Spartan girl in a joyful dance which, in contrast to the maenad's frenzied movements, is restrained. (Staatliches Museum, Berlin)*

competitive, martial dance with many a leap. But this was part of the general deterioration of taste and nobility during the second century.

As theatrical performances took place only once a year, the favorite entertainment of the ancient Greeks was the dinner party, the *symposium*. Professional dancers, often from abroad, were a major part of this entertainment, and it very often took on what we would call a night club atmosphere. We see on Greek vases dancing courtesans scantily dressed or nude, moving to the music of a flute as the male guests watch or sometimes even join them. Several literary sources described impromptu dances and contests staged by guests who brought their own dancers with them. Sometimes, of course, such a symposium provided much more elevated entertainment, such as Xenophon describes in his *Symposium*.

Throughout the Hellenistic and Greco-Roman periods professionalism was not something one thought of highly. During the Golden Age the Greek artists avoided being ranked with those who used their craft and skill to make a living. A clear distinction was made between the artist and the professional; the latter was usually a slave, a freedman, or foreigner. These professionals were hired out and were paid for their services. There were a few exceptions. Actors and members of the choruses in dramatic presentations in a city such as Dionysia were paid performers, but as ministers of the god Dionysus they were held in high respect and not considered professionals. But in general the poets, actors, members of the choruses and musicians were private citizens who dedicated their talents to serve a divinity on special occasions, such as the Dionysian festivals in spring. Their social status may best be compared with that of the passion players of Oberammergau or other contemporary amateur groups, with the distinction that their artistry was on the highest level.

From Thespis to Aeschylus, Sophocles and Euripides, the poets were their own choreographers. The earlier dramatists were called dancers since their plays were chiefly a matter of choral dancing. But even Aeschylus was known for his invention of many dance figures, and Sophocles was famous for his solo dancing. Through their connection with the production of plays these artists had many privileges. They could cross battle lines when cities were at war with each other, and they were exempt from military service, although only a few made use of this privilege.

In about the third century before Christ, performing artists were members of an association

*Etruscans danced with abandon,
using agile movements
and broad gestures. (Alinari)*

called "The Artists of Dionysus," a "trade union" with religious overtones. This organization had a shrine of its own, and its annual meetings were sacred ceremonies. From that time until the Greco-Roman period we come upon many complaints by Greek writers that the dance is deteriorating. The orderly beauty, restraint and dignity characterizing the dance on stage and at banquets during the fifth and early fourth centuries vanished and artistic standards declined. Only the Roman pantomimic art

attained high sophistication during the period of the empire. But the dancing during spring processions and on other ritual and festive occasions added little to the development of the dance. In the field of entertainment the performances in the symposia were cheapened. The Ionic dances during the Greco-Roman period were notorious for their burlesque character, their lack of form and their obviousness. Professional male dancers who performed in Italy and in Greek cities were particularly effeminate and degenerate. It was probably their dancing that caused Cicero to say in one of his famous speeches:

> Cato calls Lucius Murena a dancer. If this be imputed to him truly, it is the reproach of a

violent accuser; but if falsely, it is the abuse of a scurrilous railer ... for nobody dances, unless he be drunk or a madman; nor in solitude, nor in a moderate and sober party; dancing is the last companion of prolonged feasting....

It was the time when dancing, strongly influenced by Etruscan and Greek dance teachers, had become fashionable in private and public life in Rome. The conservative Romans warned in vain against the growing dance craze. About 150 years before Christ, Scipio Aemilianus Africanus ordered the dancing schools closed. The leading Romans did not consider the dance an expression of their way of life. But the Roman populace was captivated by the art, even though it was alien to its nature. In Nero's day—he prided himself on being a great dancer—we find no less than three thousand dance teachers in Rome, all foreigners from Greece, Alexandria, Sicily or the Orient. In many cases they were Etruscans. It is the first time that we encounter "social dancing," separated from ritual, stage and entertainment—dancing, that is, as a social accomplishment of a people.

## Ritual as Theater

There was always a desire to lift the dance from its entertainment level to its function as spectacle. Ruins of a theater were found on the island of Crete. It must have been built about 2000 B.C., that is 1500 years before the Greeks built their Dionysian theater. Phaestus and Cnossus had court theaters with a capacity of four to five hundred seats. These are the oldest playhouses known to us. But, unfortunately, we are not quite sure what took place on those stages. On some frescoes we see the audience, but we do not know what enchants it. But since a painting from Cnossus shows a group of aristocratic ladies, surrounded by a few gentlemen, viewing a dance by gaily petticoated girls in an olive grove, and another painting presents a dancing woman with extended arms and flying tresses, we may assume that a combination of dancing and music may have been part, and perhaps the main

part, of the entertainment on these stages. Homer speaks of the "dancing-floor which once, in broad Cnossus, Daedalus made for Ariadne of the lovely hair; there youths and seductive maidens join hands in the dance... and a divine bard sets the time to the sound of the lyre."

We know how the orgiastic dances in honor of Dionysus were gradually channeled into formal ceremonies which were performed as late as the second century of the Christian era. We also know that maenads were instructed in the dance in preparation for these bacchanalia; and that male dancers in goatskins with horned masks and even with cloven hoofs imitated the mythological companions of Dionysus, who were visualized as satyrs. We know how the dithyramb, a song-and-dance performance and one of the favored features of the god's spring festival, gradually took the place of improvisation and, finally, how Arion gave the dithyramb dance its circular form, with the dancers moving around the altar of Dionysus. Then Thespis came and created the first form of theatrical dialogue, thus taking the decisive step from the dance to the spoken drama.

But we do not know too much about how the Greek chorus moved on stage. We may assume with a degree of certainty that a Greek play resembled far more a semi-operatic spectacle than a drama as we know it today. Like the actors, the chorus consisted only of men. They wore masks and for the

*Greek athletes perform dance leaps. (Staatliches Museum, Berlin)*

female roles impersonated women. The costumes of the chorus were less elaborate than those of the actors. Their shoes were low and soft to facilitate movement, while the actors wore *cothurni,* thick-soled shoes.

*Emmeleia,* the dance of tragedy, was dignified and adjusted to the mood of the play. It followed a code of symbolic gestures, the *cheironomia,* which would impress us as obviously mimetic. Not unlike the conventional gestures of yesterday's classical ballet, the movement was descriptive and easily legible.

The chorus entered the orchestra area at the beginning of the play, usually singing and moving in a solid rectangular alignment of three by four, or three by five persons. After the entrance song, *parodos,* the chorus reacted visibly to the dramatic episode with groupings, movements and gestures. Then came the choral ode, *stasimon,* relieving the emotional tension with beautiful lyrics and corresponding movements, followed by three or four more episodes until the chorus filed out in its *exodos.*

In several plays we find the remark at a certain point that there a dance commences. The leader of the chorus would then call on a deity to join in or lead the dance. Hymnlike processions, paeans, victory dances, and wedding dances were performed. Euripides asks for an ecstatic dance of maenads in his play *Bacchae.* The choreographic designs were varied and free. The great dramatists were their own choreographers and also danced in their plays. Sophocles was praised for a ballplaying dance in one of his tragedies.

The dance in Greek tragedy went through several artistic phases that more or less corresponded with the development of the dramatic form. Aeschylus introduced the dance in his plays as a device for heightening of the drama. Sophocles used it to give emotional expression to a characteristic change in a plot situation. Euripides went one step further and had the dancing chorus express in pantomime the feelings evoked by the play. The chorus had to dance the essence of the drama. And it is very likely that Euripides was the first one to use solo dancing. Aristotle summed it up by saying that the dance

must not only express the action, but also the pathos and ethos of the characters.

Comedy developed somewhat later than tragedy, emerging from phallic or fertility processions, from village revelries full of horseplay, animal dances and mummery. The old comedy was a brilliant spectacle, usually with twenty-four members in a chorus portraying animals, cities, clouds, humans and allegorical beings with singing and dancing, in masks and costumes. Aristophanes and his contemporaries delighted in attacks on famous people, and the victims loved it, for in Athens it was far more ignominious to be ignored than to be derided. Obscenities and invectives made the day.

The characteristic dance of the old comedy was the *kordax*. Befitting the mood of the comedy, the dance was ignoble and obscene. One of its main features was a dancer who lewdly rotated his abdomen. Anything lively went into it. The dancer would kick his own buttocks, leap, slap his chest and thighs, stamp his heels, and even beat up his fellow dancers. Stamping of the heels, rapid foot work with a quiet torso was also a feature—one that is reminiscent of Spanish dancing. The *kordax* became a solo dance, both in and out of the theater, and was performed until its lewdness aroused the ire of the Christians.

The dance employed in the satyr plays was called *sikinnis*, and was essentially an exaggerated *kordax*, but exceeded it in vigor and lewdness and probably was a bit more acrobatic. It used more stamping than the *kordax*, swift leaps, high kicks and whirling motions. It had a touch of the burlesque, and it finally disappeared along with the *kordax*.

The great contribution of the Romans was the pantomime. A people given to mimicry and gestures, the Romans liked the dance-drama without words and developed it to such a fine point that one could rightly say that the mime-actor's body spoke, or as Demetrius said to one of the mimes after a performance: "Man, this is not seeing, but hearing and seeing, both: it is as if your hands were tongues!"

Mimicry and pantomime were, of course, not new, they existed as inherent parts of dancing throughout the Greek culture. But a peculiar fusion between old and new elements, Greek and Asiatic concepts, made pantomime into a new genre. Pylades of Cicilia and Bathyllus of Alexandria are usually considered the inventors of Roman pantomime. The date is set at 22 B.C. Performances of the new dance form were first seen in Rome and Italy and then on the Greek islands. Whether or not the two representatives of pantomime were of Greek origin, the themes of their dances were.

It was a highly stylized movement sequence, usually a solo performance, with the stress on gesture. The dancer wore a characteristic mask, with the mouth closed to indicate that he would tell his story without speaking. The performance was generally introduced by an actor who summarized the story to be enacted. A chorus sang offstage before and between the episodes. There was no longer the lyre or flute alone, the pantomimes working with an orchestra of hand drums, castanets, cymbals, metal rattles, and the scabellum, a loud percussion instrument of wood and metal, operated by the foot.

The pantomimists wore long cloaks and also a series of costumes richly embroidered with gold and precious stones. They leaped and crouched, twisted and turned, executed dazzling feats of acrobatic or statuesque beauty. Bathyllus favored what was called the *saltatio hilara*, the hilarious comedy. Although at times it had a touch of burlesque, his style remained delicate. He also liked to appear in female roles and, being very beautiful, he is supposed to have danced Leda with uncanny grace and femininity. Pylades was also famous for his beauty and incredible skill as a dance-mime. He developed the grand gesture of the tragic actor and the style he created was called *saltatio Italica*.

Later this art form declined, the performers becoming corrupt and their performances erotic and cheap. The public, however, remained devoted to them. And so did some of the Emperors. Nero wanted to be a mime, Caligula loved them, Commodus took part in some of their productions. But other emperors opposed them, Tiberius banishing them and Claudius putting one of them to death after he had become involved in a scandal with the Empress Messalina. The politicians resented the fact that the pantomimists stood high in popular esteem. Marcus Aurelius cut their high fees. And the Christian Church waged relentless war against them. Wherever the influence of the Church grew, as it did in the big cities, they were forced to leave. First, they lived and worked in smaller towns; then they became wandering entertainers, going off in all directions.

They acquired a second responsibility, of equal importance with the creation of pantomime: they helped to keep the Hellenistic tradition and the Roman spirit from perishing and carried the concept of theatrical dance, or the remembrance of it, through the Middle Ages into the days of the Renaissance.

# 3 *Body and Soul*

It was not only the leaders of Rome who lashed out against the dance. From the rise of Christianity, the Church Fathers tried their best to suppress dancing and to stamp out "this evil, this lascivious madness in man called dance which is the devil's business." In the fourth century, St. Augustine complained in one of his sermons: "It is preferable to till the soil and to dig ditches on the day of the Lord than to dance a choric Reigen. Oh, how times and manners change! What once was the business of lute-players and shameless women only, namely to sing and to play, this is now considered an honor among Christian virgins and matrons who even engage masters in their art to teach them."

This tells us, among other things, that teaching of dance and music continued in some form in the early Christian era. It may be important to note that the attitude of the Church toward dancing was divided in itself. In the Mediterranean countries and the Orient, the people never really gave up dancing, and the clergy applied less stringent measures to curb the dance. In the third century A.D., St. Gregory Thaumaturgus conducted dances and holy pantomimes within the space of the choir and, a century later, St. Johannes Chrysostom used to dance himself, but was adverse to the mimes.

Dancing played a great part in Byzantine art, and the Church in the Orient could not easily have done

*Above: Dancing fool. (Victoria and Albert Museum)*
*Right: Maypole dances, as seen in this English needle-work, are vestiges of ancient fertility rites. (Conzett and Huber: Untermeyer Collection, New York)*

*"Wild men" in a masque represent the unruly and passionate side of human nature. (British Museum)*

without it. In the southern parts of Italy, in France and in Spain, dancing in the churches never stopped until well into the seventeenth century. In the Cathedral of Toledo one can find church ballets to this very day. The heritage of the Greco-Roman culture was too strong in these countries, the Church could not deny the past and did well not to deny it.

In bringing Christianity to the north, the clergymen faced other tests. Its inner strength lay in the fact of utter asceticism and austerity. It had to compete with and to overcome the deep-rooted rituals of pagan peoples with their wild fertility dances, their mummeries with animal masks. Time and again, masked dancers tried to invade the churches, and we know of such an incident in Paris as late as 1445. In the early centuries of the Chris-

tian era, it was an uphill struggle, and the clergy could neither displace nor completely eradicate the pagan rites, the Druid cults, nor invade successfully the mythological *Reich* of Wotan. In the course of time, the priests succeeded in making these northern tribes give up their more cruel and crude customs without depriving them of all their superstitious rituals. With the Christian way of life taking root, the heathen quality was lost, but the people retained what they liked about the old way. How many things in which we still indulge nowadays have their roots in ancient pagan rituals, such as the idea of the June bride, Halloween, or Yuletide! Or who would think today of the Maypole as a phallic symbol and of the dance around it as a fertility dance?

The Church turned against dancing since it saw human goodness only in the soul and all evil in the body, conforming to St. Paul's conception of the spirit as opposed to the senses and his contempt for

38

the body and its functions. It was this division between soul and body that laid the groundwork for the extremes of medieval life.

In this long period of clashing contrasts the most obvious phenomena were seen by the people either in a beautiful light or hellish darkness. The days were filled with processions and executions; both were spectacles that rivaled the most realistic theater. And it was to this drama that people flocked to express their sentimentality in tears, with what may be called a cruel compassion, or to go through the catharsis of pity and fear, what may best be described as sensual excitement.

In between, they observed the behavior of princes, who created fear through their splendor, or they listened to the many itinerant preachers who created fear through their diatribes against the vanities of the rich as much as of the poor. "Fear of Judgment Day" was the motto of the first six hundred years after the fall of the Roman Empire. The clergy maintained that the millennium would be the day of reckoning, but when the year 1000 passed without any visible changes, some of the fear subsided.

The Church remained powerful and the spirit of medievalism lingered on, even while man awakened to a new inner freedom. From the crudeness of his carnal lust and mortal fear of it, he escaped into chivalry; checking his growing freedom, he forced himself into the straitjacket of ideal codes.

It took medieval man a long time to reach a balance between the memory of Christ and His passion, which was so overpowering as a living reality for many centuries, and reality itself. From self-mortification he turned to extreme sentimentality.

The Church was part of the new humanistic spirit; it remained a partner in the very revolution it had to fear most. It became the patron of the visual splendor with which the Renaissance unfolded. The masses had only a small share in it; for them medievalism did not fade overnight nor over a century. The emphasis gradually shifted during the eleventh and twelfth centuries, but in essence, the Middle Ages took a long time in waning. Or we could say that the Middle Ages themselves had been a Renaissance in many ways. They helped to lay the foundation for feudalism, they gave birth to political concepts of Roman magnitude, and with the militant crusades they checked the power of Islam, while completing the process of civilizing the pagan tribes in the north.

## Death and the Devil

Death and the devil are two of most common symbols used in the Middle Ages. Antiquity was already familiar with the image of death as a dancer. An Etruscan tomb shows a bas-relief of dancing skeletons. A relief on a tomb in Cumae, an early Greek settlement on Italy's west coast, displays three corpses dancing, and Roman vases show similar images. Death as the focal figure in dances appeared in many primitive societies and to this day is a prominent figure in voodoo dancing.

But it was left to the Middle Ages to turn the image of death into a symbol of frightening force. Death was rushed out of the charnel house and endowed with satanic reality. The skeleton became death personified. We cannot say when the "Dance of Death" idea began, but it is already present in primitive and archaic dancing in a more or less overt form. The dance itself preceded, of course, the many visualizations of this concept by the great painters and sculptors of the Renaissance such as Holbein and Dürer. Through the centuries it flared up here and there, usually beginning with people dancing around tombstones in a churchyard and then moving through a town, attracting more and more people as they went. This dance, also known as *danse macabre,* reached a climax during the time the bubonic plague swept all Europe in the fourteenth century.

"Dance of Death" ( *Totentanz* or *Danse des Mortes)* is the common designation of this dance, but the name *danse macabre* reminds us that "macabre" is here generally thought to derive from the Arabic *makabr,* meaning churchyards, and that the dance goes back to the Arabs.

*Peter Breughel the Elder's pen drawing shows epileptics dancing on the way to a healing well. The dance mania affirmed life in the face of death. (Albertina)*

The Dance of Death also had a social significance since it enabled the poor to see the rich as their equals: Before death all men are equal. It was thus a release for those who suffered at the bottom of the social ladder: this dance gave them a chance to impersonate the rich, living and dying. Then, there was the age-old conception of man visualizing his own dead image. This theme was often treated visually and also found its way into literature. A thirteenth-century French poem, "The Three Quick and the Three Dead," describes a confrontation in which the dead tell the living of their foolish vanities.

For a thousand years the Church Fathers tried to stamp out this "obscene" dancing in their churchyards, but all their attempts failed. During the years of the plague, when death was a daily guest everywhere, men tried to drive out the devil by catching him. Then the Dance of Death was often a dance of hysteric gaiety. Usually it started with animated dancing, then suddenly someone would

fall to the ground and play dead, while the others would dance around him with gestures of mock mourning. If it was a man, he would be kissed back to life by the girls, whereupon a round-dance followed. Then a girl would feign death and be kissed back to life by the male dancers. In this interplay of dying and living again, the joy of life was underlined. Certainly, no one realized that he was spreading the plague germs through kissing.

At times, dancing turned into a craze, and the Middle Ages are full of stories of uncontrollable dancing. At Christian festivals people would suddenly begin to sing and dance in churchyards, disturbing divine service. And it often happened that the priests could not stop these mad activities and finally cursed the dancers, which was only a further stimulus to go on dancing.

Hans Christian Andersen tells of little Karen who was cursed to dance without stopping and who could not find rest until the executioner cut off her feet. These dances of violent nature occurred everywhere. In Germany, they were called *St. Vitus* dance, in Italy, *tarantella*, which was strongly related to the *sikinnis*, the dance of the Greek satyr plays. These and similar dances indicated the tenor of the time, and particularly the period of the plague. Dansomania has been common at all times from the pre-Hellenistic days to the twentieth-century post-war periods; it seems generally to be called forth by cataclysmic events: war, famine, plague.

One of the variants of this mania, the dance of death, had lyric components, especially when it was pursued by the nobility. The painter Piero di Cosimo designed a *danse macabre* pageant for the Duke of Florence in 1507 while the city was besieged by enemies and disaster loomed. According to Vasari's description of this magnificent pageant, there was a huge triumphal car, painted with skeletons bearing the gigantic figure of death with scythe in hand. Skeletons sang songs, all attendants wore the vestments of the grave, and voices sang in dismal unison the psalm of David called *Miserere*.

Sometimes the nobility, fleeing the plague-infested city, escaped to a country house where they whiled away the time by telling stories and by dancing "a stately carole" as Giovanni Boccaccio about 1350 described it in the *Decameron*:

> Breakfast done, the tables were removed, and the Queen bade fetch instruments of music; for all, ladies and young men alike, knew how to tread a measure, and some of them played and sang with great skill; so... they struck up a dance in sweet concert; and the servants being dismissed to their repast, the Queen, attended by other ladies and the two young men, led off a stately carole.

Dancing was not only a release and entertainment at fairs and folk festivals, it was also part of all social gatherings of the nobility and the increasingly important upper layer of the middle class. When Boccaccio mentions the *carole*, it is very likely that he does so because by then this dance had become the favorite of all classes. As a matter of fact, to carole and to dance was then used interchangeably. The *carole* was a Provence dance-song, originally performed in May only. But its popularity grew with the help of the traveling minstrels. *Caroles* were danced and sung throughout the year and certainly on all festive occasions.

The meaning of the *carole* is to dance in a ring to singing voices. But it was in essence a processional

in which the dancers turned from right to left in marching steps, beating one foot against the other. There were variations of it: The minnesingers in Germany called it *Springtanz* and put into it a great many hops and small leaps. The people identified the *carole*—today known only as a Christmas song—with religious images as they appear in many "Last Judgment" paintings of the early Renaissance which show angels in heaven enjoying a *carole*.

Related to death and the devil was the medieval fool. The Church was not kindly disposed toward the fools; the canon law contained strict ordinances against them. That these ordinances were rarely enforced was at least in part due to the tremendous popularity the fools enjoyed not only among the nobility, but also among the town merchants and the peasantry. There was even an annual celebration, called the Feast of Fools, which the Church tolerated half-heartedly, although it usually had a touch of the sacrilegious, with the people feeling free to get rid of their repressions, their boredom and their annoyance with the ecclesiastical caste. This once-a-year revolt was led mainly by the lay clergy whose grievances against their superiors were manifold and justified. In the Feast of Fools there was a great deal of merrymaking, dancing and singing. The Church tried to keep these feasts under control by sanctioning them; when they got out of hand, they were banned, but with little success. No one was safe from ridicule during the *Fête des Fous*, and the jesters and fools were the heroes of the day.

The figure of the medieval fool as we know him from such plays as *King Lear* has appeared on the stage in many guises: as Hans Wurst in the German theater, as Arlecchino in the *commedia dell'arte*, or as the simpleton in many plays. The medieval fool was usually clad in red and yellow clothes and with a cap that fell over his shoulders in the form of asses' ears. His costume was hung with bells, and he was not only allowed to make caustic remarks, but also to inflict blows with an inflated bladder at the end of his baton, or bauble.

The fool's function was as dramatic and painful

"*The Dance for the Ring,*" *an allegorical etching by Israhel Van Meckenem, shows a Morris dance to the tune of flageolet and tambourine. (Bibliothèque Nationale)*

## The Not-So-Dark Ages

In no other epoch besides the late Middle Ages has the dance been more indicative of social phenomena. It reflected frightening aspects of the plague and the fear of death, but by the same token, it showed man's affirmation of life.

Our main sources for the reconstruction of what was danced in the minnesinger period are some contemporary works of literature and the visual arts. Still in the eleventh century, dancing at the feudal courts and in the houses of the rich went on for hours without any form or structure. Most often what then passed for dancing, we would hardly call so today. The participants walked, stepped about, and jumped from time to time. There was some swinging of the hips and a turning inward of the feet, as we learn from the miniatures in the Manesse minnesinger manuscript in Heidelberg. In essence, people enjoyed chain dances, in no way defined, and not ruled by any feeling for etiquette. It was a way of wooing, with the sex motif as a driving force. All these dances were accompanied by the human voice; harpists were rarely used. In these choral dances the participants sang together while moving in the simplest manner.

During the twelfth century the pendulum swung to the other extreme. Feudalism with its codes of piety, bravery, loyalty, and honor came into being. The motives of romantic love and chivalry became predominant, sex was subordinated to symbol, and etiquette became the guiding rod to living. Politeness and suggestiveness were the key words with which the codes of chivalry revolutionized dancing. It was a part of the philosophy of knighthood which in the twelfth century crystallized as a class into which one could not be born, but for which one had to be trained. It was in the same century that the knight was inspired by the myth of Tristan and

as a primitive exorcism. He was tolerated, however cruel his jokes and acid his wit may have been; he was the cheery counterpart to the flagellants, of whom there were many in the Middle Ages. He was kept by his master who wanted to be reminded of his own follies and weaknesses. The hunchbacked and dwarfed fools were permitted the freedom to utter what they pleased, letting the lords pretend they believed the fool mad. As with primitive tribes, madness was holy to medieval man, who also enjoyed the thought of the wise man being as much a fool as the fool himself. The dancing image of death and the dancing fool were two characteristic figures of the darker and not-so-dark Middle Ages, reminders of the frailty of human flesh and the transitoriness of human life on earth.

*Death dances with highborn and lowborn alike, here selecting a queen as his partner. (The Metropolitan Museum of Art)*

*A thirteenth-century manuscript illumination shows
medieval entertainers. (Giraudon)*

Isolt which made passion triumphant over conjugal
union. The myth of love as escape and dream, as
suffering and death became a characteristic product
of the time and characteristic of the complex nature
of courtly love. It also determined and colored the
course dancing took.

As the counterpart to the tournaments, dancing
had great significance in chivalric activities and
concluded all festivities and gatherings. A knight
who was admired for his strength and skill during
the day was expected to show equal ability during
the dances in the evening. In general, we can
imagine a leading couple being followed by others
who joined the dance, stepping around the room in
a form that might seem to us like a polonaise. The
trend was gradually toward a more representative
dance. The rhythm was sometimes so slow that one
could have balanced a glass of wine on one's head
during the dance. In fact, as late as the sixteenth
century, the French philosopher Montaigne having
arranged a ball in the Italian town of Lucca, described how a lady with a bowl of water on her head
danced without spilling a drop.

There were pantomimic dances, too. Roodlieb
wrote in his Latin poem in the eleventh century
about a couple that never touched each other while
dancing: he danced around her in the manner of
the flight of a falcon and she imitated a pursued
swallow; he tried to seize her, and she glided away.
This is no longer an imitation of an animal dance,

but has the imprint of courtly wooing. And in the
first half of the thirteenth century we find the verbal
tapestry of a choral dance woven in Guillaume de
Lorris' *Roman de la Rose:*

> And then a dance you might have seen,
> The maidens and the men in joy have been
> To tread a measure and to turn their rounds
> On grassy green of spring, and to the sounds
> Of flutists and of minstrels with a strain
> They sing of beautiful Lorraine...
> Then came two damsels, young and neat,
> Their kirtles showed their forms sweet.
> In gaiety the two began to dance
> With queenlike leaps and furtive glance;
> Their bodies, lithe and limber, now adavance
> And give their lips to kiss but half a chance.
> And then once more did they retreat
> To turn a dancing measure with their feet.
> What more could I describe and tell
> Of all their dancing, done so well?

The choral dance remained the favorite dance
form of the populace, while the "couple dance" at
the feudal courts developed very slowly and did not
become really popular before the early days of the
Renaissance. During the late Middle Ages we may
generically distinguish between the "courtly couple
dance" and the "rustic choral dance," but not
sociologically because these two forms mixed with
each other. Occasionally, the villagers would imi-
tate a court dance and the knights were fond of
joining a choral round.

The difference was in the manner of execution.
The peasants danced with fervor and intensity. It
was unrestrained exuberance that took them out of
their everyday existence which was still marred by
many aspects of a lingering medievalism.

The knights were the harbingers of a new world. They had their hunting parties and tournaments to prove themselves. Dancing, in its purely physical aspect as a means of wooing, had to bow to the notion of *cortezia,* the court etiquette. Also, the costumes worn by the nobility helped determine the dance. The heavy velvet and brocade skirts did not lend themselves to exuberant movement. But what the dance of the nobility lost in vitality, it gained in subtleties and delicate shadings. It was not yet the beginning but the preparation for the beginning of our theatrical dancing.

Late medieval sophistication among the aristocracy, supported by the troubadours, found its best expression in the so-called "Courts of Love." They were favorite banquet games, which originated in Provence as amorous tournaments and spread into the north. These Courts of Love were the stage setting in which competing troubadours engaged in intellectual combat like the knights in the tournaments. The questions discussed were mainly the nature of passion and love. After the battle of tongues was over, the winner was decided by the ladies. We read, for instance, about such an affair taking place on April 29, 1174, when the Countess of Champagne presided over a "Court of Love" whose subject was: "Can real love exist between married people?" Since the decision was made in the negative, the dancing which followed the banquet may well have been rather amorous. These poetic and dialectic dialogues, mounted like court dramas and climaxed by dancing, had all the elements of a theatrical performance.

Two opposite poles developed in Europe in this last medieval phase between the twelfth and fourteenth centuries: the peasants, or the populace at large, stood for the earthiness and crude joy, while the nobility replaced the primary impulses with refinement and polished sparkle.

Antiquity had developed a fine distinction between theater dance on the one hand, and the dance of ritual and entertainment on the other. The same division took place in the late Middle Ages with the separation of the people's dance from a newly developing theatrical form that had the face of feudalism but a baroque shape. The following juxtaposition shows the dividing line:

| *Folk Dance* | *Theater Dance* |
| --- | --- |
| extemporaneous (merry, active) | studied (expressive, passive) |
| choral (ring-shaped) | figure dancing |
| multitude | couple dance, solo |
| unrestrained joy | courtliness, refined pleasure |
| participants sing | instrumental accompaniment |

The spontaneity that marked the dances of the peasants was not totally eradicated in the dancing of the nobility. But the court dance was subjected more and more to rules. Contributing to this development was, no doubt, the reliance of the nobility on professional entertainers.

Such entertainers must have been of great importance since they enjoyed all kinds of privileges. Among them were members of the aristocracy, often impoverished, and all sorts of artists who had some skill in dancing, juggling, miming and acrobatic feats. These entertainers had great influence on the life at the courts and were judges of etiquette and fashion.

Of course, they did not appear overnight. With the fall of the Roman Empire, the mimes had taken to the road, going eastward and northward. They kept a tradition of entertainment alive, however corrupted and tailored to the taste of the masses. Through many centuries, these so-called "joculators"—who performed at fairs and village festivities, but hardly ever for the nobility—were seen as actors and jesters, acrobats and dancing mimes, poets and musicians. In Germany, they were called "Spielmann." They were an important link between the Roman pantomimists and the players of the *commedia dell'arte* in the sixteenth and seventeenth centuries. Miniatures show how expressive were the "hand" dances of these joculators who brought the southern culture to the north. Above all, these entertainers remained mimes. Their more elaborate numbers would be based on Greco-Roman mythology or, from time to time, a vulgar-

ized version of a scene from Seneca or Terence. The German minnesingers and French troubadours could never have come into existence without the tradition of the joculators.

"Minne" means love, but the minnesingers did not restrict their themes to romantic love, they also sang about war and many political issues of local interest. Some of these wandering entertainers, such as Walther von der Vogelweide, Wolfram von Eschenbach, or Heinrich von Morungen have become historic figures. The "von" in their names indicates that they belonged in the lower nobility. This was also true of the troubadours, who even include some of the upper aristocracy such as Alfonso II, King of Aragon, Richard Cœur de Lion, and Folquet de Marseille who became bishop of Toulouse.

The minnesingers and, even more, the troubadours, traveled in grand style from castle to castle, followed by a train of minor entertainers, the minstrels and jugglers. The minstrels were the instrumentalists who accompanied the troubadours and executed their notions for entertainment. Sometimes, the minstrels traveled alone to perform their masters' works. Most often the troubadours made their appearance with the entire group—like a medieval touring company; and the expenses were so high that, at times, they found themselves stranded without means. To recoup their losses, they sometimes joined the crusaders.

On the lowest social rung among these entertainers stood the *letzim*, the Jewish minstrels, who could dance, sing, play the fiddle and were comedians with a sad, biting humor. Some of them had broken out of the ghetto life and taken to the road. The ghetto institution of the *Tanzhaus*, or dancing hall from which they came, plays a far greater role in the history of the dance than is generally realized.

The need in the ghetto for the *Tanzhaus* was obvious. The extremely limited living space made it

*The elegant courtly medieval dances utilized slow, formalized movements. (Bodleian Library)*

necessary to celebrate all festivities in one place. Having been cut off from the world, the inhabitants of the ghettos felt the need to be gay and to express the joy of life more acutely. Weddings were frequent and the festivities were not restricted to one day. Dancing formed a major part of all such celebrations. Men and women danced in lines or circles, mostly without any prescribed steps. When they danced together, particularly according to the rabbinical rules, a rather elaborately designed dance became necessary. Moreover, the limited space of the *Tanzhaus* required someone to keep order among the dancing couples.

Thus, very early in Jewish ghetto life a new character came into being: the dance leader, a forerunner of the square dance caller. He had to be musical, have a good singing voice, be able to improvise a rhyme or a song and demonstrate a few dance steps. He was a master at organizing groups of people. His role became traditional and grew in importance, particularly after the inquisition in the thirteenth century when all Jews had to live in the ghetto.

The *Tanzhaus* and the dance leader created a new situation. The dancers and the dances had to be organized. Since spatial limitations were set by the dance hall and the number of participants, the *letzim* had to learn how to think in terms of space. Forced to improvise, the dance leaders often tried new steps and variations while leading the dance, and when they pleased, such steps were repeated.

Thus the Jews in their ghettos created an excellent platform for the training of dance teachers. Because there were too many of them in the ghettos, some dared the dangers of the outside world and joined the many wandering entertainers. Some of them established a reputation and even received permission to settle down. This is why at the very beginning of the Renaissance in the fifteenth century we find so many Jews among the dancing masters in northern Italy. One of them, who proudly called himself Guglielmo Ebreo, or William the Jew, was destined to play a major part in the creation of the balletic art.

# *4* *The Dances of the East*

Ever since man's discovery of the world during the Renaissance, the influence of the East has been reflected in the culture and art of Western man. From the many *ballets géographiques* of the eighteenth century to the Oriental influence on Martha Graham and the strong impact of Zen Buddhism on such dancer-choreographers as Merce Cunningham and Erick Hawkins, Western man has been inspired and attracted by the "otherness" of the East. He senses what William Saroyan meant in saying the surprise of art lies not in shock but in wonder.

It is not surprising that a culture such as ours

*An Indian dancer enacts the god Shiva's eternal dance of creation and destruction. (Brian Brake: Magnum)*
*Above: Cambodian dancer. (Dominique Darbois)*

which has embraced external reality with scientific intensity should lean in its art toward the philosophic-artistic expression of the East. There is deep harmony in the Eastern approach to art and to expressiveness as such. Eastern art traditionally has been a religious experience for the Asiatic and thus has formed an integral part of his life. Even when no religion is involved, his art, and particularly his dance have the function of deepening his communication with the universe. When the fire dancer of Ceylon—to choose an extreme case—holds a flaming torch down his throat, we regard it as a daring feat to be applauded. To him, however, it is a symbol of his mastery over demons, and his dance, designed to drive away evil spirits, proves that a man can conquer his own fears.

Asiatics are accustomed to see in symbols. To

49

depict spring for instance, he may paint only a small branch, with a few delicate brush strokes spreading into his canvas. To express the same emotional experience, a Western artist would be far more apt to paint the whole tree, or even a blossoming landscape.

## The Difference Between East and West

The Oriental dance is essentially a gesture dance. Through their idolization of God, the Asiatics turned the human body into an instrument of gesture and symbol, while we, as heirs to the ancient Greeks who idealized man, have made the human body a crucible of energy. This is why the dance in the West has become an expression of action, whereas Eastern dance is basically focused on contemplation.

Western dance is designed to show the causes of man's inner conflicts in their relation to the world, but mainly as they reflect his being. Thus, his dances are descriptive because they are dramatic. Eastern dances are descriptive because they are reflective. They are enacted as a totality within a stable world which accepts conflicts as basic to all existence. Therefore, the Asiatic is concerned with giving a stylized depiction of the eternal actions caused by these inner conflicts.

Unlike the forced separation of drama and dance in the West when in the Middle Ages the Church split body from soul, dance in the East never severed its ties with religions rites and it never gave up being an essential part of all theatrical performances. Moreover, dance has always been so great an expression of communal life that even children play games related to dancing.

The dances of Western man have been shaped by

*Dancing Apsaras, celestial water nymphs of Indra's heaven, in a thirteenth-century sandstone relief from Rajasthan. (The Metropolitan Museum of Art)*

50

*A figure from the Madurai temple in South India showing the Bharata Natyam dance as performed in the twelfth century. (M.N. Swaminathan: Courtesy Lalli)*

well have injected subtle variations into it. They delighted in the mastery of their art. This alone was their professional reward.

The differences in approach and technique are the logical results of the two different worlds of East and West. We pride ourselves on our imaginative creativity, on the individual artist's inventiveness. In the Oriental dance this is controlled by the framework of the traditional form. In Western dance, the female-male relationship is shown explicitly in its profane, purely human sense. The love-sex aspect in Eastern dance is always associated with a higher, sacred love. Human love, abstracted into stylized gesture and facial expression, symbolizes love for the divine.

Our whole ballet history has developed with the aim at conquering space, at making the best of floor design, in which the interplay of the dancers gains meaning and in which the ground is not only a point of departure but an active participant, particularly with the modern dancer's dominant use of the floor as a new dimension. In contrast to our active and aggressive approach, the Eastern dancer is not space-conscious; he does not conquer the ground but rather integrates it into his dance pattern. With the tremendous emphasis on gesture and facial expression, the slightest change in movement language indicates a whole new world of emotions. To duplicate a similar range of expression, the dancer in the West needs an incomparably wider scope of movements.

Technically speaking, the Oriental dance puts the burden of interpretation on the upper part of the body. A central line, like a rod, runs through it, giving the trunk a rigid appearance and underlining the stylization of the dance. Generally, the hands play the most important part, and each country has its characteristic style. The *pataka,* or flat hand, of India is the prototype for the expressive hand in all countries of the East. More than any other gesture, the use of the hands reveals the country of origin. The Hindu religion spread throughout Asia the cult of the dance, which, by fusing with folklore, has adapted itself to the people's needs.

individuals; they carry the stamp of personality. In an endless flow of innovations they have changed and come to reflect each age. The dances of the East were shaped collectively and successively by dance masters who did not try to put the stamp of their personality, or even of their epoch, upon their art. On the contrary, they endeavored to preserve and perfect the conventions of an existing style. However, by perfecting their art, by preventing it from deteriorating or becoming sterile, they may

## India: Embodied Soul

The center of the cult is India. Indian dance, in the words of L. S. Ramaswamy Sastri, "is not mere activity of the human limbs resulting from high animal spirits or love of rhythmic movement. It is the embodied soul's attempt to express not only through the mind or the senses alone ... but through the mind and the senses and the body acting together, its nature and its visions. It uses the hand and the voice and the mind for expressing its passions and desires. The whole body becomes so expressive that one might almost say the body thought."

According to Hindu legend all this began in heaven: the world was created by Lord Shiva in a dancing mood, and with a divine dance Shiva annihilated his monster enemies. Ever since then, the gods have danced. And with the principle in mind that "what delights the gods, must delight man," dance was received from the gods as their great gift to man. Probably in the fifth century, the sage Bharata established artistic principles and a system of training—the rigid rules for the gesture language called the *natya shastra*.

Sanscrit has a single word for dance and drama: *natya*. Bharata speaks of *nritya*, the expressive dance which tells a story through pantomime; *nritta*, the pure dance, dance for the sake of dancing giving itself up to intoxicating rhythm; and added to these are *gita*, the song, *vachika*, speech, and *vadya*, the musical accompaniment. There are 24 movements for single hands, 13 for combined hands, 10 arm movements, 5 chest movements, 5 movements each for waist, thigh and hip, there are movements for neck and eyebrows as well as 36 glances to express different feelings. The gesture language of the hands, the *hasta-mudras*, is most beautiful in the complexity of its symbolism. For example, the hand position in which the thumb is bent across the outstretched fingers expresses such things as the beginning of the dance, clouds, woods, bosom, river, night, bravery, clemency, waves, walking on the street, month, year, rainy season, day, and sparkling water.

For centuries the *natya shastra* was the dancers' bible, but it often had to go into hiding during the many invasions of India. The invaders ranged from the Moguls in the north between the twelfth and fifteenth centuries, who suppressed the dance for religious reasons, to the British who outlawed it out of Victorian prudery. But also the temple dancers had contributed to its deterioration. The art long faced obliteration, and the renascence did not come until the turn of the twentieth century.

The dance tradition, nevertheless, was preserved mainly by the *devadasis*, temple dancers, who, particularly in the south—which survived both invasion and stifling restrictions better than the north—kept the *Bharata Natyam* alive. Leaving their families in early youth these servants of the gods dedicated their lives to the temple service and were trained in the art of the temple dance. A comparison with Christian nuns whose lives are also committed to a

*India's Republic Day is celebrated with processions and dancing. (Government of India Tourist Office)*

*Lamas dancing in front of Ghoom monastery, Darjeeling. (Government of India Tourist Office)*

divine purpose illustrates how the austerity of Christianity is pitted against the sensuousness of the Oriental world. When an Indian maiden has achieved perfection in the temple dance, the stone phallus of the god Shiva takes her virginity. And with this act she enters into the possession of the priests, the god's representatives. Thus, in an odd exchange of symbols, the vestal virgin becomes the sacred harlot. This tradition was common from the ancient East to ancient Mexico.

Another trend in most Hindu cultures was the development of the royal court ballet from the chorus of the temple dancers. Once the beloved of the god, the dancer now becomes the concubine of the prince. Since human love was regarded as a symbol of divine love, this is in no way surprising and it certainly did no harm to the magic and

religious ideas of the cult itself. Central to the dance was its retention of a ritual character, and no dance was ever begun without prayer.

Besides *Bharata Natyam*, the style practiced by the *devadasis, Kathakali* is part of the great tradition. Mainly danced on the west coast of South India, it could be called the passion play of Hinduism. Pantomimic in its dramatic presentations, the dance borrows mainly from India's mythological literature, the *Ramayana* and *Mahabharata*. The performers are usually boys and young men who often play the roles of women and wear very elaborate make-up and costuming.

The highly stylized dance of the south differs

*Overleaf: American-born Lalli dances a* padam, *in which she prays to Krishna to aid a love-stricken friend. From left to right the gestures say, "Her suffering is pitiful to see...," "You will come," "Expecting you...," and "Resplendent Lord, come soon and cast her not away." (Herbert Migdoll)*

greatly from the other two classic dances, whose origins lie in northern India. The *Kathak* was first performed by Brahmin priests who illustrated the legends of their faith with dance and pantomime. The Muslim invaders, opposed to god images, suppressed all religious dancing and caused the *Kathak* to become a secular dance. Far more spontaneous than any other Indian dance form, the *Kathak* is a strongly rhythmic dance with exciting turns. The tapping of the feet is accelerated to the accompaniment of the drums. Men dance it in their wide-skirted coats, women mostly in saris. In this northern version, the spectators are seated on all sides; in the southern version it is conceived rather as a stage dance to be watched from one or three sides and at a lower level.

The northeast brought forth the *Manipuri,* which is probably closest to the Far Eastern dance in style and feeling. Some of these dances need great vigor and even acrobatic skill, and others have a modest dignity and the graceful, swaying movements of a folk dance. Rabindranath Tagore chose *Manipuri* as the style best suited for Santinikitan, the first school, which gave a strong impetus to the renascence of Indian dance.

The *guru,* or teacher, considered the incarnation of wisdom, has always been the center of the dance development. This is shown in a letter written by the Indian dancer Lalli:

> "I've settled down in Lucknow for at least six months of study with my former teacher, Vikram Singh. We've had two weeks of lessons— two or three hours each morning, five or six days a week, with two musicians playing continuously. Vikram teaches in the traditional manner, by demonstrating a step, part by part, while I follow, with little or no explanation. When I ask a question, Vikram affects good nature but reminds me that a student's question is a sign of little faith in the teacher. He does not want me to analyze or bring my own ideas to the dance. Whatever I dance is to be his creation totally, his vision. In this way only is the true art passed on. I am fortunate that Vikram is taking great pains to teach me the true art—the nuance, the heart and soul

of each movement—even without benefit of the customary initiation ceremony which binds the Indian pupil and master (by a thread tied around their wrists, which symbolizes the slender thread of mutual trust). Vikram's art is a beautiful blend of strength and grace and there is such a rare quality in his movement that it has the color and brilliance of an image in stained glass. I hope and pray that I will become his vision of the dance, for it is my vision, too."

The *guru* may be one of the most important dancers of his time or he may never take a dance step, but he knows the traditional dance thoroughly and he has the ability to communicate his knowledge. The Indian dancer's art is a way of living, a complete dedication which she will learn in the home of her *guru*. He teaches not only an art but also a philosophy of life.

To sum up, it can be said that each part of the body has its own dance, but that all are parts of one dance, in other words, the body is an assembly of highly disciplined autonomous limbs. To understand the Indian dancer we should try to see Western dancing through his eyes. We would soon find that we are deficient in many ways. There is no life in our faces, heads, hands, fingers and toes. We would miss the strength of angles in our postures and gestures, in the knees, ankles, elbows, and wrists. And we would look in vain for the magic of the eyes, whose changing directions project into time and space the impetus of each movement.

## India's Neighbors

Ceylon was conquered and invaded many times before it achieved its present independence. First there were the Indians and then the Portuguese, Dutch and British. The result has been an enriching

*With intricate hand-gestures and ceremonious poses these Cambodians perform traditional dances formerly seen only at royal courts. (Dominique Darbois)*

of Ceylon's culture without changing its character.

The dances of the Ceylonese show the strong individuality of the people. In vigor and activity, they differ from all other Asiatic dances. The use of acrobatic leaps and turns in air is decidedly not Oriental. The Ceylonese dance has a rare, sophisticated humor that is peculiarly realistic.

The dance renascence in Ceylon dates only from 1947, but its dance culture reaches back—some say a thousand years—to a time when no foreigner had set foot on the island. By that time Ceylon was already the home of the fire-, devil- and mask-dances. From these ancient rites the Ceylonese had learned how to envelope themselves in flames without being burned, and secrets about the nature of demons handed down from father to son, from witch doctor to medicine man.

All their dances are rooted in ancient wisdom and traditional folk humor. Whereas the fire-dancer proves his power over the elements and intimates that he can frighten off the demons, the mask-dancer tries to match the ugliness and ferocity of the demons and force them to be good toward their tormented victims. The mask-dancers also try to heal through clowning and laughter. The gift of the Ceylonese for mimicry is astounding, and since most of their dances tell stories, the dances represent theater at its best, combining realism with ritualism.

The *Devil Dance,* directed against the twenty-seven demons which frighten and harass man, is a virtuoso dance that leads with dazzling whirls and leaps into paroxysms of ecstasy. On the other hand, the *Kandyan* dance which originated about four hundred years ago in the highlands of Kandy is full of grace and elegance, of delicate movements recounting history or legend. So dance-conscious is this island that the dance is a compulsory subject in all schools.

The neighbors to the east of India have kept their own identity, although their style and approach to the dance show the influence of the two giants, India and China. In Burma the dance drama emerged from primitive rites, and during that early period dance rituals were performed by women in a trancelike state in order to invoke the thirty-seven "nats," the gods of pre-Buddhist days. Vestiges of these dances can still be found in Buddhist pageantry, and the gay Burmese is very fond of these. All his folk festivals, both in his animal dances and in the clowning scenes added to the early passion plays on the life of Buddha, show his predilection for mimicry.

Probably some of the strongest influences came from the Siamese in the eighteenth century during the Burmese conquest of Siam. As usually happens, the conquerors brought back with them the culture of the conquered and surrendered some of their own identity in the process. In this case, Burmese art succumbed to the Siamese dancing and acting tradition which, although it did not develop quite as complexly as the Hindu gesture language, was nevertheless very rigid.

Dancing remained the most popular art form in Burma and despite the fact that the professional dancers were mostly men, their technique was based on those early Burmese "maenads," the god-inspired, mad women, who performed the dance to the nats. This tradition was so strong that it survives to this day in the dance of the "posture-girls," who perform in what we could call the curtain-raisers to all theatrical events. The characteristics of the Burmese dance are an out-curving backbone and bent knees. The dancers' faces are usually smiling. The hands are not too restricted by set rules and poses, but their language is of the greatest subtlety.

Unlike the dance drama of Siam and Cambodia, which took wholeheartedly to the *Ramayana* and the *Mahabharata,* the Burmese is not based on the two great Indian epics. In Indo-China, the cultural influences of India and China met and merged; the Hindu influence is predominant in the dances, while the Far East has contributed mainly to the costum-

*A dance lesson in Bali. (Dominique Darbois)*
*Overleaf: Graceful dancing girls of Bali execute the formal steps and gestures of a centuries-old tradition. (Ernst Haas)*

ing of the dancers. The pointed caps on the shoulders give the dancer a pagoda-like shape. The costumes are bedecked with gems and rich golden embroidery. As in Burma, masks are rarely worn except by the villains of the dance dramas. In both countries dancing was under the control of the princely courts for many centuries. The dancers were housed and educated in the royal palaces, and the ballets were performed in the palace itself or with the temple as a background.

The Siamese underline action in their dances far more than the Cambodians, who are more descriptive in their approach. The dances of the Cambodians are unforgettable because of their extreme delicacy, their dreamlike quality and the unique hand gestures. As with most Eastern dancers, the body line is rigid and there are the customary bent knees and up-pointing toes. But the arms, hands and fingers of the Cambodians are among the most subtle dance contortions known to us. The arms and fingers of the dancers are methodically wrenched out of joint. Part of their training consists of bending each other's fingers backward while seated by twos in the practice room. They force back each other's arms which are naturally loose-jointed, until their elbows give way to a backward arm position of forty degrees. Through such exercises the bone sockets are widened and the ligaments expanded. Every joint of the body undergoes a similar training in distortion. The result is a convulsive dance which gives these dancers a marionettelike but resilient and poetic movement. Rainer Maria Rilke succeeded best in translating into verbal imagery the visual magic of these dancers:

> There they were, these gracile little dancers, like metamorphosed gazelles. Their long, slender arms as if in one piece drawn through the shoulders, through the slender and yet sturdy torso (with the full slenderness of Buddha pictures), arms thinly hammered into one piece down to the wrists from which the hands emerged like players, agile and independent in their actions. And what hands! Buddha hands knowing how to sleep, how to lie down easily, finger next to finger, to rest for centuries on laps, with the palm upward or standing straight up from the joint, demanding quiet ceaselessly. Then imagine these hands awake! The fingers spread apart, open like rays, or turned inward like the petals of a Jericho rose; these fingers enraptured and happy or alive with anxiety at the very end of the long arms—fingers dancing. And the entire body alerted to keep the ultimate of this dance suspended in the air, in the atmosphere of the body itself, in the richness of the Oriental world.

## The Islands: Art as a Part of Life

For the Javanese, dance is as serious and integral a part of life as churchgoing is to the devout Westerner. The most famous dance drama, *Wayang Wong*, is one of the most finished theater pieces ever created, with a rigidly prescribed code of movements and expressions. It has never forgotten its ritualistic past, and in the spiritual exaltation with which it is performed and watched the actor and spectator become one. The audience is there not to be entertained but to be enlightened, to be imbued with the elation of worship.

Before the Hindu invasion in the second century A.D., the Javanese believed in ancestor worship and had magic rituals, with primitive dance movements executed by masked actors. When the Hindus brought the shadow play *Chaya-Nataka* with them, it found an immediate response and has remained the most popular theatrical form in Java. First, the figures were cut out of palm leaves. Then, marionettes made of leather were used in profile only, and from them developed wooden marionettes. The *dalang*, as the operator of the puppets is called, chants the stories and directs the musicians. Many believe that the dalang is only a modern version of the shaman's rites, whose purpose is to summon the spirits. Out of all this evolved the *Topeng Dalang*, in which the operator speaks and the masked actor dances. All these forms have helped create the *Wayang Wong*.

While the common people had their puppet plays, the *Wayang Wong* was the exclusive property

*"Singkil," as executed by members of the Bayanihan Philippine Dance Company. (Courtesy Bill Doll)*

of the royal house. The dances were strongly influenced by the marionette, as reflected in the dancer's rigid torso and the little staccato movements of the knees and elbows that are occasionally brought into play. But, in the main, the Javanese dance has become famous for its slow movements and for a swaying and a spiraling rhythmic surge, that creates a soothing quality. The gamelan, an orchestra of tuned percussion instruments adds to the mesmerizing effect.

The characters are distinguished by five different styles of dancing. The lyric hero is noble and calm; the dramatic hero embodies strength; the technique of the giants and demons is broader, more strongly accentuated. Only the clowns are allowed to improvise. The dance of the women is very soft and feminine.

Nearly four hundred years ago when Islam began to make itself felt on Java and tried to suppress the dance theater, many of Java's traditions were lost. As with so much of the Oriental dance, the Javanese renascence started at the beginning of this century when a systematic search for abandoned customs reclaimed this old dance culture from oblivion. No

63

longer the monopoly of princes and their courts, it is now being enjoyed by all the people.

The Balinese in their naiveté and innocent gaiety, have never cut themselves off from the dance, and it continues to play an important role in their daily life. Just as Balinese music is impetuous and noisy in contrast to the soft tranquil Javanese music, so their dancing is strong, vigorous and compelling. One would think that dancing, as an integral part of their lives, would be a communal affair. But it is essentially a dance for exhibition, necessitating rigorous training for a mastery of the quick and difficult movements. Especially in the most famous dance, the *Legong,* the whole body seems to be in movement, from eyebrows and neck to wrists and fingers, from shoulders and elbows to knees and feet. Although the Balinese dance is said to derive from Indra, the Hindu god of the heavens, it can be traced back to the primitive rituals of the people. The dances are accompanied by gamelans, in which xylophones for melody and gongs for metrical accent hold the central position.

The *Legong* is a pantomime dance performed by two young girls dressed in rich and flowery garments set off by beautiful headdresses and fans. (The closer one comes to the Far East, the greater the part the fan plays.) Only in recent days has a modernized version of the *Legong,* the *Djoged,* become more of a communal affair. In the *Djoged* a girl dances in the *Legong* style and boys from the audience join her. In the traditional repertoire is the *Kebiyar,* a modern and intensely virile form of the *Legong* which is executed mostly in a sitting position.

No islands in the Pacific show more clearly than do the Philippines the influences of foreign conquest on their dance. Here the earliest settlers emigrated from China and later were joined by people from India and the Arab countries bringing an Islamic infiltration. In the sixteenth century, the Spanish conquistadors exerted their influence, and Christianity began to put its stamp on the Filipinos.

The mountain tribes had magic dances in which a priestess sacrificed a pig to the ancestral spirits and invoked their power to give the tribe brave head-hunters. This feast, called *canyao,* as well as the victory celebration which followed the head-hunting expedition, was accompanied by dances that imitated animal movements. Dancing was the Filipino's natural expression of joy at weddings and births, at planting and harvesting.

Strongly akin to Hindu-Arabic movement patterns, the Mohammedan dances are characterized by their emphasis on the torso, by vivid facial expression, by inner intensity and mystic grace, by the flowing movements of the arms. All-pervading is a genuine playfulness. A famous dance of the Muslim princesses, the *Singkil,* tests the dancer's agility and grace as she dances between two pairs of bamboo poles which are clapped together in syncopated and ever-accelerating rhythm.

It is difficult to say whether the Filipinos adapted many of the dance steps of the Spaniards, or whether the latter modified those of the natives. In this happy blending of two cultures, the warm climate helped the Filipinos to slow down many of the European steps such as the polka, the rigadoon and the waltz.

In the Philippines, too, a renaissance began in the 1920's and with the foundation of the Bayanihan company ("Bayanihan" is the Tagalog word for the ancient custom of working together), the folk dance of the Filipinos was raised to a theatrical level marked by a spectacular simplicity. Indigenous props, such as bamboo poles clapped together without catching the dancing feet, and drinking glasses or lighted oil lamps balanced on the dancers' heads, were used. But these props have their roots in folklore and they are entertaining because the dancing itself has atmosphere, rhythm and the native innocence of the people, lost in the joy of movement.

This joy of feeling the human body in motion to the muted thud of drums—which sounds like a distant echo of the pounding of breaking waves—

*The dance of Muslim dervishes, now outlawed but still performed, may lead to a trance and is an expression of religious devotion. (The Metropolitan Museum of Art)*

is symbolized in Hawaii's hula. In fact, hula is the whole body praying and laughing.

The night club hula, or what is shown as a tourist attraction, is a poor facsimile of what it once was—the expression of primitive beauty wrapped in joy, a part of Polynesian folklore. The hula began as a dance of worship, as a means of identification with the forces of nature. Invoking the gods with sensuous contortions of the entire body, with the weaving of the arms and the rippling play of the muscles, the people besought fertility. In the early days the dancers were priestesses. With the advent of the white man, beginning with Captain Cook, who was followed by the missionaries, the hula was outlawed, but not forgotten.

Whether it was to the rhythmically alluring beat of the drum or to Christian hymns, the Hawaiians could not help dancing. The solemnity of hymnal music was clandestinely changed to a gayer tempo in which the swaying hips of the hula dancer felt more at home. Later in the nineteenth century, the Hawaiians waltzed with the languor of the Oriental on a hot night. In their naive gaiety, these people could neither understand the ambitious Japanese nor the practical white man. To both they have lost their innocence but not their joy in living, of which the hula is like a remembrance of things past.

## China: Technique and Imagination

The scholarly actor-dancer Dr. Mei Lan-fang has made painstaking studies to piece out our fragmentary knowledge of the classic Chinese dance. In spite of the erudition and artistry of this one man who gave the long-dead Chinese dance new life, there can be no doubt that what is now known and danced in the classic style is only a very small part of a once great repertoire of gestures and steps.

We know of the ecstatic rain dances of the primitive Chinese. Religious ecstasy was also a component of the circle dances through which they formed a tie between the living and the dead as part of their ancestor worship. It is said that Yü, the god

of fertility, hopped ecstatically on one leg, but it is difficult to determine whether the limping dance had its beginning in ancient China or was adopted from other mythologies in which the concept of the limping god appears, symbolizing growth from initial weakness.

There was no clear division between dance, drama and opera as the Chinese theatrical arts developed. Both opera and drama are most stylized forms, and singing, music and movement make equal demands on the performer's skill. Since almost no scenery and only such props as a chair or a table, a fan, an umbrella, a whip and a pole are used, movement and gestures are all-important. On the other hand, the most is made of the symbolic significance of these props. Thus, a candle in an outstretched hand indicates utter darkness, although the stage is brightly lighted; a cup or a pitcher may lead to the most astounding acrobatics (Chinese dancers are the world's best jugglers and acrobats); and pheasant feathers or fans require a special technique to convey a great variety of meanings.

Each character type has its own hand postures and movement pattern. The complex symbolism also involves fingers and feet, with the technique of the "rippling water sleeves"—three feet of white silk sewn into the *mang*, or *Teih-tzu*, sleeve—representing the most delicate and difficult movements in the history of the dance.

When completely understood, the gesture language is most eloquent. The shades of expression are endless. There are seven different female types, each with her own gestures and traditional costume. The straightness of the back and the tiny, almost invisible steps are arresting, and the head is always very expressive, while being completely unobtrusive.

In the twentieth century it is mainly the *Peking Opera* which has developed to artistic perfection. The demands it makes on the performer to be actor, singer, dancer and acrobat are extraordinary. The plots either deal with a brave general, wise emperor or loyal citizen overcoming the enemy or they recreate simple situations. For instance, an innkeeper mistakes a guest at his inn for an enemy. He

*Dancers of the Peking Opera in one of their legendary dance-dramas. (Serge Lido)*

enters the man's room at night and the illusion of their sparring in a pitch-dark room is created on a brightly lit stage. Or a girl on one side of a lake wants to be rowed over to the other side. The ferryman approaches her, she steps into the rocking boat, he rows her across, and helps her out of the boat. All this is done without props but with the most minutely worked out gestures and movements. The illusion of reality emerges from the convincing performance of the two actors. The world of make-believe triumphs over its real counterpart.

## Korea: Subtlety and Playfulness

Most mountain people hold to their traditions, and the Koreans are no exception. In spite of civil wars and conquest by their neighbors, they keep their old dances alive, so that some of them can be traced back to a millennium before Christ. While Buddhism and, later, Confucianism became the official religions, earlier Taoist beliefs and even shamanism never quite died out. Their influence is seen in the many fairies, demons and animal ghosts depicted in Korean dances. The workings of magic can also be seen in *The Farmers' Dance* as the ground is beaten to drive the evil spirits into it: or when with high leaps the dancers invoke the good spirits to make their plants grow tall. Even more vigorous jumping movements are part of *The Sorceress Dance*, a folk version of the dances of the medicine man—which supposedly help the medium to invoke the spirits.

The court dances, characterized by elegant movements, were once performed for the women of the royal household, which may account for the graceful restraint of the dancers and the tasteful color combinations of their costumes. Prince Hyomong, one of the last of the Yi dynasty (which ruled until the Japanese annexation in 1910) excelled as a choreographer and composer and is credited with many dance creations. *A Nightingale Singing in the Springtime*, one of the purest examples of subtle

67

formality and measured elegance, is attributed to him, although chronicles indicate that it was known much earlier. A solo dancer represents the Nightingale, an extremely exacting role in which the slow movements of arms and feet as well as the slightest movement of a finger has great significance.

The crane as a sacred bird led to another favorite court dance that became part of the Korean tradition. Basically, *Hahk-Mu, The Crane Dance,* is a miracle play in which two dancers in subtly stylized movements represent cranes attracted to two lotus flowers. They peck at the flower until the petals open and two angels, originally danced by children, emerge and engage the cranes in a dance of playfulness and gentle joy.

*The Nine Drums Dance* is the most popular and spectacular dance of the Korean people. Its origin is the Buddhist *Monk Dance* in which a dancer in a monk's robe rises as if from meditation, lowers his long sleeves as if his faith were shaken and starts beating a drum. Then a solo dancer beats out his syncopated rhythms as he moves among nine drums.

## Japan: No and Kabuki

Not until the end of World War II were the Japanese court dances seen outside the Imperial Palace. The *Bugaku,* which came from India via Tibet, China and Korea to Japan, became the most popular form of entertainment at the royal court. It was preceded by the *Kagura,* the oldest known dance, which was brought from China during the seventh century. A dance related to Japan's sun goddess, the *Kagura* was followed by another import, the *Gigaku,* a dance with masks, which found a place in the Buddhist ritual.

A more acrobatic form of the stately Bugaku was the *Dengaku,* which appealed to the general public for the first time and made the dance a popular medium of entertainment. Next in line was the *Sarugaku,* the "monkey dance," which relied heavily on mimicry. Originating in the ancient Shinto and Buddhist festivals, the *Sarugaku* was the first native

dance of Japan. The importance of this rather comic dance lies in the fact that it played the same role in Japanese culture as did the dancing during the Dionysian festivals of ancient Greece. In the fifteenth century it gave birth to the Japanese drama called *No* or *Noh*—with the difference that the *No* drama never divorced itself from the dance. On the contrary, this highly symbolic and stylized theater precedes the dancing with dialogue and singing that give the dramatic situation, and then uses the dance as the climactic form of expression.

The *No* drama, a very esoteric form even for educated Japanese, puts its emphasis on a finished performance. The timing of precise movements and the exact expressiveness of the miming are of the utmost importance. The *No* drama is performed on a platform roughly twenty feet square, supported by four pillars, open on three sides and covered by a roof. Chorus and musicians have their places at the right and at the back of the stage. The painting of a tree on a wall represents pine trees near the shrines.

The five basic positions used in the *No* drama are: an erect stance and movement to the left, right, forward and backward. The erect stance is the primary position and from it the actor unfolds his own variations. The symbolism is further accentuated by the wearing of wooden masks which, like the elaborate costumes, have a specific meaning.

Just as comedy and the satyr play developed from the Dionysian revels to furnish comic relief in Greek drama, the *Kyogen,* a broadly played one-act farce, served to amuse the spectators of the *No* dramas. It emerged from the *Dengaku,* or "rustic music," dance. These comic interludes—there are still 280 *Kyogen* extant while only 250 *No* plays have come down to us—were badly needed not only to relieve the tension and the demands made on the audience's imagination, but also to allow time for the actors to change their elaborate costumes.

There has always been a variety of folk dances in

*Juvenile Kabuki actors rehearsing in an 1801 print by Shuntei. (Honolulu Academy of Arts)*

68

Japan: the rice-planting and fishermen's dances, the famous lion dance and such temple dances as the *Bon Odori,* in which the people give vent to their feelings during religious holidays. But until the seventeenth century there was no popular theater for the unintellectual, entertainment-hungry audience. This gap was filled by the *Kabuki,* a vulgarized offshoot of *No.* O-Kuni, ritual dancer of the Shinto shrine of Izumo, is credited with having given birth to the *Kabuki.* In 1596—so the legend has it—she gave a dance recital on the dry bed of the Kamo River in Kyoto and added her own variations to the simple Shinto-Buddhist dances. To collect money

*In a Kabuki scene by Kayonaga, the hero Sukeroku—the Japanese Robin Hood—strikes a defiant attitude against corrupt authority. (Honolulu Academy of Arts)*

for reparing the Shinto shrine, she went, so to speak, on a dance recital tour, but when at last she arrived at Kyoto, her desire to dance was stronger than her urge to serve the shrine. She was joined by her lover, Nagoya Sansaburo, who combined her simple religious dances with a rather elaborate *Kyogen* and gradually reduced the religious elements in their dances. When one day O-Kuni dared to appear in the guise of a Japanese warrior, Sansaburo gave her performance the title, *Kabuki.** A description of O-Kuni by the playwright Tamenaga Icho reveals that "she was beautiful, she was skilled in calligraphy—an important female accomplishment— had a sympathetic nature, love for flowers and the moon, and that a snowy evening or a maple scene in the autumn inspired her to poetry."

There are four major variations of *Kabuki* which of course is not all dance and subsequently developed other dramatic forms: (1) The *Kyogen Zyoruri* is a dance with dramatic content; (2) *The Dance from the No Drama,* a variety of dances whose material is largely taken from the No drama, but given a greater range of freedom (the wooden masks of the *No* plays gave way to a bizarre make-up in the *Kabuki* dances); (3) The so-called *Transfiguration Dances,* a combination of various dances with little story or plot, but characterized by a variety of impersonations, often with rapid transformations, and (4) The comic dance, *Zyoruri,* whose chief purpose was to arouse laughter. This group also contains some dramatic dances from the *No,* but their presentations are combined with various comic features, humorous situations and actions and are spiced with witticisms and puns.

In the beginning the *Kabuki* theater employed mostly young and very handsome youths. It was only later that the actors impersonating both male and female figures, were of an adult age and, no longer being able to rely on their physical charms, had to hold their audience's attention by skill alone. The basic principle of Japanese dancing is a natural line movement with no straining for form. There

* The word, *Kabuki,* stands for: "Ka"—song, "bu"—dance, "ki"—technique.

was a strong emphasis on posture, with a straight line running from the neck to the heels and the line of the shoulders and feet diagonally placed toward the audience for support of the dancer. The performer also employed the *Aragota*, the technique of exaggeration, which gave the power of emphasis.

With the *Kabuki* limited to male dancers, the female dancers entertain at banquets with music and dancing. These professional girls, known as the *Geisya* dancers or *Geishas*, receive their training from the masters in the great dancing schools of Japan. Their dances are usually derived from the *Kabuki* and performed without stage setting or costuming. Twice a year, however, the *Geisyas* perform on a stage with dress and make-up like any other Kabuki dancer. Of their dances, the *Spring Dance* has become popular and the oldest of them is called *Miyako Odori*, known as the *Cherry Dance*.

The Japanese have shown considerable interest in the dancing of Western man. The first introduction of ballet technique can be traced back to 1912, when a Musical Comedy Department was opened at the Imperial Theater in Tokyo. The department soon closed again, but some of its students went to America and France and brought back with them a better Western technique and renewed enthusiasm. Also, for more popular consumption, a combination of the ballet and the *Kabuki* dance resulted in the *Kabuki Revue* which, with a touch of both styles, turned out to be an entertaining girl show.

After the Second World War the modern expressive dance found many admirers among the Japanese. Many of their dancers have studied the Martha Graham technique in New York and some American teachers have been invited to spread the gospel of the modern dance in Japan's major cities. A young Japanese choreographer approached the story of *Rashomon* in the modern dance idiom, and the result was a strange fusion of two different worlds. Subject matter and technique remained alien to each other and succeeded only in making the contrasts of two ways of life even sharper. The Japanese will have to create new ideas for the adopted medium of expression, ideas born of their

*Japanese ivory sculpture of a mythical angel dancer. (Collection Ruth Schneidman)*

contemporary life. For theirs is a world of fine sensibilities in which the fleeting touch of a paint brush or the slightest movement of a fan can conjure up images for which Western man needs many more means of expression.

In the East the art of the dance functions in a sphere of tradition-bound enchantment. It tries to wrap up the essence of things in a conventional language of gestures. Its significance is hidden in its symbolism. Its aesthetic effect and beauty lie beyond the obvious. It is a magic world to which few Western men have the key. All they can do is look through the keyhole and catch glimpses of its incomparable beauty.

# 5  *Folklore and Theater*

The way of all dancing seems to lead from folk dancing to ethnological as well as to ballroom dancing, and all three have found their way in modified forms onto the stage. Dancing is deeply rooted in the people, in their folklore, their national peculiarities and racial temperament. To renew their artistic strength and to find the most effective ideas, movement patterns and images, choreographers have returned to these roots time and again.

Fokine used the English *Morris Dance* in his ballet, *Don Juan;* the Italian *tarantella* was incorporated by Bournonville in *Napoli;* we find gypsy dances in Leonide Massine's *Aleko,* and Spanish dancing in Ivanov's and Petipa's *Swan Lake;* Balanchine created a long ballet consisting only of waltzes in his *Liebeslieder Walzer;* Agnes de Mille's work is unthinkable without its folkloristic material, or Jerome Robbins' without the jazz influence. When one considers the polonaise, the polka, the fandango or bolero, the Basque or Negro dances, the minuet or quadrille as basic material for ballet creations, the list becomes endless.

We must accept the concept of a basic dance as something deeply embedded in the needs of man. It began with the magic dances of primitive man, and many popular folk dances through the ages show their close relationship to or dependence upon man's beginnings. Even what has come to be known as the "modern" dance, one of the artistic expressions of our time, has returned to the principles of the basic dance, however intellectualized and psychologized it may appear to us.

Every epoch in history and every part of this globe developed its own dance images and idioms

*Left: A member of the Moiseyev Dance Company.
(Hurok)    Above: The stately* allemande *is caricatured
in a 1772 English engraving. (Courtesy of the Dance
Collection, New York Public Library)*

through which the people expressed themselves.
Dances have their sociological and historic connotations. They often foreshadow a new cultural trend.
As soon as a dance reflects its age, the folk dance
material has by then gone through a process of
refinement. The *basse dance,* which was called the
"queen of all dances" during the Renaissance, was
a quiet, gliding dance of which the *pavan* became the
favorite form in the sixteenth and seventeenth centuries. It was then the perfect expression of the
dignity and form-fulfilled somberness with which
the new feudal lords opened their balls and was in
keeping both with their etiquette and the rich,
heavy materials of the ladies' costumes. There is
little known about the origin of the *basse dance,* but
many scholars believe that it dates from the *estampie*
of an earlier century. Etymologically, the name
seems to indicate that it was once danced with
stamping feet and only later, in the fourteenth
century, turned to a more quiet pace.

Through the centuries, we will find that dances
undergo a similar process. An example of how
dances become "tamed" is the *saraband.* Whether
its origin is Arabic-Moorish or Persian, it came to
the European courts through Spain. At an early
period of its existence it was considered wild and
vile, highlighted by "pantomime of unparalleled
suggestiveness." Legislation had to be passed against
it in Spain where the sentence for dancing the
*saraband* was six years' service in the galleys for boys
and exile for girls. Ben Jonson still exclaims: "How
they are tickl'd with a light ayre! The bawdy

73

*Vignettes showing variations of the* mazurka. *(Courtesy of the Dance Collection, New York Public Library)*

Saraband!" When Spanish influence grew all over Europe during the seventeenth century, this dance found many friends at the court of Louis XIII. There, however, it had little in common with its original form.

For more than 150 years, the *minuet* was the social dance most expressive of its age. But it too went through many changes. Whether we want to trace it to the *courante* of the sixteenth century, or the *branle of Poitou*, it began as a gay fast dance. When it was introduced at the court of Louis XIV, it became "a dance of only moderate gayety and tempo," according to Louis Horst in his study, *Pre-Classic Dance Forms*. In the late Baroque and Rococo periods, it had all the artificiality of the time, becoming more and more static, unemotional and totally mannered: a mirror image of the decline at the French court and of that graceful emptiness ruling the people. Voltaire ridiculed the *minuet* when he spoke about the metaphysic philosophers and compared them to dancers "who, most elegantly adorned, bow a few times, mince daintily across the room exhibiting all their charms, move without

progressing a single step, and end up on the very spot from where they started...."

Towards the second half of the eighteenth century, the world was bored with the shallowness and affectation of the minuet and turned to the *waltz*. For decades this dance had been known in the mountain regions of southern Germany and in Austria as the *weller* or *spinner*. There was a refreshing, natural spirit in this fast, sliding peasant dance which had nothing of a superficial politeness. The waltz, it was said, helped at least as much as Voltaire and Beaumarchais to undermine the slowly fading spirit of a feudal society.

The waltz became the craze of the latter part of the eighteenth century and is still with us to this very day. In the beginning, it was considered vulgar and lewd as were so many other dances in their crude form while still in the process of breaking from the pleasant routine of the past. This turning dance with its intoxicating rhythm, executed in enrapturing closeness of the dancing couples, was a gyration into oblivion, a joyful, almost ecstatic expression which later became an escape from reality. At its beginnings, however, the emphasis on the first beat contained the hidden connotation of challenge, of the assertion of the ego. The waltz outlived the quadrille and cancan, both children of the

minuet, and it went through many metamorphoses —such as the skipping French waltz or the slow, gliding Boston—but it has never changed its true face as one of the most symbolic expressions of the bourgeoisie. Balanchine's *Liebeslieder Walzer* recreates the nineteenth-century bourgeois atmosphere.

Whatever dance we may choose as an example, the trend of the development from folk to social to theater dance remains the same. Ballroom dancing, as we know it now, was born with the first dancing masters of the Renaissance who arranged the entertainments for the self-styled dukes and princes. And with their desire to move the entertainment from the hall of their palaces to a better defined area, the ballet theater came into being. The former event took place at the very beginning of the Renaissance, the latter, at its climactic end. But, while all this happened, the common people continued to enjoy their folk dances.

The strength of folk dancing lies in the participation of the individual who gains a sense of oneness with the many. This collective feeling goes beyond the mere joy of moving within a group. It goes back to the ritual dances of primitive man. It is through the reassurance of belonging to a certain group or community that men attain their collective identity.

Originally peasant or country dances, they have since conquered the cities, too. But folk dancing, in spite of and because of its national and racial characteristics, has universal appeal. Dance steps know no barriers and with all their differences dictated by their respective heritages, they have many things in common. Like human beings, they are far more interrelated than they may be willing to admit. Some of the variations have resulted from purely geographical differences. Thus, the dances of people living in the mountains all over the world are more closely related to one another than those of the people in the lowlands, although they may belong to one and the same country. And, all of them are united by the oneness of emotional joy in moving together.

We must not forget that all dance steps emerge from the same physical mechanism, from such basic locomotor movements as the walk, run, hop, skip, slide, gallop, or leap. Their combinations wedded to a certain rhythm have become traditional steps: the two-step, polka, waltz, or mazurka.

Folk dances come into being without the influence of any one choreographer and merely for the pleasure of those who execute them. They show certain characteristics of the environment and peculiarities of a racial temperament. In some instances,

*The* Spring Symphony *danced by the Czech Ballet Company. (Czechopress: Black Star)*

it may be difficult to draw an exact line between folk and ethnological dances, but the latter have developed a distinct traditional style, a technical terminology and a clearly defined school of instruction. No longer done as a communal experience, they have become art dances executed for the enjoyment and edification of spectators. The ethnological dance was a folk dance first before it became the art expression of a race. Most of the Eastern dances have grown from popular dances into art forms.

Although the will of a people fashions the ethnological dance, the will is expressed by trained artists and through the influence of teachers who act as the molders of talent and the guardians of tradition. While primitive or folk dancing is by its nature repetitious, to a great extent unconscious and limited in scope, the theater dance is selective, conscious and unlimited in its range of expression.

## Spanish Dance: The Art of Passion

The Spanish dance is a good example of an ethnological theater dance fashioned by traditional

style which has still retained all the earmarks of its folkloristic base. Since it has come of age as an exciting theater art, it has enjoyed tremendous popularity all over the world. It could be said that after the First World War, the South American dancer, La Argentina, conquered the theater for the Spanish dance, and it was said by the great Russian-born French critic André Levinson: "She alone has revived and developed an art form too long debased by the gypsies of the music hall." But we could also say that it antedates all theater dances in Europe since we know of Spanish dancing during the Golden Age of Hellenic supremacy in the fifth century before Christ, and at the time when the

Romans had established their empire, "las Andaluces delicias"—those dancing girls from Cadiz—were already touring the then-known world. With the invasion of the southern parts of Spain by the Moors, the province Andalusia became the nerve center of the Spanish dance. Music and dance were part of the social entertainment in the caliph's palace. When Spain became reunited and culturally important again under Ferdinand and Isabella, the dancer entered the theater with the help of the drama. Even the Church, particularly in Sevilla and Toledo, opened its door to the dance and—this is mentioned as an ironic twist of history—Jewish dancing masters were quite active before the

Inquisition. Curt Sachs, in his *World History of the Dance*, tells us that as early as 1313, Rabbi Hacen ben Salomo taught the Christians to perform a choral dance around the altar of St. Bartholomew in Zaragoza.

The need for emotional relief through dancing has always been a driving force in the Spanish dance. The Spaniards were the great and daring navigators of that time and, from their discovery of other hemispheres, they brought to Europe dances from America and India. Some of the influences can even be traced back to the Phoenicians. The *fandango* is related to the *Reinos de las Indias* of the American Indians and turned into a rage on Spanish soil, especially during the late seventeenth and the eighteenth century. Even Mozart asks for a fandango in *The Marriage of Figaro* in 1786, although he visualized this courtship dance in triple time in a somewhat tamed form. But in 1767, Casanova, strongly impressed by the fandango when he saw it danced in Madrid, records in his *Memoirs*:

> Each couple, man and woman, never move more than three steps as they click their castanets with the music of the orchestra. They take a thousand attitudes, make a thousand gestures so lascivious that nothing can compare with them. This dance is the expression of love from beginning to end, from the sigh of desire to the ecstasy of enjoyment. It seemed to me impossible that after such a dance the girl could refuse anything to her partner.

By the end of the eighteenth century, the fandango was replaced by the *bolero*—the dancer, Sebastian Cerezo, is usually credited with having introduced it—which no longer had the intense suggestiveness of the fandango. Retained, however, was the innuendo of the sex game, with the two dancers challenging each other: the woman slipping away, approaching and then escaping again. The *bolero* gained in importance when, in the middle of the nineteenth century, Théophile Gautier, after a visit to Spain, helped spread its fame with his enthusiastic endorsement for this basically romantic dance.

A substantial part of Spanish dancing is a the-

*A gouache by Marc Chagall depicts a Spanish dancer. (Gemeente Musea, Amsterdam: Permission* A.D.A.G.P. *1966 by* F.R.R. *Inc.) Right: José Greco and partner do a flamenco dance. (Benedict Fernandez: Nancy Palmer Agency)*

atricalization of the regional dances. When Argentinita continued La Argentina's work to give the Spanish dance theatrical stature (organizing in 1932, in collaboration with the poet Garcia Lorca, the Madrid Ballet), she became famous for her productions of traditionally communal dances. There is the *jota* of Aragon, the *seguidillas* of Castile, the *sevillanas* of Andalusia and many more which found their way onto the stage.

In the eighteenth century, the so-called "school dances" borrowed the refined intricacies of the French ballet and applied them to certain routines of folk dances which, in this way, became theatricalized. The *bolero* is a good example in which

one of the steps, the "cuarta," is identical with the *entrechat quatre* of the classic ballet while the sudden stops of the *jota* are reminiscent of regional folk material. A series of dances went through this process of refinement and during the earlier part of the nineteenth century, a great many dances were thus "invented" which also used the heel work of the gypsies.

Goya painted such groups of lighthearted gypsy dancers who would sit in a semicircle by the wayside, one or two of them playing guitars and singing. One by one, the gypsies would rise and dance, clapping hands and thighs, snapping fingers instead of castanets, and stamping their heels in an intoxicating rhythm. Spanish dancing is often erroneously equated with the *flamenco* of the gypsies in southern Spain. The gypsies consider themselves the descendants of the Moors and their name is derived from the idea that gypsies came from a certain "Little Egypt." But these nomadic people, who are usually handsome, are at least partially of East Indian origin as seen by some of their typical names, such as Maya or Amaya, which are Sanscrit.

A great number of these gypsies live in Spain, with headquarters in Granada and Sevilla. The Granada gypsy calls himself *gitano* and lives in mountain holes in the Sacro Monte; the Sevillian gypsy lives in clean adobe houses and is more often referred to as *flamenco*. This word may go back to the Flemish people, the Fleming, whose name, in turn, is related to *fleme*—to banish, to drive away. The Spanish have another explanation for calling the gypsy "flamenco." They looked down on the Flemish people as crude and ill-bred at the time of the Spanish occupation of the northern part of Europe during the fifteenth century and, in a bowdlerized form, this word had come to mean any rowdy, ill-bred person. It is understandable that this epithet should be applied to this carefree, wilful, traditionally independent group.

The gypsies probably did not bring the *baile flamenco* with them to Spain; rather, this dance has developed elements of Moorish influence into which were mixed their own rebellious spirit and traditional feelings, best expressed by their uncanny sense of rhythm. One of its major sources is the strongly Oriental sounding *cante* which dates back to the pre-Spanish days of the gypsies. This inimitably rhythmic singing sets the mood for the flamenco, supported by guitar playing, called *toque*. The guitar is certainly associated with Spanish folklore. The flamenco singer and guitarist inspire the dancer, but must also adjust to him since the baile, the flamenco dance, is characterized by the freedom of its form and by its improvisational, spontaneous performance. Each dancer develops his own style based on the fundamental technique. The heel work is its most dominant feature. With the striking of the half-toe, the heel and the full sole, the flamenco dancer conjures up an endless variety of tone and rhythmic combinations. But also, the carriage of head and torso as much as the movement of the arms and fingers are basic to the projection which is unequaled by any other dance in its emotional fire and fury. The complete harmony between the upper part of the body with the position and action of feet and legs is the key to flamenco's subtle nuances. Certain rhythmic forms of flamenco dances are: *alegrias, bulerias, farruca, tango, zambra,* and *zapateado*. Flamenco's mystery lies in the style of delivery, but the most theatrical impact is derived from the *zapateado*, the footwork, to which Cervantes already referred as "the shoe-sole beater" and whose close relative is the *Schuhplattler,* mainly danced by people in central European mountain regions.

Castanets are often used to heighten the effect of Spanish dancing. However, many male gypsies consider castanets effeminate. This tiny percussion instrument whose origin is undoubtedly in Asia Minor—although it was also used by the ancient Greeks and Egyptians—has come to be identified as being part of the Spanish dance. It is now often used by the female dancer, and it is surprising how varied the nuances are and how intricate its musical range is when played to artistic perfection.

In general, it can be said that Spanish dancing is a mixture of Eastern and Western dance with a dash of exoticism added for good rhythmic measure. It is

Calaucan, *choreographed by Patricio Bunster of The Chilean Ballet, creates the impression of a folkloric dance without using a single Indian dance movement. (Department Fotografico de la Universedad de Chile)*

not dancing with the feet alone; even the fiery zapateado uses the stamping or striking of the floor as a point of departure to electrify the legs, which, in turn, set the whole body on fire. The Spanish dance is the most physical expression of man's emotion. It is, whether danced with utmost abandon, fast and forceful to the point of animalistic nakedness, or with the restraint of tender passion, the epitome of sensuality.

There are several aspects of Spanish dance which overlap and manifest the essence of folk as well as theatrical dancing. Although it is danced to fasci-nate and excite the spectator kinetically, it can apparently accomplish this only through self-excitation. By dancing himself or herself into a state of frenzy, the dancer enables the audience to feel the ecstatic experience vicariously. The specific vocabulary of the flamenco dance best lends itself to such suggestive power. The dancer's hips move from a hardly perceptible rotation, slowly lighting the flame of her feelings to the most lascivious readiness. Her shoulders and head can spell coldness and rejection while her hands, turning and twisting, beckon and promise. The male dancer is more than a match to her luring vitality. There is hardly any other male dancer who can show pride and dejec-tion, or the awareness of his virility and violent passion, as intensely as the Spanish dancer. The symbolic power in all its naked suggestiveness, how-ever, is rarely crude or offensive because the dance, forced into a strict, stylistic frame, is protected by

81

*Above and Right: The Deer Dance, part of a hunting rite, imitates faithfully the movements of the hunted animal. Still danced by the Yaquis of Sonora, it is one of the rare examples of practiced imitative magic, here done by the Ballet Folklorico de Mexico. (Hurok)*

conventions which do not permit indecent gestures. One could also say that the implications of the natural demands of nature and the play on the emotional tit-for-tat are so unashamedly admitted and so frankly displayed that their obviousness disarms the skeptic. The Spanish dance restores the

lost innocence to the natural expressiveness of the human body.

## The Theatricalization of Folklore

That the Spanish dance has most easily made the arduous journey from being a folk art to becoming a theatrical experience is due to the fact that its original qualities are sufficiently exhibitionistic, and inherently dramatic or theatrical in mood, content and style. It only has to be removed from the atmosphere of the cafés and music halls and to be elevated onto the magic platform behind footlights. What it needed was the genius to liberate it from its native environment, from the source, and to approach it with the eyes of the artist. There is no isolated phenomenon in history, and if La Argentina had not had the artistic daring and greatness to bring about this transformation, others would have. And others have too, because in the 1920's and 1930's the time was ripe for the renaissance of the neo-Spanish dance.

One of the finest dancers of this art form was Vicente Escudero, who first partnered La Argentina before he set out on his own. If we speak of a pure classic style of the flamenco, then he was undoubtedly in possession of it with all its subtlety and elegance. The star of Argentinita shone for a very brief span of only about fifteen years. When she suddenly died in 1945, her sister, Pilar Lopez, formed the *Ballet Español* which featured Carmen Amaya and José Greco, who both established their own companies in 1950. But, while Amaya—who was, by the way, the first woman to dance in male costume—went back to her gypsy sources time and again and became the epitome of dynamism with an uninhibited temperament on stage, José Greco's approach turned more toward entertainment and seems to lack the necessary contact with the sources of his art.

Many names succeeded one another, but they all have their very personal peculiarities. Among the more famous dancer-choreographers, Antonio

fused the Andalusian and classical into a style very much his own. Roberto Iglesias and the Ximenez-Vargas company—without losing their own personality—followed the concept of Carmen Amaya. Luisillo is not only a passionate dancer, he also used story elements with a touch of the poetic and literate.

But not all folk and ethnological material is equipped to retain all—or even part—of its innate quality when transplanted onto the stage. That the individual artist will always have to find his way to his roots to replenish his art has been proved by choreographers of the classical ballet as well as of the modern dance. From Petipa to Balanchine, from Martha Graham to Agnes de Mille, they have all absorbed folk material whenever their topics needed it, but they did so only with the intention of personalizing and stylizing it, of using it as a vehicle for their artistic vision.

With the rapidly progressing mechanization and standardization of life, the trend toward folk art has almost turned into a flight from a too technical and sophisticated reality. Man in an over-industrialized civilization must, of necessity, seek redemption by returning to the soil. This explains the vital interest

in bringing folk and ethnological dances into the theater, an interest that has become symptomatic of the ills of the twentieth century.

Here the choreographer faces the difficult task of the translator: to betray neither the original nor the natural demands of the theater. The danger is equally great in that the folk quality may overshadow the necessary theatrical effectiveness or that the theatricality of the dance presentations may make us forget its folkloristic background.

Ethnological dancers from the East, who bring the magic of another world to Western man, most often heighten certain aspects of their art and, above all, cut the length of their dances to fit them to our theatrical customs. Most Eastern art presupposes an esoteric knowledge and a sense of its heritage which the foreigner lacks. But the secret of its fascination lies in its strange beauty which is universally understandable because its language is so highly stylized. Dances of faraway people and even further-away cultures also create a kinetic reality which is readily understood by everyone everywhere.

When Amalia Hernandez shaped a program out

*Macuilxochitl, the Aztec God of the Dance. (Courtesy Merle Armitage)*

of Mexican folklore, she faced the problem of three cultures that have put their stamp on Mexican art expression. There is no answer to the question of how to restage dances of the Aztec period to maintain their folkloristic credibility. In this, we can hardly succeed; we are also unable to visualize properly a facsimile of an ancient Cretan or Greek dance. In general, such dances will always lack authenticity and glaringly manifest an empty gesture, however colorful the image may appear. We know too little about the dancing of these cultures, and the little we know leads to too many assumptions. On the other hand, where the folk material is still alive, it creates a stage reality mainly by being what it really is. In the *Venado Dance* of Mexico's Yaqui Indians, a deer runs through the forest, is hit by an arrow and slowly dies. This pantomimic dance is still executed in its genuine environment where the Indian creates this imitative dance. Staged without any particular theatrical awareness, this dance is strong and vital because its movements are as genuine as its basic idea is universal.

Inbal, the dance theater of Israel, encountered similar problems when it tried to recreate Biblical dances. The moment Sara Levi Tanai, its artistic director, moved from the realm of conjecture into the folklore of the more recent past, she recaptured the spirit of a people who have brought with them many influences from their former homelands. Shepherd dances, or ritualistic material upon which were based such dances as *Yemenite Wedding* or *With Drum and Flute,* showed the primary concern with native symbolism and a convincing simplicity. The artistic risk for all these companies lies in trying to explore a past beyond our grasp because we lack substantial information, or in using a symbolic gesture related to its folklore for a story or fictitious theme that usually appears pale and synthetic.

To those countries which have more or less successfully attempted to translate their folk dances into theatrical forms belong the Russians and Poles, with the Yugoslavians and Bulgarians trailing close behind. In most cases, the folk music with its native instruments has more appeal than the dancing. The reason for this is the genuineness of the indigenous music, which is little, if at all, tampered with, and the temptation of the choreographers to add trick steps, turns and lifts to the folk dances. Spectacular as it may be, the strength displayed by the Polish girl in lifting her male partners, or the often breathtaking leaps and other feats of the Russian dancers are calculated far more to get applause than to attain a genuinely folkloristic character on stage.

Even Igor Moiseyev, who, from an artistic point of view, showed the most convincing feeling for his

*The Ballet Folklorico de Mexico tries to preserve the native grace of its material by extracting the essence of national tradition and local character. The picture above shows the* Fish Dance *from " The Tarascans."* *(A. R. Goldring)*

*The Moiseyev Dance Company exhibits its great technical skill and its power to create an atmosphere of nationality. Famous for being athletic, its acrobatics are an integral part of its folklore material. Above: Igor Moiseyev's* Partisans, *based on World War II events. Right: A scene from* Ukrainian Suite *(Hurok)*

native dances, fared better when his dances mirrored folk idioms and native forms rather than when he undertook more ambitious works. But what creates the strong impact in such works as his world-famous *Partisans* is sheer abandonment and dazzling stage tricks. Seen in perspective, the Moiseyev Dance Company undoubtedly represents the folk-dance turned stage-image at its best. Igor Moiseyev has the necessary sense of theater which he combines with a reverential bow toward the indigenous art

86

forms. Despite his leaning toward virtuosity and the spectacular, Moiseyev is saved from deviating too much from a faithful transport of the genuine spirit simply because he keeps close enough to what he calls "root movements."

In the September, 1958, issue of *Dance News,* Moiseyev explained his basic approach thus:

> If we analyze the movement of the dance of any nation we find that, in its basis, each system of folk dance possesses only a limited number of different movements. The movements upon which is based the entire system of the dance we call root movements. If we know a number of fundamental movements, a number of the roots of which the language of the dance is composed, and are familiar with the laws of connecting movements, our own fantasy will make it possible to add a number of new movements ... in the same system.

It could be maintained that when folklore leaves its immediate environment or place of origin, it must of necessity lose its character. Through breathing the air of a world of make-believe, it is tempted by the artificial and spectacular. How to preserve its basic characteristics, its rudimentary powers, its emotional impact while shifting from the healthy joy of participation in a folk dance to the pleasurable edification of viewing it as a spectator may depend on the innate theatricality of the material. Also of importance is the skill of the choreographer in finding a happy balance between being inspired by a source he uses without imitating it and keeping intact that source which inspires imagination.

However useful the theater dance may be in serving and preserving the folk dance—theater always claims victims and crowns its victors—folk dance will remain a life-giving force.

# 6 The Renaissance Man

When the curtain slowly fell on the Middle Ages, European man felt as if he had rediscovered his own being. He found himself surrounded by an atmosphere in which he could not help but become creative.

At that time, the power and purposefulness of the individual became more decisive than laws and customs. It was a time when *condottieres*, leaders of a handful of mercenaries, became dukes, when bankers founded dynasties and their sons were anointed popes, whose sons in turn rose to the title of princes. Ability—or often enough, ruthlessness

*An Italian Renaissance couple dances the* galliard. *(Henry E. Huntington Library and Art Gallery.) Above: Morris Dancer by Erasmus Grasser. (Stadtmuseum, Munich)*

—counted more than the cleanest pedigree. Aeneas Sylvius spoke of Italy as a country "that loves change, in which nothing is solidified.... Small wonder, then, that it is easy for servants to become kings!"

However, to show their might, these "kings" did a great deal for the arts and particularly for the dance. Thus, we find the cradle of the theater dance in Italy, although it received its polished stylization and, later, its baroque beauty in France. It was at the courts of a few little tyrants—the Medici, Sforza, Este and Gonzaga—that social activities became spectacle and theater. The dance was first on the social calendar of this elite.

A great many developments outside the dance contributed to its growing theatricality. Above all, Renaissance man had a visual mind, as his accomplishments in painting, sculpture and architecture prove. The eye became used to seeing in patterns. And it was geometric design which inspired the first attempts at ballet. Louis Horst pointed out that we owe to the Renaissance the transfer of the allegiance of art from the principles of religion to those of architecture. This new allegiance introduced solid forms and definite patterns, a formulation of steps for each dance, a set vocabulary with certain inviolable rules. To enforce discipline and to limit spontaneity, the dancing master appeared and played the most important part in creating a theater dance.

The musical aspect was of equal importance. At that time, almost all great compositions were written with the dance in mind. Since dance needs change in pace and pattern, this gave birth to the musical concept of the *suite,* which, in turn, influenced the classic sonata form. We read mainly of "dance-songs" and "dance-tunes." Medieval music is at best characterized by the Gregorian chant, the linear style with its irregular rhythm, borrowing in the main from Byzantine music. It created a mood of austerity, of otherworldliness. This was not the right music for the architecturally-minded people of the Renaissance who saw vividly in color and design. This demanded musical composition with a melodic line and a definite rhythmic accompaniment. Thus, *ars nova,* the new music of the fourteenth and fifteenth centuries—in contrast to the *ars antiqua,* the medieval style—was born, and polyphony reached an unprecedented complexity. It was an inventive style and created many new forms of which the madrigal* was the most important.

The madrigal went through many phases and reached a climax in Orazio Vecchi's famous *L'Amfiparnaso,* consisting of fourteen madrigals put together with a narrative of two parallel plots, the *lirico tragica* (a love story) and the *grottesco comica* (which portrayed the clowning of some *commedia*

* Gian-Carlo Menotti tried to capture the spirit of the madrigal in his "The Unicorn, the Gorgon and the Manticore, or the Three Sundays of a Poet," which John Butler choreographed in what may have been the manner of sixteenth-century madrigal dancing.

*dell'arte* figures). It was composed in 1597 and is considered a forerunner of the opera. The singers often danced to the madrigals.

Their main topics were love and nature. Thematically, the madrigal was influenced by the pastoral which had had a remarkable revival in the latter part of the medieval period. Pastoral romance with its bucolic simplicity was an escape from reality, from the world of violence, scheming and careering. This escape into a light-hearted treatment of Greco-Roman mythology at the very beginning of the history of ballet seems to have left a mark that has endured.

Masquerades, mummeries, and pageants had been an important pastime of all the people in the late Middle Ages; as private entertainments of the nobility during the fifteenth and sixteenth centuries, they became refined and finally turned into extravaganzas and spectaculars. At the courts and in the houses of the leading families, the nobility loved to revel in masques. If it was not carnival time, there were always suitable occasions, most often the wedding of an aristocratic couple.

The mask assumed a special significance during the Renaissance. People would travel in masks to remain incognito, and even among feuding families the mask blotted out the identity of the wearer. In Shakespeare's *Romeo and Juliet* we have a classic example of masked dances being arranged on all possible occasions, or of people coming masked to any kind of entertainment. Disguised as a pilgrim or palmer, Romeo joins "the night's revels" in Capulet's house. Tybalt, enraged by Romeo's presence, "cover'd with an antic face," asks for his rapier, but is prevented by Capulet from starting a fight in his house. Rooted in such masked dances, *le grand ballet* in France and the Masques and Anti-Masques in England lifted those danced masquerades to a level of sophisticated elegance.

One of the most frequently executed dances of that period was the *Morris* dance, or *Morisco,* which remained a favorite at the courts for a long time, but was certainly a part of all great festivities between 1550 and 1650. It also never lost its popularity

*Thomas Rowlandson caricatures the ribaldry of what he calls "The Last Jig, or Adieu to old England." (Courtesy Dance Collection, New York Public Library)*

with the common people; it is still danced in Spain today and is kept alive particularly in the British Isles as a folk dance, a jog-trot.

Morisco was the Spanish name for a Moor who stayed in Spain and became a Christian after the country was reconquered by the Spaniards. The dance emerged from romantic memories of the Moorish domination. It crystallized in two forms, as a solo and group dance. Its original form consisted of six dancers in two rows, with some having their faces blackened. Sometimes a man was dressed as a fool, a boy as a woman, and another would carry a hobbyhorse with him. All of them were

usually costumed in an antic way with many bells around their legs. The movements were very manly, mostly one leg was vigorously thrust forward while the other skipped lightly, although high leaps occurred, too, from time to time. There was hardly any use of the whole body, the stress being on legs and arms, which were swung simultaneously. The dancers waved a handkerchief. It is a dance of strength and precision, whether done in groups or as a solo. It was originally accompanied by flute, a small drum or a bagpipe and much shouting. Today, a violin or an accordion is used.

One of the most famous Morris dancers was Will Kempe, the comedian in Shakespeare's company, who "spent his life in mad jigges," as he claimed after his nine-day dance from London to Norwich, or when he danced his Morris across the Alps.

A minor contribution to the theatrical dance

*The god Apollo joins a circle dance with the Nine Muses in a painting by Giulio Romano. (Alinari)*

came from the pageants. Having had their roots in the miracle plays and the representations of the medieval trade guilds, pageants with floats and decorated cars can still be seen today on various occasions. Living pictures are often seen on these floats and costumed dancers and singers are part of the train. From the earliest recorded pageant in London, held in 1236 in celebration of Henry the Third's marriage to Eleanor of Provence, to the various Mardi Gras, the history of pageantry is full of splendors.

The greatest pageants during the Renaissance were the *Trionfi,* those mythological masques, the triumph of artistic design; and, to a lesser degree, the *Carri,* pageants arranged by the craftsmen and tradesmen in the Italian cities, with a multitude of masked people following the symbols of their activities, singing, dancing and roaming the town until late in the morning.

But it was the *Trionfi,* in the main the Triumphs of Lorenzo de' Medici, which created wondrous outdoor spectacles. The Florentine Carnivals were traditional festivities going back to the early Christian Lent celebrations (carnival is derived from *carne vale,* meaning O flesh, farewell!). Lorenzo engaged the greatest artists of his time, among them Filippo Brunelleschi, the architect, whose arrangements of the floats were based on classic models. Every duke and prince in every Italian city tried to emulate him, including Milan, where no one else but Leonardo da Vinci organized festivals at the court of Lodovico Sforza.

These open-air extravaganzas, featuring verses, music and dance and, above all, visual marvels paved the way for the indoor spectacles which gave birth to the art of ballet. At the same time banquets and festive gatherings going on indoors were equally important for the theater dance. During these feastings in Italy and France it became customary to have small groups of mostly masked dancers appear at intervals. These *entremets* in France and *intromesso* in Italy turned up in the ballrooms and later in the theaters as *intermezzi* or *intermedii*. They were the danced interludes that became the respected and self-contained ballet "entries."

## Guglielmo Ebreo: The Formula for Ballet

Only in the fifteenth century and only in northern Italy, could we have found the roots of modern theatrical dancing. The atmosphere was laden with the excitement of the coming, of the new. Each of the little "town" republics in Italy was a microcosm vibrating with the genius of the time. The exuberance of the people was bound to find all kinds of expression.

The ordinary people had their own little joys, their games, fairs and carnivals and, at all of these, their rustic dances. Many must have felt that there was something contagious in the air, and what better way was there of expressing a sense of liberation than through one's body? The dance was no longer considered evil. It was raised to one of the creative manifestations of man.

The lively rustic dance was not becoming to the ladies and gentlemen at the courts. Their garments, the halls, or gardens in which they danced and even their thoughts would have been in complete conflict with such movements. The dance, like every other art form of the period had to be perfected, had to be studied and performed with dignity and grace.

For the creation of a dance art, a vocabulary of steps and a choreographic pattern or design is necessary. To achieve this, one needs dance teachers, dancing masters. And with them was laid the foundation for dance theory. The dancing master ruled out all spontaneity, natural inclination, or learning from observation, and left them to the masses. For him, dance was a matter of restraint and refinement designed for people of taste and culture. His dances had to consist of steps striving toward elegant movements. There was no longer anything folksy in it, it was dancing created for theatrical effect, though the stage was the ballroom floor of

princely courts. For the first time, a clear distinction was made between folk dancing and this complicated, refined art of movement pattern.

If we treat the dance of the Renaissance as the groundwork for the ballet, we may easily be misled concerning both. The dances of those days were no doubt closer to today's social dancing rather than to artistic dance. But attempts at achieving coordinated steps within a pattern, the rehearsing of steps and figures, the growing importance of professional dancing masters and the arranging of dances for groups watched by the other courtiers: all this became the first step toward theatrical dancing.

Country dances have never ceased to be the source material for the theatrical dance, and they certainly had a strong influence on the beginning of the theatricalization of the court dances. A growing number of dancing masters used the country dances for their own purposes. While the court dances more and more took on the appearance of a "show," with their studied steps and the refined bearing of the noble court dancers, the lively and vigorous country dances remained compatible with the rustic life.

Some of the painters of that period provide us with vivid images. For instance, Mantegna's *Parnassus* and Giulio Romano's *Apollo Dances with the Muses* show the lively large movements of the peasants, their wide steps, contrasting sharply with the restrained and well-defined movements of the court dances.

There were both slow and fast dances, and often a strange mixture. Lively rhythms would suddenly interrupt a movement which had had a very ceremonial start.

In the main, there were three dances. The favorite, particularly at the courts, was the *basse danse,* or *bassa danza,* literally meaning "low dance." The entire fifteenth and the greater part of the sixteenth century can be called the "age of the *basse danse,*" as we today speak of the beginning of the nineteenth century as of the "age of the waltz" or the early twentieth century as of the "age of jazz." In other

words, this dance was mostly without jumps or lively movements. The dancers were supposed to move slowly and solemnly, but their feet hardly ever leaving the floor. Dignity had to be preserved. The joy of life and the erotic element were only hinted at. But not for long, because suddenly the lively rhythms of the *saltarello* would burst forth.

The *saltarello* was a vigorous three-beat dance which was supposed to be done with leaps or jumps. It is probably a feebler or more urbane version of the wild tarantella. Curt Sachs links the *tarantella* with the Roman *saltarello* or the Tuscan *tresca*. "What a dance," exclaimed Rainer Maria Rilke once, "as though invented by nymphs and satyrs, old and as rediscovered and rising up new, wrapped in primeval memories—cunning and wildness and wine, men with goat's hooves again and girls from the train of Artemis." Of all this we find at the Renaissance courts little more than a gay dance with an occasional leap. But the *saltarello* was no doubt a welcome interruption of the ceremonial, gliding *bassa danza*.

The third dance in fashion was the *piva*, which required double steps in a rapid tempo. But whatever the dance, the movements were constantly combined in different ways and given such fancy names as *Bel Fiore, Angello, Venus, Cupido, Mignotta, Zaura, Piatosa,* and *Lioncello*.

Up to this time, there had been no professional dancers but only wandering mimes, jesters and jugglers who also danced. The greater artists among them settled down as dance teachers. A surprisingly large number were Jews, and one of the greatest of these was a certain William of Pesaro—his full name was really Guglielmo Ebreo of Pesaro—of whom it was said that he "excelled all men in the dance." His reputation for agility as a dancer and skill as a musician is substantiated by the fact that his work, which survives in a number of manuscript copies, was used in several places at the same time.

*The Three Graces dance in a detail of* Primavera *by Botticelli. (Alinari)*

Putti, *messengers of the Goddess of Love, and symbols of Dionysiac abandon, dance in a Renaissance painting by Francesco Albani. (Alinari)*

He was one of the first to write on the dance. He was probably born about 1440 or somewhat earlier and he seems to have traveled extensively, especially in Italy, but not too much is known about him.

Guglielmo hailed from Pesaro on the eastern coast of Italy. He was the son of Jewish parents who probably had come the long way from Spain. Or he may have been one of the many *letzim*, those callers in ghettos, who also were wandering entertainers.

Guglielmo wandered northward to become the pupil of a certain Domenico of Piacenza, who had made a great name for himself as a dancing teacher. He was accepted and served his apprenticeship. In his own work, the famous *De praticha sue arte tripudii vulghare opusculum*, which is one of the earliest and most complete works on the art of dancing, Guglielmo refers to himself as Domenico's devoted disciple, and many of Domenico's dance compositions can be found in Guglielmo's compilation.

Antonio Cornazano, later a famous dancing teacher and poet, was also a pupil of Domenico's and also wrote a book on the dance. How difficult it is to write on an art so visual and fleeting, was recognized by Cornazano when, after trying to make a dance clear to his readers, he retreated into the statement: "This cannot be well explained unless you are present and made to do it." Although both Guglielmo and Antonio did their best to describe in detail a choreographic technique, their explanations remain rather obscure in places. How difficult it must have been to keep the many variations of the three main dance forms in mind becomes evident in Guglielmo's stress on *memoria* as one of the essential prerequisites of the dancer. And Antonio bragged that he needed only to see a dance once to be able to repeat it without a mistake.

The Wedding Dance *by Peter Breughel the Elder captures the exuberance of peasant festivities. (Detroit Institute of Arts)*

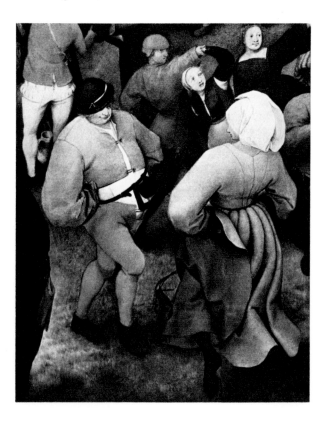

When Guglielmo left his master, he soon established himself as one who "excelled all men in the dance." His must have been a strong and proud character, for he did not at first follow the example of many other Jews of his time who converted to make life easier for themselves. However, there are indications—according to Arthur Michel's research—that at a later age Ebreo did bow to pressure and accept baptism. But there can be no doubt about one thing: in the scheme of theatrical dancing, his contribution is of great importance.

At that time, when violence and passion ruled in a country of so many rakes and cynics, platonic love was personified in a few women—above all in Vittoria Colonna. Ruthlessness and power needed a counterpoint in personal life. Personal purity and sublime love was thought to be one of the antidotes to the corrupt life of these self-styled aristocrats.

Guglielmo must have spent some time in Bologna since one of his dance compositions reads: *"Alis nominata Caterva composta in Bologna."* Another entry proves that he had access to members of the most powerful Roman family, the Colonna, although it is not certain that he ever went to Rome. But his famous dance, *Colonnese,* was composed for Madonna Suena di casa Colonna, a relative of the celebrated Vittoria Colonna.

Guglielmo could not have done better than to compose a dance for a respected and adored woman. The dance, so long defamed as carnal stimulation, had to fight hard against the prejudice piled up against it through the centuries. Dance and purity had to be made synonymous. Guglielmo fought ardently to raise the dance to a level where it would be beyond criticism from an esthetic viewpoint. He tried to free the dance from the motif of love and sex, and to elevate it to beauty and grace.

During one of his short sojourns in his home town of Pesaro, Guglielmo was recommended to the great Federigo, Duke of Urbino, and no doubt remained in his service until death overcame the Duke in 1482. Federigo was probably the most perfect representative of the Renaissance. He had the political morality of the condottiere, and yet, at

*The country dance* Thread-the-Needle *as it appears in Rubens'* La Kermesse. *(Anderson)*

the end, he presided over the most accomplished court in Italy. No other ruler of his time was so much beloved by his people. Taste was the keyword for his approach to knowledge and the arts and he was willing to spend freely to maintain it. Among the 350 to 500 people on his payroll were:

| | |
|---|---:|
| Teachers of grammar, logic and philosophy | 4 |
| Architects and engineers | 5 |
| Readers during meals | 5 |
| Chaplains | 2 |
| Singing boys | 5 |
| Organists | 2 |
| Fencing masters | 2 |
| Dancing masters | 2 |

and so forth. One of the dancing masters was Guglielmo Ebreo of Pesaro.

When Duke Federigo died, Guglielmo may have gone to Florence. He must somehow have been in touch with Lorenzo de' Medici, because two of his dances, *Venus* and *Zauro*, were incorporated in Guglielmo's work. The Florentines were fond of the pageants, festivals and processions arranged by Lorenzo, and dancing masters played a great part in them. Their work went far beyond merely teaching dance steps and composing "dance variations." Today they would also be called masters of deportment. In one paragraph in his manuscript Guglielmo says:

Her glance should not be proud nor wayward, gazing here and there as many do. Let her, for the most part, keep her eyes, with decency, on

97

the ground; not however, as some do, with her head sunk on her bosom, but straight up, corresponding to the body, as nature teaches almost of herself.... And then at the end of the dance, when her partner leaves her, let her, facing him squarely, with a sweet regard, make a decent and respectful curtsy in answer to his.

Guglielmo's writing makes clear that he did not see his final aim as a mere compiler of dances. Above all, he attempts to explain the fundamentals of dancing.

He has given a great deal of thought to the relation between the dance and music. At that time, music for the dance was based on four *voci principali* which, strangely enough, were linked with the four elements of earth, air, fire, and water. Properly balanced, so he says, the four voices of the music fill the ears of the hearer with a most gentle sweetness. "The dance is derived from this melody, as an act demonstrative of its own nature. Without the harmony and consonance, the art of dancing would *be* nothing and could *do* nothing."

The teaching of the dances was not always as simple as we may imagine. People were used to dancing spontaneously, with steps more or less dictated by the mood of the moment. Now for the first time dancing teachers aimed at precision striving for elegance of movement and the memorizing of a well-defined vocabulary of steps. Any dance thus performed on a stage instead of on one of the courtly ballroom floors would have contained all the elements of theatrical dancing. Guglielmo must have given much thought to coordinating music and dancing, and translating the imageless music into dance figures. He says for instance: "Let the dancer try a measure or two against the musical time. If he carries through, it will afford him much pleasure, will sharpen his intellect and make him attentive to the music... for everything is known and better understood by its contrary." There are still other tests, all of them showing whether or not the dancer has grasped the principles of *misura*, that is the ability to keep time.

A classical example of one of those early Renais-

sance dances is a *bassa danza* by Guglielmo. His *piatosa* belonged to those dances most widely known and done all over Italy at that time. His explanations are not always too clear, but they give us a fair notion of the dance's conception:

> The *piatosa* begins with two simple steps and one double step, commencing with the left foot. Then the dancers make a *ripresa* (a stepping backward) on the right foot, while the man makes two *continenze* (a kind of leave-taking wherein the man bows before the lady, then takes her by the hand and leads her back to where the dance began). During the *continenza* the lady goes from the under hand of the man with two simple steps, beginning with the left foot again. Then the couple joins hands and make two *riprese,* one on the left foot, the other on the right, and follow it with two *continenze*. Then they repeat all they have done so far and the gentleman returns to his place. The next step is a curtsy on the left foot, whereupon the gliding *bassa danza* is interrupted by two bars of the livelier *saltarello* followed by a curtsy by the man on the left foot. During his curtsy, the lady makes a half turn, then they go contrariwise, one to the other, with two double steps, again beginning with the left foot. After a half turn on the right foot and two *riprese,* one on the right and the other on the left foot, they curtsy on the left. Now they go opposite each other and, taking hands, make a *ripresa* on the left foot and then a full turn with two simple steps, commencing with the right foot this time, and a *ripresa* on the right followed by a curtsy on the left. And when all is done, it is repeated once more.

Whatever we may think of such dances today, they were revolutionary for the fifteenth century. A new style was created, the foundation laid for our ballet. The word ballet itself derives from *balletti,* a diminutive for balli, a technical term for all livelier dances in contrast to the low, the *bassa,* dances. In the beginning, of course, the term *balletti* carried no theatrical meaning; it referred simply to dance figures. However, after the Medici had brought the Italian art of dancing to France where it was destined to reach undreamed-of perfection, the term *Balletti,* or in French *ballet,* acquired

significance. Guglielmo wrote a great many *balli*, among them the famous *Colonnese*. But, still most concerned with the basic needs of the dancer, he outlined six prerequisites for all dancers:

*Misuro:* the dancer's ability to keep time to the musical rhythm.

*Memoria:* the ability to recollect steps in correct sequence.

*Partire del terreno:* the ability to judge the limits of the dance floor, that is to do the right movement in space.

*Aiere:* a somewhat obscure term which seems to denote a certain swaying and upward movement of the body with the corresponding settling down.

*Maniera:* a certain movement in the style of that time ("When one performs a single or a double step he should turn his body, as long as the movement lasts, towards the same side as the foot which performs the step, and the act should be adorned and shaded with the movement called maniera.")

*Movemento corporeo:* probably the ability to move gracefully.

Guglielmo was, of course, outlining the basic requirements for the artistic dancer of all times, yet all he intended was to compose dances for courtly balls.

## Beaujoyeulx and the Cultural Explosion in the Sixteenth Century

After the birth of ballet in northern Italy, the theater dance came of age in France. And yet it was mainly Italian talent that helped give it shape and substance.

99

or Spain without such increasingly theatrical entertainments. Mythological themes and figures were often mingled with popular dance and folk concepts. The best example of this is an entertainment arranged in 1521 at the Vatican for Pope Leo X, a son of Lorenzo de' Medici. First, a lady appeared and addressed a song to Venus asking her for a lover. Suddenly, heaps of old clothes on the floor rose and became eight hermits; they were about to

*The 1581* Ballet Comique de la Reine *performed in the Petit-Bourbon Palace is the earliest-known ballet combining dancing, music and acting with a dramatic theme—the story of Circe.   Left: A siren which appeared at the first interlude. (Collection George Chaffee: Harvard)   Right: The procession of satyrs. (Bibliothèque Nationale, Paris) Below: The prologue. (Collection George Chaffee: Harvard)*

Catherine de' Medici, the great-granddaughter of Lorenzo il Magnifico, came to France as the bride of the Duke of Orléans, later King Henri II. Catherine was an exceptional person and well equipped for her significant part in developing the *ballet de cour* into a theatrical form. The political need of the Medici to keep the French nobility entertained at the Court was also of great help to the dance.

The ballet de cour has a long history. Its roots can be found in all dancing that followed each tournament or hunting party, or served as the grand finale to social gatherings. The desire for more showy interludes during banquets resulted in those miniature spectacles of posing and dancing, the *intermezzi*. They usually involved savages fighting for the possession of a beautiful woman, whereupon the Goddess of Love would appear and set her free. Or a girl riding in a chariot drawn by a unicorn would enter and unchain a few captives. All the *intermedii* allowed for a great deal of dancing.

With the growing influence of Italianate humanism toward the end of the fifteenth century, these interludes shifted to mythological themes. By that time there was no court festivity in Italy, France

whip Cupid when Venus came to his rescue. The hermits threw off their garb and revealed themselves as handsome young men, who started a Morisco dance, with swords in hand, fighting for the favor of the Goddess of Love.

This has all the elements of an exciting visual show, although not yet with a fully developed story line. As with the Morris dance here, such entertainments used the favorite social dances of the time. The *pavane*, for example, was expressive of the courtly dignity with which most social dance events opened. Its name comes from the Latin *pavo*, meaning peacock, and suggests the pompous walk of this fowl. Rooted in the Spain of the Inquisition, this dance has a sombre mood which recommended it as a ceremonial dance. More or less a walking dance with simple steps in a slow 4/4 or 2/2 rhythm, it joins grace and stateliness. The pavane was usually followed by the *galliard* (originally meaning a gay and dashing person), a vigorous lively dance. In contrast to the pavane's gliding movements, it was full of leaps and kicking steps. There were innumerable variations of the galliard, some quiet, others violent. One variation, the *volte* or *lavolta*, was a favorite among younger, more agile dancers because it required turning and lifting of the girl by her partner.

Shakespeare refers to the galliard in *Twelfth Night*: "Why dost thou not go to church in a galliard and come home in a coranto?" The courante was a swift dance marked by a great deal of running and gliding, with a few slight jumps. Other fast dances were the *gigue*, whose origin is traced to England, and the *sarabande*, a bawdy Spanish dance that had to be tamed for use at the French court under Louis XIII.

Most of the social dances of the Renaissance were originally folk dances. The vigorous *bourree* in 2/2 or 4/4 time was danced by peasants of Auvergne, the *passepied*, light and playful, came from Brittany, and the merry *branle* from Poitou. In Germany, the branle was another version of the *Reigen*; it was danced in the round with everyone holding hands. In England, this dance was best known as shepherd hey, and the hay branles were danced very much like a courante. There are records of various branles in France, which were mimed and danced with rich gesture patterns. For instance, the Maltese branle was done as if devised as part of a court masquerade in which the dancers, dressed in Turkish costume, moved in a round with many lively gestures and twisting movements.

All these dances, of course, constituted the basic

Ag.no Ricci In. Del ballo

The equestrian ballet, a favorite entertainment of feudal
society, reached perfection in the sixteenth and early
seventeenth centuries. With the growing vogue of opera and
ballet it lost its importance. Only the Spanish and
Hapsburg monarchs have kept it alive, as in the world-
famous Vienna Riding School ("Spanische Reitschule").
The horse above is seen performing a jeté. (Fred Ward:
Black Star)   At left, the Horse Ballet plays a major part
in a festival of the Grand Duke of Tuscany. Details
of the choreography are shown in the margins. (Courtesy
Dance Collection, New York Public Library)

CARRO D AMORE

FIGVRE DELLA FESTA A CAVALLO, RAPPRESENTATA NEL
TEATRO DEL SER.mo GRAN DVCA DI TOSCANA
il di 15. Luglio 1637

Felice Gamb.ai Ing.re fe   Str. de.lo be.lle dd. c

*Costume design by Inigo Jones for a character in a masque.*
*A description reads, "A Crier of Mousetraps, Buy*
*a Mousetrap." (Geoffrey Clements: Columbia University)*

duced the vogue of the figure dance in France. When Catherine de' Medici arranged a grand spectacle to welcome Polish ambassadors, the masquers of *Le Ballet des Polonais* delighted in the most complex steps. The Poles "marveled at the orderly confusions, the well-formed numbers of the ballet," and declared that the dance of France could not be equalled by those of any king on earth.

An even greater event took place in 1581 on the occasion of the marriage of the Queen's sister. The Italian Baldassari de Belgiojoso who changed his name to Balthasar de Beaujoyeulx was charged with the arrangement of part of the festivities. Having come to France in 1555 as a violinist, he was admired as a musician, but even more as a courtier with esprit and imagination. Beaujoyeulx worked out an entertainment, called "Circe," which was known as *Le Ballet Comique de la Reine Louise.* He explained the terms *ballet* and *comique* in his introduction to a printed edition of the libretto, saying that *comique* stood for "the lovely, tranquil and happy conclusion by which it ends," and that *ballet* meant to him "a geometric combination of several persons dancing together."

The concept of a geometrical arrangement was a vital step forward in the direction of choreographic principles. Beaujoyeulx was the first to think of ballet architecturally in terms of space and an unbroken line. And the relation of this ballet de cour to the comedy (it was not comic in our sense) created the first link between ballet and comedy in what was to be a long chain of *comédies-ballets.*

About ten thousand guests of the French royal family saw this spectacle, which lasted from ten o'clock in the evening until half past three in the morning. Jacques Patin designed the scenery much in the manner of the medieval stage with its various mansions. The garden and castle of the enchantress Circe stood opposite the seats of the royal family, with a golden cave to the left and the Arbor of Pan to the right with illuminated trees. A niche for the musicians was framed by clouds and lighted within. There were wide passages on both sides for the dancers to enter on cars, resembling the floats used

material that went into the entertainments at the various European courts. But two major social events in France set the scene for the future development of dancing. The Italian dancing master Cesare Negri, who was among the loot the French brought back after conquering Milan in 1554, intro-

for the Trionfi. The music was composed by a relative of the Queen, Sieur de Beaulieu, and all the actors, dancers and singers were of the nobility.

After the overture, Sieur de la Roche, a gentleman-in-waiting, fled Circe's castle, rushed in terror to the center of the hall, and addressed the King in verses, requesting help against Circe who had transformed him into a lion, but had then given back his human shape. He had hardly finished his plea when Circe appeared and sang "The Complaint of Circe Having Lost a Gentleman." She withdrew, and a procession of sirens followed, announcing a float with water nymphs who stepped down and danced.

There were twelve geometric figures in the first entry, but Beaujoyeulx left no detailed record of it. Then Circe rushed out of her castle, struck the nymphs with her magic wand who, arranged in two lines *en croisant*, stood in arrested movement in a perfect choreographic design. Then the nymphs, freed by Mercury, continued to dance, whereupon eight satyrs moved through the hall, singing couplets. Another chariot rolled in with four pastoral virgins who began to dance and were joined by the satyrs. After the entry of the Four Virtues singing and playing the flute, a monstrous serpent dragged in another float with the goddess Pallas, who asked for the aid of Jupiter. He came riding down on an eagle. Pan headed a troop of satyrs, who, together with lesser spirits, assaulted the palace. Circe defied them, but Jupiter struck her down with one of the thunderbolts and freed all captives. The finale was a grand ballet, or great figure dance, performed by the nymphs.

The historic accomplishment of this ballet de cour lies in the fact that Beaujoyeulx utilized every courtly amusement, from the pastoral to masquerades, from mythology to the spectacular intermezzi. The use of all these elements in a fully integrated "show" was a unique and invaluable contribution

*For another masque, Jones designed a costume with wings of flame for "A Page like a Fiery Spirit." (Geoffrey Clements: Columbia University)*

*Headgear helped in identifying roles; here are notes by Inigo Jones for a turban and Medusa's wreath of snakes. (Geoffrey Clements: Columbia University)*

to the theater dance. This event was too lavish, costing 3,600,00 francs, an expense prohibiting any repetition of it. But the many ballet-masquerades that followed it kept its memory alive. Sometimes, ingenious mummeries were shown at these ballet-masquerades, pieces of pantomime and acrobatic feats, after which all masquers joined in a grand ballet.

The emphasis in the world of the arts again shifted for a few decades to Italy. The Italian courts never stopped trying to give artistic expression to what was considered a true revival of antiquity. Where to entertain was a question of prime importance to feudal lords. The two great French ballet events had required huge halls, but the scenic image was still the medieval multiple stage. The problem of creating an auditorium that allowed for intimacy and was at the same time big enough to stage spectacles was solved in 1580 when Andrea Palladio began to build the Teatro Olimpico at Vicenza, the first horseshoe theater, a type of theater that outlasted its usefulness in the second half of this century.

From then on, Italy began to build theaters rapidly and export its theatrical innovations to the whole civilized world: ballet, opera, and the horseshoe theater. The ten volumes of *De Architectura*, written by the Roman Vitruvius in the first century, were the bible of the academicians of the Renaissance who, of course, desired to recreate the Roman theater. But Vitruvius' influence turned out to be a point of departure rather than a goal. In 1545, architect and painter Sebastiano Serlio set forth to publish the idea of a definite set, with lofty palaces for the tragic play, ordinary city buildings for the comic play and landscape of trees, hills and cottages for the bucolic play. Gradually, the perspectives turned into arches and columns. The first wings were built in 1606 to accommodate the surprising stage effects that were more and more often employed. It was no longer a matter of the classic *deus ex machina*. People began to appear in clouds or to walk through fire. Giacomo Torelli was the master magician of scenic décor, and artists came from everywhere to learn his stage tricks. Illusion was the aim of the Renaissance designer. The wonders of perspective as known from the canvases of the great painters had to be imitated. A twentieth-century audience, of course, would be hard put to accept the artificiality of this "theatrical" perspective. It is significant that only in the ballet, and only in the romantic ballet, can such a décor still be successfully presented.

Theaters were built with boxes from which one could withdraw into an adjacent room to feast or to play cards and to which one could return to see a favorite dancer or hear a beloved singer. They were particularly useful in a theater that depended on the patronage of high society. And with opera coming into being and dominating the Italian scene, theater architecture became keyed to spectacular productions, but always with the emphasis on the dollhouse view, the proscenium stage. The final separation between the audience and the performer began. The participation of the nobility was reduced to a minimum, and the professional dancer entered the scene. Framing the stage like a picture demanded the constantly growing enhancement of this picture, or staged illusion. It also created the feeling for those beyond the footlights of no longer being necessarily involved. An esthetic and social distance resulted from this separation.

But it was the right framework for both ballet and opera as they developed into a stylized art form. In 1597, the opera emerged from the attempt of a few Florentine noblemen to revive the Greek chorus. And nine years after Jacopo Peri's *Dafne,* the first *dramma per musica,* Claudio Monteverdi created his *Orfeo* and broke the tedium of the recitative with duets and trios. Monteverdi turned the spectacle of the Florentine nobility into modern musical drama. He developed the aria as a substitute for the movement-supported chorus.

This separated the Italian opera from the ballet. On Italian soil where they were both born, these two art forms went their own ways. Sometime later in France, they became inseparable, wedded to each other for better or for worse.

## Shakespeare, Jonson and Jones

The spiritual and physical awakening that occurred in Europe during the Renaissance did not stop at the Channel. The English, about to become the world's greatest merchants and destined to rule the waves for a long time, had frequent contact with the peoples of Europe. French dancing masters and Italian actors often crossed the Channel, and entire companies of English players went to the continent.

As a matter of fact, a great many of them felt obliged to go abroad since there were always more players than parts to be had in the London theaters.

Dancing was a necessary accomplishment for all actors. Shakespeare and his contemporary playwrights indicated through such laconic notes as "Dance" or "They dance" in their stage directions that they took the actors' dancing ability for granted. At that time no director had to worry about finding an actor who could also dance or a dancer who could also act. This was the spirit of the *commedia dell'arte,* which at that time had reached its peak in Italy, and the very same spirit dominated the training of the English actor. The demands on the actors' versatility of the *commedia dell'arte* stagger our imagination today; the best of them were excellent mimes—continuing the tradition of the Roman mimes—acrobats, accomplished dancers and musicians, men of superlative swordsmanship, and of no slight education. The English actor abroad faced comparison with his Italian colleagues and, on the whole, fared pretty well. His skill as a dancer was especially acclaimed time and again.

It was customary to end the performance of a play with a dance by some of the members of the company. There is a record of a medical student from Basle named Thomas Platter who described his stay in London from the 18th of September to the 20th of October 1599:

> After dinner on the 21st of September, at about two o'clock, I went with my companions over the water and in the strewn roof-house saw the tragedy of the First Emperor Julius with at least fifteen characters well acted. At the end of the comedy they danced according to their custom with extreme elegance. Two in men's clothes and two in women's gave this performance, in wonderful combination with each other. On another occasion, I also saw after dinner a comedy... at the end they danced very elegantly both in English and in Irish fashion....

In Elizabethan days a play performed at court entertainments was often followed by a masque. And on the public stages the playgoers after the

play expected to see a jig, or one or two of the company's members concluded the spectacle with a dance, as borne out by the closing lines in *Much Ado About Nothing*: "Strike up, pipers. Dance"; or when in *As You Like It* the banished Duke announces to the happily united couples:

> Play, music! And you, brides and bridegrooms all,
> With measure heap'd in joy, to the measures fall.

This invitation to the "measures," a stately, pavane-like dance, mostly followed by livelier steps, culminates in the Duke's last words:

> Proceed, proceed: We will begin these rites,
> As we do trust they'll end, in true delights.
>
> A dance.

The playgoing public usually considered the epilogue a natural lead into a dance or jig. Even amateur performances, of which there were many in England, ended with dancing. Shakespeare, parodying amateurs in *A Midsummer Night's Dream*

*Above: A ball given at the court of Henry III in 1581 for the marriage of a courtier. (Giraudon) Right: Queen Elizabeth in mid-air, as she does the leaping turn of the* lavolta, *assisted by the Earl of Leicester. (Viscount De L'Isle, Penshurst Place, Kent)*

in the artisans' performance, has Bottom ask Theseus, Duke of Athens, in his malapropos way: "Will it please you to see the epilogue, or to hear a Bergomask dance between two of our company?" Whereupon Theseus asks for a bergomask, or more correctly, a *bergomasco*, a popular round dance.

The Elizabethan playgoer's participation in whatever was spoken or shown on the stage was intense. There was a kinetic reaction to it, often violent—an experience which electrified both players and spectators. The Elizabethan still knew the innocent joy of being a part of the magic of word and movement. In fact, he had no choice, he had to give himself up completely to the play and players,

since the greatest demands were made on his attention and imagination. Although the acting was more often realistic than not, there was no, or scarcely any, scenery; the spectator depended entirely on the word to identify the location of each scene, and it was the word and the poetry which painted the emotions of each character and mounted the events of the play. Words alone had to create the magic of love-making, especially since younger boys played the parts of the women. Moreover, the listener's ear was subjected to a rapid delivery of the lines.

Therefore, it becomes more understandable that so much stress was put on dancing and that, as relief for the audience, musical interludes were scheduled between the acts, and not seldom a boy came forward to dance. In Fletcher's *Faithful Shepherdess* we find the lines:

Nor wants there those who, as the boy doth dance
Between the acts, will censure the whole play.

And, seen in this light, it is quite conceivable that the audience demanded to stay a short while longer after the play to see a dance. Sometimes, as in the Second Part of *King Henry IV* the epilogue was even spoken by a dancer. When, today, we hear him say toward the end of his speech, "my tongue is weary; when my legs are too, I will bid you good night...," it makes no sense to us who expect the curtain to fall after his last word. In those days, he then began to dance until his legs were actually weary.

Shakespeare mentions twelve different dances and concerns himself fifty times with dancing in his plays and poems. As Shakespeare so often used the simile of life being a stage and felt that a play held a mirror up to nature, we may safely assume that the music- and dance-minded stage of the Elizabethans was the true reflection of their life. Even Queen Elizabeth's great passion was dancing; she was an experienced dancer with a strong sense of rhythm. It is said that she exercised each morning by doing six or seven galliards and that when she watched a dance she followed the cadence with her head, hand and foot. This love of the dance endured

to the verge of her grave. Her share in the Twelfth Night revels of 1599 was reported to Spain by its ambassador with biting sarcasm: "... the head of the Church of England and Ireland was to be seen in her old age dancing three or four galliards." And in April 1602 she danced yet two galliards with the Duke of Nevers.

Elizabethan London was full of dancing schools, frequented by the nobility as much as by the citizens. The Duke of Bourbon declares disdainfully in *Henry V* (III, v), "They bid us to the English dancing schools and teach lavoltas high and swift corantos." Of course, he who could afford it went to France, which was a center of the dance. The dances then in vogue were not easy, and the many dancing schools in London profited from the fact. The taste of the time was for the theatrical, the spectacular, for dances with intricate steps, with leaps and lifting of one's partner, as we are now used to see on the stage rather than on the ballroom floor. But we must not forget that these were originally court dances imported from France and that these very same dances had led to figure dancing and to the dramatic *Ballet Comique de la Reine*.

The French dances dominated the English social scene and, in spite of their intricacies, won more and more popularity after the middle of the sixteenth century. A visitor to one of the London dancing schools in 1585 watched a performer do a galliard and remarked how "at our entring he was beginning a trick as I remember of sixteens and seventeens, I do not very well remember, but wonderfully he leaped, flung and took on." The London citizenry did as well in these French dances as the courtiers. Of course, the surprised visitor was watching an amateur practicing for his own pleasure. And if nonprofessionals were such excellent dancers, we can imagine what expert performances were expected from the actors on the stage.

We get the best conception of the Elizabethans craving for the dance, and their indulgence in it, from those who opposed this rage and from the writers who satirized it. Most outspoken were the Puritans, the preachers and self-appointed moralists, and the London Council, which always used the spectre of the plague as a pretense for its anti-theatrical actions and which eyed any diversion of youth with disapproval, fearing for its morals as well as its industry. Philip Stubbes railed against the dancing madness in his *Anatomy of Abuses* in 1583: "Some have broken their legs with skipping, leaping, turning and vawting ... men and women together ... in publique assemblies and frequencies of people, with such beastly slabberings, bussings and misdemeanors ... every leap or skip in dance, is a leap toward hell...." The record of the Middlesex Justices shows that, in 1612, they made a special order for "Suppressing jigs at the end of plays on the ground that the lewd jigs, songs and dances so used at the Fortune led to the resort of cutpurses and other ill-disposed persons and to consequent breaches of the peace." The Puritans were most concerned with the many women who indulged in those dances, which demanded agility and acrobatics rather than dignity. A deaf person, unable to equate the music with the dancing, watched a galliard dancer in a London dancing school and thought "verily that he had been stark mad and out of his wit."

The dances mentioned in the Shakespearean plays were the favorites of the age. But it is difficult to define precisely how the various dances were done, for there seems to have been general confusion in the use of dance terms in late-sixteenth-century England. In fact, even as late as 1728 Soame Jenyns wrote in *The Art of Dancing*:

> Long was the Dancing Art unfix'd and free:
> Hence lost in error and Uncertainty:
> No Precepts did it mind, or Rules obey,
> But every Master taught a different Way.

Also, the good dancers varied their steps and devised their own variations. Thomas Morley, one of the foremost composers of the age, said that dancing had "come to that perfection that every reasonable dancer will make measure of no measure, so that it is no great matter of what number you make strain." Richard Brome, Stuart playwright and disciple of Ben Jonson, made fun of this state of

*A 1768 English caricature "Grown Ladies Taught to Dance" satirizes pointedly dances and dance masters. (Courtesy Dance Collection, New York Public Library)*

confusion in his play *The City Wit* (IV, 1), in which one of the characters speaking of the dance asks his friend, "... I prithee teach me some tricks," whereupon his friend answers: "Ha! Tricks of Twenty: Your Traverses, Slidings, Falling back, Jumps, Closings, Openings, Shorts, Turns, Pacings, Gracings,—as for Corantoes, Lavoltoes, Jigs, Measures, Pavins, Brawls, Galliards or Canaries."

The light-footed and nimble Elizabethans who so willingly surrendered to the fashionable continental imports, took great pride and delight in their many home-grown country dances. These dances were taught in the dancing schools beside the imported French dances, although they could be danced with simple steps. At Court, they were often preferred to the French dances which needed far more practice and, above all, talent. A courtier could easily cut a bad figure in a French dance, and one of them, during the reign of James I, made the

111

Carro di Teti fatto in firenze nella festa a Cauallo per la
uenuta del Serenissimo Principe d'Vrbino.
Era su quest Carro Teti con le tre Sirene, con le Nereidi
ei Tritoni, caminauano a pie del Carro Otto Giganti
in forma di tanti Nettunni che figurauano i principali
Mari del Mondo. an 1616.

Iul. Parigi I dallot F.

*An engraving of a masque design by Jacques Callot.*
*(Courtesy Dance Collection, New York Public Library)*

sarcastic remark that it was easier to put on fine clothes than to learn the dances of the French and that therefore "none but country dances" were seen at the Court.

This, of course, was an exaggeration, but it shows that we cannot draw a clear line between the English country dances and the French court dances because they constantly crossed the social border lines. And on the stage we naturally find the same fusion and confusion.

The major contribution of the English court to the dance was its growing enjoyment of the masques; they began to play a great part during Queen Elizabeth's reign, but became most fashionable under the Stuarts. The dances were arranged by the dancing masters who were the choreographers of that time; they drilled the dancers, who

were members of the nobility. The rehearsals for such a masque usually lasted many weeks. The dancing masters tried, of course, to please His Majesty, and James I favored vigorous and sustained dancing at such masques.

At a certain point of the entertainment, the masquers "took out" the guests of the opposite sex to dance. This "commoning" between masquers and spectators was one of the highlights of these spectacles. Ben Jonson says in his *Masque of Queens* that after the masquers' second dance, "they took out the men and danc'd the measures, entertayning the time, almost to the space of an hour, with singular variety," which mainly was made up of lavoltas, galliards and corantos.

The masque, as a variant of the ballet de cour, brought two of England's masterminds together: Ben Jonson, the poet-dramatist, and Inigo Jones, one of the most impressive stage designers, or scene masters, as he was then called. Both succeeded in lifting the ballet de cour to a level of fine artistry.

The European courts rivalled one another, and the masques were an efficient instrument of political propaganda to display the power of the throne and the richness of the realm. For a short period the English nobility was able to create a court entertainment that outshone everything else on the continent. Jonson and Jones found the key to the theatricalization of the masque: the anti-masque.

Ben Jonson alone wrote about thirty masques. He developed the anti-masque as the logical answer to a theatrical need. In a rudimentary form it was already evident in some of the ballets de cour. Since the masque was to praise beauty and to pay compliments to the ruler or a member of the aristocracy, there was an unavoidable sameness, however heightened the splendor may have been. The anti-masque became the dramatic counterpoint, working on the principle of contrast. They discovered how much stronger was the effect of beauty if set off against the grotesque and ugly. Also, antic faces of boys, old hags and witches could easily utter funny lines and add a touch of humor to the strangeness of their appearance. The anti-masque was theatrical dancing and clowning at its best.

A stage description in Jonson's masque of 1608, *The Hue and Cry After Cupid,* pictures such merriment:

> ... from behind the trophies, Cupid discovered himself and came forth armed, attended with twelve boys, most anticly attired, that represented the sports and pretty lightness that accompany love.... Wherewith they fell into a subtle, capricious dance, to as odd a music, each of them bearing two torches, and nodding with their antic faces, with other variety of ridiculous gesture, which gave much occasion of mirth and delight to the spectators. The dance ended, Cupid went forward.

For Ben Jonson, the masques offered an opportunity to write an integrated theater piece in which the poetic image could be composed of drama, music, movement and color. But it was inevitable that the visual splendor should soon take the spotlight away from his intentions, and this ended, in 1631, Jonson's collaboration with Inigo Jones, whom he called a "maker of properties ... whirling his whimsies."

Jones had traveled on the continent and seen the technical marvels of the new theaters, he had also studied the scenic engravings of Jacques Callot, when he returned to London and tried to translate the Italianate splendor and French finesse into the English idiom. He brought the idea of the proscenium stage with him and designed a new frame of ornaments and symbolic figures for each masque. He delighted in stunning stage images and magical scenic changes. Also, Jones was the first to employ theatrically effective group scenes. These courtly masques were imitated on many occasions on a far more modest scale by the lower nobility and the London citizenry. How common the masques were is best reflected in the many contemporary plays which made them part of the plot.

The Puritans under Oliver Cromwell put a halt to any further development of the theatrical aspect of the masques. Not that they did not have their own masques. One was called *Cupid and Death,* devised by James Shirley in 1653, and another was John Milton's *Comus,* a verse morality with incidental dancing. Even Oliver Cromwell danced till five o'clock in the morning on the occasion of his daughter's wedding—but it was what he would have called a purified dance totally lacking in eroticism.

Thus, a great theater conception of the dance came to a sudden end. From then on the English who, of course, always enjoyed their country dances, continued to import what the continental ballet companies produced. England had little to contribute to the development of the dance until it caught up with the new dance renaissance of the twentieth century.

# 7 *Ballet Comes of Age*

Although ballet and opera were born of the genius of the Renaissance, they became children of the baroque. After many highlights of accomplishment, mainly in the visual arts, these two art forms carried the signature of the feudal society of the sixteenth century. The ballet, with its inner tenderness and outward splendor best reflected the society that gave life and shape to it.

Close to seventy years after the *Ballet Comique de la Reine,* the dance entertainment of the aristocracy and the rich citizenry in France had little social meaning, and its relation to the arts was negligible. The themes, mainly mythological, pastoral and allegorical, remained remote from life except when mummeries and grotesque dance numbers were included. But the people greatly enjoyed the ballet-masquerades, perhaps because these entertainments obeyed no formula or tradition. Even when put into

the frame of a stage as so-called *ballet-comiques,* the structure was poor, chiefly a loose mingling of declamation, singing and dancing that had no direction or thread of thought. However, these amusements were important since they sharpened the taste for what we would call "numbers" on certain themes. Generally, the ballet-masquerade was the favorite entertainment until the middle of the seventeenth century and also evoked response among the growing middle class.

The aristocracy preferred productions that gave more space to music, singing and pantomime. They called them *ballet-mélodramatique* which in many ways resembled the English Masques of the same period, only without the genius of a Ben Jonson and Inigo Jones to lift them above the ordinary. Both mirrored the mood of the time and showed the influence of the opera; the latter was by far a newer

*Left: M. Dumoulin. (Collection George Chaffee)*
*Above: Design by Daniel Rabel for the "Musiciens de Campagne" scene in* Les Fées de la Forest de Saint-Germain, *danced in the Louvre in 1625. (Collection George Chaffee: Harvard)*

art experience than the dance of which the people had always been fully aware. The *ballet-mélodrama-tique* was closer to opera than ballet, and the English Masque underlined the singing voice.

From all these variations of the ballet-masquer-ade emerged the classic form of the *ballet à entrées* which is nothing else but our divertissements\* and which became, in its diverting lightness, the favorite balletic entertainment in the mid-seventeenth century. The nobility delighted in dancing the *ballets à entrées*, but the latter half of the century brought about marked changes. It was the beginning of professionalism, and the appearance of the professional ballerina changed the image of the theater dance. Until then one rarely saw both sexes dancing in ballets on stage. A lingering custom from the Shakespearean days, young boys played the female parts, a practice reaching well into the seventeenth century. Louis XIII, who ascended the throne in 1610—the year in which he appeared in several entries of the ballet *Alcine*—loved comedy parts and

\* The divertissements had a varied history. Lully and Rameau made full use of them in the seventeenth and eighteenth centuries. When Noverre proclaimed the independence of the ballet from the opera, he tried to do away with all divertissements and to present the ballet as a dramatic entity. In the Romantic era, choreographers wanted to have it both ways: to create a danced drama and enjoy the divertissements, too. And they are still with us to this day. While choreographers like Antony Tudor or Jerome Robbins are inclined to follow the example of Noverre, George Balanchine, in his romantic moods, embraces the concept of divertissements wholeheartedly. The definition of a divertissement is "a series of dances, called *entrées*, inserted into a classic ballet; or a group of dances put together for the purpose of presenting several individual dancers in a series of separate numbers."

*King Louis XIV as the Sun in the 1653 ballet* La Nuit.
*(Bibliothèque Nationale, Paris)*

good reason. The noble men and ladies vied with one another in their proficiency as dancers. They had to practice with experts, the dancing masters, who could not boast of having royal blood. But among the French aristocracy in the first half of the seventeenth century we encounter many first-rate dancers who could well compete with their middle-class teachers. Later in the century, the nobility lost its superiority in dancing skill to the professionals. From then on the aristocrats preferred to play the part of patrons and spectators, keeping away from the stage and concentrating on ballroom exercises.

But during a good part of the seventeenth century the enthusiasm of the nobility for the ballet often approached a dance craze. The dancing kings—whether Louis XIII or XIV—became indelible images in history. Louis XIV derived his famous epithet of *Le Roi Soleil*, the Sun King, from the *Ballet de la Nuit* in which he danced the role of the sun. This was in 1653, when, at the age of fifteen, he appeared with the symbol of the sun on his chest, with sun rays around his head, his neck, his shoulders, his wrists, knees, and shoes. It goes without saying that, as the sun king, he conquered the night in this ballet.

The *Ballet of the Night*, which is said to have lasted for thirteen hours, is also memorable for the fact that the twenty-one-year-old Lully danced in it together with the King, and the monarch took a great liking to him. Lully appeared in five different roles, which started him on a fabulous career, not as a dancer, but as the artistic dictator at a focal point of European culture.

## L'art c'est moi: Lully

All great—and also the less important—decisions at the French court were made by the ruling minister, not by the king; at first, by Richelieu and then by Mazarin. The decade preceding Richelieu's death was a barren period in the dance field. One was enamored with the *ballets à entrées* which deteriorated more and more into insipid comedies making no demands on intellect and emotions. It

also delighted in dancing female roles. Men partnered men disguised as women, or when the queen danced a ballet with princesses and duchesses we find that some of them in tights appear male. The baroque ballet discovered the usefulness of tights and these, since then, have never left the ballet dancer. This transvesting of the sexes had an erotic charm, however perverted it may seem; it was employed in many operas, but lost its fascination for the choreographer.

Whenever men were permitted to appear in ballets danced by ladies of the aristocracy, we find many nonaristocratic members among them with

*Design by Daniel Rabel for the "Danceurs de Sarabande" in* La Douairière de Billebahaut (The Dowager of Bilbao). *(Collection George Chaffee: Harvard)*

was the lowest point in the development of the French ballet since the days of Beaujoyeulx. Mazarin was determined to remedy this situation and, having not forgotten his Italian past, he tried to bring as many Italian artists to Paris as possible. Between 1645 and 1647 he produced one Italian opera after the other. The most lavish production was Luigi Rossi's *Orfeo* which, at a cost of four hundred thousand livres, was presented at the Palais Royal. But the nobility had come to like the easy entertainment and diversion of *ballets à entrées*. Although the records refer to superb dancing and singing in this opera, the people were bored since they understood no Italian and it lasted over six hours.

Now, France had everything she could borrow or buy of the fragments left by Italian Renaissance genius. It had started with Belgiojoso who had become Beaujoyeulx. Another such striking metamorphosis was needed. This happened when in 1646 fourteen-year-old Giovanni Baptiste Lulli became *garçon de chambre* to Mademoiselle de Montpensier, cousin of the King of France. He was a youth of tremendous agility and many talents, not the least important of which was his ability to ingratiate himself with the right people.

His preoccupation with music soon brought him a post with the house orchestra of Mademoiselle de Montpensier, and after six years, having called sufficient attention to his talents—not only as a musician, but also as a dancer—he left Mademoiselle's service. Soon, he appeared with the King in the *Ballet de la Nuit*. As a virtuoso in the dance as well as on the violin, he gained Louis XIV's favor and the King asked him to write ballet music and made him the conductor of an orchestra of twenty-four strings, "Les petits violons du roi," founded for Lully. As the King's *maître de musique,* he stood in such high honor that when he married a French lady, Madeleine Lambert, in 1662, the King and Queen were his witnesses.

Loved by the King, furthered by Mazarin, his compatriot, nothing stood between him and an almost dictatorial power in the musical-balletic-theatrical field. But in 1662 Mazarin died, and his successor, Jean Baptiste Colbert, was a French chauvinist, particularly disdainful of Italian influence. Lully conveniently forgot his Italian origin and clandestinely helped Colbert clear Parisian art of Italian influence, and kept himself at a safe distance from his former friends. By the time Lully died in 1687 his fame had spread all over Europe.

Lully's ambition and ruthlessness in no way affect his greatness as an artist. He was brilliant as a composer, conductor, dancer, mime, promoter and organizer. He understood public taste perfectly. He had an uncanny sense for the dramatic in whatever medium he worked. He was the founder of the French opera—nothing can be more French than Lully's approach to lyric theater—and, oddly enough, it was an Italian's work that had the most profound effect on him. Francesco Cavalli—who was the most gifted student of Monteverdi and who created the term *opera scenica*—was invited to Paris to help produce *Serse* in conjunction with the marriage ceremonies of Louis XIV in 1660. Cavalli's work became a point of departure for Lully, although he went in another direction.

As a professional dancer, Lully knew the problems and needs of ballet music. His style with its luminous clarity, gay overtones and graceful melodies held together by simple counterpoint, was just right for it. Simplicity, the avoidance of unnecessary ornament, and coherence in the musical and dramatic line were new concepts at that time and basic in Lully's work. He did not immediately embark on writing big operas. He wisely sensed that he could form a profitable partnership with Molière and

*Costume designs by Jean Bérain, Jean Baptiste Lully's scenographer, costumer and "machinist." (National Museum, Stockholm)*

*Two dancing positions from Cesare Negri's* Gratie
d'Amore—Nuove Invenzione di Balle, *1602.*
*The rope seems to have served as a barre. (Collection
George Chaffee: Harvard)*

create a light comedy including a series of ballet
entries which the eyes would enjoy as much as the
intellect. Lully aimed at a fully integrated entertainment with music and dance related to action
and words. He thought, as he wrote, that this was
"new to our stage, but one might find authority for
it in antiquity; and, as everybody was pleased with
it, it may serve as a suggestion for other performances which can be worked out more at leisure."

Their partnership, starting in 1664 and lasting
about six years, brought forth a new genre, the
*Comédie-Ballet,* the musical comedy of the French
baroque. Such masterpieces as *Le Mariage Forcé, Les
Facheux,* and *Le Bourgeois Gentilhomme* resulted from

it. Unfortunately, these plays when done today fail
to retain the flavor of the period by omitting music
and dance. This new kind of entertainment could
not have evolved without the influence of the *ballets
à entrées* and the *commedia dell'arte.* The spirit of
the *commedia dell'arte* with its stock characters,
earthy humor and vitality, and the wit of improvisation can be found in Molière's characters and Lully's
musical stylization. Harlequin slipped into the costume of Louis XIV, and the burlesque humor of the
Italians received its refined Gallicized treatment in
these *comédie-ballets.* Lully gave substance and
meaning to the *ballets à entrées,* and the dancing
often eclipsed the comedy part in these productions.
He not only wrote the music for them, he himself
danced with the major ballet figure of his time,
Pierre Beauchamps. The importance attached to
the ballet can be best measured in the satiric remarks Molière made in *Le Bourgeois Gentilhomme:*

All the ills of mankind, all the tragic mis-
fortunes that fill the history books, all political

blunder, all the failures of great commanders, have arisen merely from lack of skill in dancing....

When a man has been guilty of a mistake, either in ordering his own affairs, or in directing those of the State, or in commanding an army, do we not always say: So and so has made a false step in this affair...?

And can making a false step derive from anything but lack of skill in dancing?

From the light musical touch, Lully proceeded to write operas. In collaboration with the librettist Philippe Quinault he wrote fifteen operas which enriched the recitatives, developed the aria as well as the harmonic and rhythmic vocabularies. Some of his best operas such as *Cadmus et Hermione, Alceste,* or *Armide et Renaud* remained in the repertoire of most opera houses for over a century. Lully made the ballet an important feature in his operas, and from then on opera-goers in Paris expected to see dancing, chiefly in the second act of each opera. Lully's greatest fame was as a composer of ballet music, and his songs were heard everywhere, in the salons as much as in the streets.

For the dance historian, his greatest importance lies in his realization that dancing was the strongest physical and visual counterpoint to the pirouettes of French esprit; that it best fitted a period of growing extravagance in dress, speech and behavior, of conspicuous waste, and of an artificiality manifest in everything happening in the salons, from conversation to love-making. Lully's interest was focused on the dance in whatever he did and with whomever he worked.

He contributed most to the dance as the head of the *Académie Royale de la Musique et de la Danse.* The need for an academy seemed to have been innate with the French. Already in 1570, Catherine de' Medici gave Jean Antoine Baïf, author of many amorous sonnets, permission to found the Academy of Saint Cecilia. It exerted great influence on the music for church, chamber and ballroom. Essentially, Baïf's effort was to revive the poetic metric of the ancient Greeks. The religious wars raging in France put an end to Baïf's endeavors, but the idea

of creating a dramatic synthesis of music, dance and verse remained alive among the royal musicians and dancing masters. Two minor artists, the poet Abbé Pierre Perrin and the composer Robert Cambert, both of whom loathed Lully and the Italianate artistic climate in France, tried to create *the* French opera. They even obtained a patent to present operas within the framework of the Académie Royale de la Musique, and their work, *Pomone,* premiered in 1671, was surprisingly successful. This surprised Lully who had doubted that the French public was ready for a more serious opera *à la française.* He took advantage of the apparent change in taste and of his good standing with the men in power; and in 1672 they put him at the helm of the academy for life.

As head of the academy he fostered the idea of a unified dramatic subject and stage presentation. For him, coherence was the key to creation, and he insisted on having one librettist or poet, one composer and only one designer working on any single presentation. He worked closely with Jean Bérain, the first great scenic designer in France, who toned down the dazzling effects of the Italian school and tried to create a poetic stage atmosphere.

More significant was his work with Pierre Beauchamps, the King's dancing master and the most important choreographer of the period. Beauchamps was an excellent performer, full of vigor and famous for his pirouettes. But his historic importance lies in his technical innovations. He oriented ballet toward the conquest of space, stressed a greater use of the arms, and tried to make the entire body a part of choreography. Although his figures of dances were called noble and they impressed Lully and his contemporaries as daring and new, they were denuded of sentiment and expression (as Noverre said, two generations later) and would probably strike us as a kind of balanced marching in a geometric design. But what Beauchamps achieved was technical perfection. No attempt was made to express anything, or to achieve naturalism; everything was keyed to the classic ideals of clarity, balance and proportion, even if rigidity became unavoidable.

*A scene from* Le Nozze degli Dei, *designed in 1637 by
Alfonso Parigi, shows a ballet of sea divinities. This
is probably the first picture showing an* entrechat. *(Collection George Chaffee)*

This was both the positive and negative result of
the principles evolved at the Académie. A critic
rightly remarked about the new academic artists
that "they believe in the creative power of artistic
prescriptions."

However, this whole stylized form demanded
technical nuances and this led to the perfection of
the *danse d'école,* the classic school of dancing. Beauchamps set forth the important principle that each
leg must be "turned out" and the feet must move
to and from the five fundamental positions of classic
ballet. They become second nature to him. Beau-

champs formally established them in about 1700 as
the foundation for exercises and performance. He
also made sure that the front of the dancer's body
always faced the audience in its maximum silhou-
ette. The entire vocabulary and all choreographic
idioms evolved from these principles, which also accounts for the use of the French terms wherever
ballet is taught.

In 1681, another historic innovation took place.
Beauchamps choreographed the ballet *Le Triomphe
de l'Amour* as a court entertainment; Bérain designed
the décor and the costumes and Lully wrote the
music and Beauchamps danced with Louis XIV a
*pas de deux* in it by taking the part of the lady. The
ballet was so successful that it was also performed at
the Académie. With the general public as audience,
Beauchamps dared to give his part to a professional
dancer, the first *première danseuse,* Mlle. La Fon-
taine. Beauchamps danced the part of Mars. There

is no doubt that at that time and still for some time to come the male dancer played a more important role in the classic ballet. But the triumph of the ballerina began with *Le Triomphe de l'Amour.*

## Rameau: Elevation, Exoticism and Decadence

The dance at the end of the seventeenth century was still court-oriented and dominated by a slow elegance of movement. Although Louis XIV danced for forty-eight years with vigor and joy, we cannot visualize him as a bravura performer. But the "noble" dance—so common at that time—helped create the *adagio,* one of the mainstays of balletic art, its archetypal form, a spatial dialogue of love, originally performed by a couple and sometimes today, according to the subject, by more than two dancers. The *adagio* is inherently romantic in its relation of two persons to each other; it also gave the ballet its tender, dreamlike and elusive quality.

But faster movements—the *allegro* had to follow the *adagio*—and virtuoso technique became the natural aim of the well-trained dancers at the Académie. During the first decade of its existence it produced twelve male and ten female dancers. However, the interest in it and the number of participants grew tremendously toward the end of the century. The result was more and better-trained dancers, such as Jean Ballon, famous for his lightness and elasticity in jumps, or Louis Pécourt whose precision and grace on stage were as well known as his amorous involvement with Ninon de Lenclos, a celebrated French beauty and wit whose salon made literary history. Pécourt is also credited with the creation of the *minuet,* which became the dominant social dance of the late baroque and rococo periods. He followed Beauchamps as *maître de ballet* and designed a series of *danses galantes,* single dance numbers which were soon favored over the imaginative and integrated ballet.

Several events contributed to the creative barrenness of the fifty years between Lully's death and Jean-Philippe Rameau's rise. The academicians had eyes only for the accumulation of a perfect technique and in time their teaching became rigid and dogmatic. Through their academic approach, however, they laid the foundation for the tradition in which dancers turned into teachers of the next generation and for the creation of dynasties in the ballet world. Less than two generations later the great dancer Gaetan Vestris could say about his son, Auguste, whose mother was the danseuse Marie Allard: "Auguste—*le dieu de la danse*—is more skilful than I am because I am his father, an advantage nature denied me."

Another factor keeping the French ballet from carrying out Lully's legacy was the remarkable rise in popularity of the Italian opera and the sweeping success of singers in the beginning of the eighteenth century. Pietro Metastasio, a Roman librettist and, from 1730 on, court poet in Vienna, dominated the operatic scene with his bombastic plots, a flowery text and grandiose climaxes. The French, too, succumbed to his influence, and the ballet-opera that Lully had brought to an artistic height gave way to stage presentations which—if they were not purely operatic, full of ornaments and coloraturas —treated unrelated subjects under a general title, such as *The Ages of Man, The Four Seasons,* or *The Cosmic Elements.*

In all these presentations, the dramatic action was reduced to a minimum, and structure and content were wanting. It was a period in the marriage of opera and ballet in which the musicians called the tune. Not that there wasn't a craving for dancing! On the contrary, the light-heartedness of the age of Watteau and Boucher had a wonderful component of light-footedness. In the first half of the eighteenth century Lully's artistically balanced ballet-opera became the opéra-ballet in which theme and plot served the singers and elegant dance numbers. The opéra-ballets trifled with and overdid the pastoral and its bucolic scenes. The saccharine idols of shepherdesses triumphed over everything else and remained on stage until their heads fell along with those of their counterparts in real life.

*Swordsmanship and dancing, both emphasizing controlled and stylized movement, were part of every courtier's education. This late seventeenth-century engraving shows lessons in progress. (Collection George Chaffee)*

There were, of course, attempts at expressing the growing undercurrents of this period. The age of Enlightenment had dawned and a spirit of rationalism heralded a realistic approach to life and the arts. By 1733 the works of Rameau began to replace those of Lully at the Académie. The Académie, or its outgrowth, the Parisian Opéra, had meanwhile become a power. To be produced at the Opéra, or to dance there, was recognized as accomplishment.

Rameau, the first French-born master in opera, was the son of a church organist; he started to make a name for himself as a theorist before, at the age of

fifty, he was acclaimed as a composer. His aim was the restoration of reason in music. As a child of the baroque, he could not help but make his music sound rich even though it was not opulent and ornamental. But he was immediately accused of sacrificing melody for the sake of harmony and intricate orchestration, of putting too much stress on drama and on an integrated plot with a great deal of dancing expressing character and situation.

For some time he had searched for a suitable text. Finally, an abbé wrote for him *Hippolyte et Aricie*, based vaguely on Racine's *Phèdre*. Rameau did not set out to create a new style or taste. He wanted to restore Lully's balance between drama, music and the dance, but the Lullists denounced his complex orchestration as a betrayal of Lully's simplicity and claimed his music was cerebral and did not express emotion. The Ramists felt that he was laying the

123

*Watercolor sketch by Boquet of a costume*
*for the ballet* Medusa.
*(Giraudon: Bibliothèque de l'Opéra, Paris)*

foundation for a French operatic art, and the two factions fought violently. This struggle became more heated in 1752 when an Italian troupe presented Pergolesi's *La Serva Padrona.* It was called the *guerre des bouffons,* and this "war of the buffoons," carried on in the salons and streets of Paris, was the desperate fight of established Italian opera against a new style, a "modern" approach to opera and ballet.

Jean Jacques Rousseau, whose romanticism made him believe in the Italian method, wrote about Rameau that "the French airs are not airs at all, and the French recitative is not recitative." The musicians and singers at the Opéra gave Rameau a hard time. But there were those who realized the composer's genius. "Rameau has made of music a new

art," Voltaire wrote, and André Campra, a minor composer, said, "He will eclipse us all." In his own defense, Rameau declared in 1735:

> Forever occupied with fine declamation and the lovely melodic line which reigned in the recitatifs of the great Lully, I attempt to imitate him, not as servile copyist, but availing myself, as he did, of fair and simple nature as my model.

Rameau actually anticipated the ideas of the encyclopedists whose spokesman, Diderot, wrote: "The enchanted world may serve to amuse children. The real world alone pleases the mind." Rameau discarded the sham pastoral settings and tried to replace shepherds with human beings. It was the time when the wonders of mythology gave way to the exotic, which, of course, was anything but realistic. The oriental influence had already started in Lully's day, but toward the mid-eighteenth-century Europe, and particularly France, was swept by a wave of exoticism. Everything from far-away was indiscriminately thrown onto the stage as the image of the noble savage. The best example of it is Rameau's opera-ballet, *Les Indes Galantes,* produced in 1735, in which the gallant Indians came from everywhere. The nature of the dance changed too, the oriental influence producing an emphasis on sensuous excitement.

Rameau was not only attacked for being ballet-minded, but also for the manner in which Louis Dupré—Pécourt's pupil—choreographed for him. In the 1730's, the balletic art, having by then well-trained dancers at its disposal, took a big step toward becoming the dramatic visualization of grace at its most beautiful. The dancers began their conquest of gravity, bringing the *danse haute* (high dance) into being. The main goal of choreography was no longer to make the most of grace in well-placed figures on a horizontal plane, but to display the brilliance of a technique in which the elevation, or vertical dance, was most characteristic. The Lullists, clinging to the tradition of the *danse basse,* condemned the revolution of the *danse verticale* with its high leaps and pretty entrechats, or beaten jumps.

Maria Camargo was the most impressive tech-

*Costume design by Jean Bérain*
*for the figure of Neptune.*
*(Giraudon: Bibliothèque Municipale)*

chats to right and left and in all directions, but scarcely rising from the ground; yet she was received with fervent applause."

Camargo delighted in fast dances and gave impetus to the development of the *allegro*. Her Spanish temperament coupled with her physical abilities won many admirers for her. While she was famous for technique and virtuosity, her great rival, Marie Sallé, enchanted the Lullists with her expressiveness. They saw in her "the muse of modest, gracious gesture." For the first time we find dance for the sake of dancing pitted against dance that gains meaning through expressiveness. Sallé channeled all her energies into the expression of feelings, she found a gesture language, a pantomimic realization for all emotional nuances, and thus opened up a new world for the ballet.

She prepared the way for Noverre who, as a young man, had danced with her and who later worked most of her ideas into programmatic principles which were to turn the trend of the theater dance. And she definitely anticipated some of the concepts with which, two hundred years later, Isadora Duncan revolutionized the dance. When Marie Sallé appeared in London in 1734 in her own choreography of the ballet-pantomime *Pygmalion*, the London correspondent of the *Mercure de France* reminds of reactions to Isadora Duncan when he says: "She has dared to appear in this entrée without pannier, skirt, or bodice, and with her hair down; she did not wear a single ornament on her head. Apart from her corset and petticoat she wore only a simple dress of muslin draped about her in the manner of a Greek statue."

Marie Sallé touched the heart with her tenderness and inspired the mind with her intelligence. She was loved for her natural grace and lack of affectation and she was admired as a woman of wit and intelligence. Among her friends were Voltaire, Gluck, Garrick, and Noverre. After her death in 1756 Noverre wrote:

> Mademoiselle Sallé replaced tinsel glitter by simple and touching graces. Her physiognomy was noble, sensitive and expressive. Her vo-

nician of this period, with a sensitive ear for music and an effortless airy bravura. Still hampered by heeled shoes and long skirts, the daring deed which opened all kinds of virtuoso possibilities to her was the shortening of her skirt by a few inches. She is said to have been the first dancer to execute the *entrechat quatre*. With the skirt above the ankle, one could see much better the nimble footwork, the height of a cabriole, the vigorous beauty of a *jeté*. The Ramists extolled the gaiety and intensity that La Camargo brought to the ballet. But we must not imagine that even such a vivacious dancer as Camargo achieved any great height in her movements. Casanova said of her in his *Mémoires*: "I saw a danseuse who bounded like a fury, cutting entre-

luptuous dancing was written with as much finesse as lightness; it was not by leaps and frolics that she went to your heart.

## Noverre and Gluck: the Grand Simplicity

Jean Georges Noverre, the greatest name in ballet history, was recognized and honored at a point in his life when his innovations had become a matter of the past. He brought a brilliant mind to ballet art, and his concepts of the theater dance are as

*Jean Ballon, who was classed as a "danseur noble," was one of the leading professionals in the age of Louis XIV. (Collection George Chaffee)*

valid today as they were revolutionary in his own time. He choreographed more than one hundred and fifty ballets, but none of his choreography has survived except in form of a few scenarios. We know, however, that most of his ballets were recognized in Germany, Russia, Italy and England as the great works they were. His French colleagues were strongly influenced by his ideas, but jealousy and official inertia drove Noverre from his homeland after he had published in 1759 *Lettres sur la Danse et sur les Ballets,* his famous protest and guiding principles. Noverre addressed fifteen letters on every aspect of his art to an imaginary correspondent who was obviously everyone interested in theater dance.* These discussions are the most penetrating analyses and the most enlightened criticism ever written on theatrical dancing. The monument Noverre left was not his dancing or his choreography, of which there is hardly any clear image, but his writing, as Lincoln Kirstein pointed out.

Noverre made his debut at the age of sixteen as Dupré's pupil at Fontainebleau. He then went to Potsdam to dance for the King of Prussia, impressing Frederick with his gift for imitation and skilful parodies of other dancers. His first major opportunity came when the director of the Opéra Comique engaged him as *maître de ballet.* There, in 1754, he made his first great impression on the dance scene with a ballet, *Les Fêtes Chinoises,* which he had already tried out in Lyons and Marseilles. Even in his eyes it was a poor concoction—a concession to a passing fad, the Chinese-influenced rococo. Boucher designed a dreamlike décor and Bérain, beautiful dresses. The dramatist Charles Collé noted in his *Journal* in July, 1754:

This month, all Paris has flocked to a Chinese

* What Noverre tried to achieve for theater dance was paralleled by Christoph Willibald Gluck in the field of opera and by Gotthold Ephraim Lessing in dramatic literature. Lessing translated Noverre's letters into his native tongue. In his epoch-making *Hamburg Dramaturgy,* Lessing attacked the pseudo-classic school of French writers and prepared the way for the romantic revolt by extolling Shakespeare as the ideal dramatist; he echoed Noverre's sentiments when he tried to free the writer from the fashionable strait jacket of mechanical rules. Approaching theater art in different media, both Lessing and Noverre fought for full artistic freedom, purity, and integrity.

*Open-air ballet designed by Ludovico de Burnacini at the end of the seventeenth century. Etching by J. M. Krausen. (Collection George Chaffee)*

ballet given at the Opéra Comique. I do not like ballets and my adversion to dancing has greatly increased since all the theaters have become infected with ballets; but I must admit that this Chinese ballet is unusual, and at least by its novelty and its picturesqueness it has earned a share of the applause it is given. This ballet has been designed by a certain Noverre, a young man of 27 or 28 years. He seems to have a wide and agreeable imagination for his profession. He is novel and prolific, varied and a painter. It is not by the *pas* and the *entrées* that he pleased, it is by the variegated and novel tableaux that he achieved this prodigious success. If there is anyone who can drag us out of the childhood in which we are still in the matter of ballets, it must be a man such as this Noverre. The Opéra should secure and pay well such

talent; but for the very reason that they should do so, they will do nothing of that sort....

One could not imagine a more astute and prophetic review. The success of this Chinese Ballet must have frightened his competitors. It certainly induced the famous English actor-manager, David Garrick, to invite Noverre to London with the entire cast. But on the night when his *Chinese Metamorphosis*, as his ballet was called there, opened, the Seven Years' War broke out between the French and the English. Garrick's claim that Noverre was really Swiss—the truth is that he had a Swiss father and French mother—could not prevent a patriotic demonstration that turned into a riot in which the décor was destroyed. Noverre seemed to have stayed in England for some time and staged incidental dances, harlequinades, farces, or spectacles of the kind that were still customarily presented after plays. His brother Augustin settled in Norfolk where the Noverres remained dance teachers for genera-

*The Drottningholm Theater near Stockholm is the only eighteenth-century theater still preserved in its original condition and used for opera and ballet. (Courtesy Anna Greta Stahle)*

tions. Until recently one could hear in Norfolk the rhyme, "Mr. Noverre came from France to teach the natives how to dance."

When Noverre returned to France, he tried again for the coveted position at the Paris Opéra, but in vain. Even Madame Pompadour's intervention could not overcome the fear of his rivals. In 1758 he accepted an offer from the theater in Lyons, a prosperous provincial capital; and it was then that he wrote his *Lettres,* at once a testament to future generations and a bomb hurled at the nonentities ruling the taste of the time. But before the bomb exploded, Noverre had left for Stuttgart where he became ballet master for Karl-Eugene, Duke of Württemberg, who loved good living and the arts. The Duke's importance to the arts was incalculable: He engaged all the great artists whom he could

reach—writers, musicians, painters, singers, actors, and dancers.

Before the inevitable financial crises overwhelmed the Duke, Noverre had had the freedom to unfold his great talents. His reputation and the Duke's money attracted the star dancers of the time, among them the inimitable Gaetan Vestris and Charles Le Picq. Of Noverre's ballets, *Jason et Médée* proved to be one of the most popular and was given time and again in all the capitals of Europe.

From Stuttgart Noverre went to Vienna, one of the growing cultural centers of Europe. There he became dancing master to the Imperial family, gave lessons to young Marie Antoinette and acted as ballet master to the two great Viennese theaters, the Burgtheater, where French plays and operas were produced, and the Theater at the Kaerntnerthor, which later became the Viennese Opera. His meeting with Christoph Willibald Gluck in Vienna was for both of the greatest significance. In 1761 Gluck wrote the music for Noverre's ballet *Le Festin de Pierre,* based on Molière's comedy of Don Juan, and the following year Noverre arranged the dances in Gluck's *Orfeo*. When, in 1767, Gluck's opera *Alceste* was premiered at the Kaerntnerthor, the opera itself was considered a bit too lugubrious, but the evening was saved by the extraordinary reception given Noverre's ballet.

In preparing the operatic stage for Richard Wagner, Gluck tried to establish a closer bond between the words, action and music; he demanded that the dance express action within the action of the opera, that it further the plot. Although he began under Metastasio's influence, he soon turned against the Italianate entertainment with its bombast and bathos. "My chief endeavor," he tried to explain, "must be to attain a grand simplicity." Gluck's and Noverre's innovations were, of course, part of an intellectual revolution—paralleled by political events —that was sweeping through France, England and some of the cultural centers of Central Europe. Voltaire, Rousseau and Diderot were its spokesmen, with Winckelmann's *History of the Art of Antiquity* later adding a classic revival.

After his stay in Vienna, Noverre felt vindicated by his triumphs. He also had in Marie Antoinette, his former pupil and now Queen of France, a powerful patron. When he returned to Paris in 1776 at the age of fifty and with the coveted title of ballet master of the Paris Opéra, his revolutionary ideas had already won out. Ironically, his concepts having been usurped, modified and popularized by others, he found himself a stranger in a world built out of his own dreams. Now he was considered the tired revolutionary, the foreigner, the man who had made his name in the provinces. The intrigues of the many cliques at the Opéra brought him only bitterness and disillusionment.

The famous ballerina, Madeleine Guimard, was the uncrowned queen of the Opéra and controlled the patronage lists. Her dislike of Noverre was intense, although she triumphed in many of Noverre's ballets, particularly in *Les Caprices de Galatée*. She was joined in her schemes by the two brothers Gardel. Maximilian, the elder one, was assistant ballet master before Noverre's appointment. According to tradition he should have succeeded to the post. His animosity and vengeance went so far as to perform with obvious indifference in Noverre's first production, *Apelles et Campaspe*. Also, Gardel, a fine technician, "would rather have renounced kingdoms of the world than his entrechats."

Finally, worn out by the intrigues against him, disgusted with the poisoned atmosphere in which he had to work and live, he came to an understanding with Maximilian Gardel and Jean Dauberval, one of his finest pupils, whereby he would resign in their favor if the Académie would grant him a yearly pension of three thousand livres. The man whom David Garrick called "the Shakespeare of the dance"; for whom Mozart wrote on speculation *Les Petits Riens* in the hope of working with him on other ballets; whom Gluck embraced as a kindred spirit, had to bow to the pettiness of a few jealous contemporaries.

Noverre retired to Clermont-Ferrand, but when the Revolution came he felt that as the former protégé of the Queen he would be safer in England.

*Dumoulin's protégée, Marie Camargo, in an engraving after a Nicholas Lancret painting. (Collection George Chaffee)*

There he produced, among other works, the ballet *Adèle de Ponthieu,* which remained in the repertoire of many companies well into the nineteenth century. In 1797, he returned to France, wrote a great deal more about the dance, the function of an opera stage, and edited a final two-volume edition of his letters and libretti. He died in Saint-Germain in 1809 while working on a dictionary of the dance.

Responding to the esthetic demands of his age, he declared in his very first letter that "poetry, painting and dancing are, or should be no more than a faithful likeness of beautiful Nature." With Diderot, he insisted on a return to nature, but imitating it meant to him a synthesis of man's creative powers. He saw with the eyes of a painter, and a ballet was to him "a picture, or rather a series of pictures, connecting one with the other by the plot which provides the theme of the ballet; the stage is, as it were, the canvas on which the choreographer, who is the painter, expresses his ideas; the mechanical movements of the dancers are his colors, their physiognomy is the brush and the ensemble and variety of scenes, the choice of music, the décor and the costumes are the tones."

He may have visualized ballet with the eye of a painter, but he knew that this picture must come alive through action: "The action in the matter of dance is the art of conveying our emotions and passions to the soul of the spectator by the true expression of our movements, gestures, and physiognomy." This echoes the encyclopedists who said: "Ballet is an action explained by a dance." Along with them, Noverre repudiated pure dance, dance for the mere sake of dancing and without instructive or moral subject matter. Like them, he was a realist, the first realist in ballet, who pleaded for fewer fairy tales,

*Below left: A 1781 English caricature of Marie Auguste Vestris. The inscription reads "A stranger at Sparta standing long upon one leg said to a Lacedaemonian 'I do not believe you can do so much.' 'True (said he) but every goose can.'" Below: A famous* pas de trois *with Marie Madeleine Guimard, Jean Dauberval and Marie Allard, Paris, 1779. (Both, Collection George Chaffee) Right: The father of Auguste Vestris, Gaetan Vestris, the greatest dancer of his day, in an 1782 engraving appears with Adelaide Simonet and Giovanna Baccelli in* Médée et Jason. *(Courtesy Dance Collection, New York Public Library: Cia Fornaroli Collection)*

for less of the marvellous and unbelievable and for more truth and lifelike action. Impatient with the entries, he visualized a flow of action fitting the plot, pantomime replacing speech, and gestures prompted by deep sentiment rather than by convention. In his choreographies the *corps de ballet* ceased to be a mechanical background, it became a part of the action like the Greek chorus. "Be original!" he often said to his dancers. The true dancer puts his entire personality into his movements. The five positions are good to know but better still to forget; they must become second nature to the dancer, must never intrude on the awareness of the artist and audience.

Noverre saw himself in the role of the restorer of the true dance and good taste, of the reformer of an impoverished art, when he addressed dancers:

Children of Terpsichore, renounce cabrioles, entrechats and over-complicated steps; abandon grimaces to study sentiments, artless graces and expression; study how to make your gestures noble, never forget that is the lifeblood of dancing; put judgment and sense into your pas de deux... away with those lifeless masks; they hide your features, they stifle your emotions; take off those enormous wigs and those gigantic head-dresses which destroy the true proportions of the head in relation to the body; discard the use of those stiff and cumbersome hoops which detract from the beauties of execution, which disfigure the elegance of your attitudes and mar the beauties of contour....

Voltaire acknowledged Noverre's greatness, exclaiming: "You are a Prometheus, you must mold men and move them." The world in which Noverre lived accepted the light from him and used it, but gave him little chance to hold up his own torch.

# 8 The Triumph of Romanticism

The wave of the Romantic ballet that swept Europe in the 1820's made the world forget Salvatore Viganó's great achievements. The pendulum of taste swung away from him, and he was soon forgotten. It was almost a hundred years later that several scholars, along with the notes and letters of Stendhal, established the dancer-choreographer's historical importance.

Salvatore Viganó was born in Naples in 1769. His father, mother and several uncles were dancers and his mother was the sister of the well-known composer, Boccherini. As a boy Viganó showed no special liking for the dance; in fact, he was more interested in literature. But his love for music, inherited from his mother, was even stronger. He began to compose at an early age, and an intermezzo of his was performed in Rome when he was only

seventeen. Finally, however, he decided to make the dance his career.

He first danced in Rome, then in Madrid, where he became a pupil of the famous *maître de ballet* Jean Dauberval. It was also in Madrid that he fell in love with and married the beautiful Spanish dancer, Maria Medina. From 1790 to 1812 the couple danced with sensational success throughout Europe. To do things "à la Viganó" became the vogue. Beethoven, who later wrote his *Prometheus* for him, composed a minuet "à la Viganó," based on a theme

*Above: M. Théleur in his ballet* Figaro au Village.
*Right: The ethereal Marie Taglioni as she appeared in her London debut in 1830 as Flora in* Flora et Zéphire.
*(Both, Collection George Chaffee)*

from one of their ballets. Everything from clothes and coiffures to bonbons and cigars bore their name. During their performances in Vienna, Viganó, inspired by Greek sculptures, created a series of plastic positions in which his wife appeared naked under transparent veils. From the phallic dances of primitive man to the various exhibitionistic dances on the stage—as Viganó's example shows—eroticism has always played a great part in the history of the dance.

Becoming estranged from his wife, Viganó went to Milan, where he lived until his death in 1821. Milan was a center of both music and literature, and La Scala was not only a sanctuary for opera and ballet; it was a place where society women flirted with the men and behaved like ladies of the *demimonde*. As Stendhal put it: "At La Scala a woman's reputation...was made when her lover escorted her to her box, ruined when only a servant or her husband accompanied her." In 1812 Viganó became *maître de ballet* at La Scala and decided to give up dancing in order to concentrate on choreography. The famous opera house had all the facilities needed to put his theories into practice, and he composed more than forty ballets within nine years.

Viganó created the *choréodrame*, the dance drama in which, for the first time, each dancer characterized his part individually. There was no longer any uniformity of poses to express emotion, yet Viganó, using the principles of his predecessor, Noverre, was able to make a choreographic unity out of these individual expressions and continually changing pictures.

Pantomime, alive and natural, played the greatest part in his innovations. "It expresses...the movement of the soul," he said, "it is the language of all peoples, of all ages and times. It depicts, better than words, extremes of joy and sorrow... It is not enough for me to please the eye: I wish to engage the heart."

We learn a good deal about Viganó's ballets and working methods through Stendhal's passion for the ballet and his many references to the "immortal Viganó," as he called him in his writings. Stendhal,

who had made Milan his headquarters, said: "I pass each day from seven to midnight hearing music and seeing two ballets...." Some of Stendhal's utterances and analogies are typical of romantic exaggeration. He went so far as to say: "I challenge all classical writers of the world to draw a single ballet from the entire *œuvre* of Racine which could be compared to the great ballet *Othello*." Othello was one of Viganó's famous ballets. Or we come across such sentences as, "the tragedies of my God Shakespeare actually are ready-made ballets."

His enthusiasm knew no limits and even his God Shakespeare had to be dethroned one night when he left the Scala after "having seen this ballet (Viganó's *Myrrha*) for the eighth or tenth time, still quite excited." In his exaltation he also exclaimed: "... Shakespeare's best tragedy does not impress

*Marie Viganó in three etchings by Gottfried Schadow. (All, Staatliches Museum, Berlin)*

me half as much as Viganó's ballets. He is a genius who will make his art grow with him and who has no equal in France...." Though it is obvious that Stendhal's emotions generally got the better of him at La Scala, his critical faculties had not forsaken him. On December 1, 1817, he dared to censure Viganó for having done *Psammi, King of Egypt,* "quite an amusing ballet" but a "mediocre work of a great artist."

From a brief biography, published anonymously in Milan in 1821, one can piece together an image of Viganó's personality. He seemed to have been a rather short man with a shapely body, a man who liked well-mannered people, who enjoyed gay, sleepless nights as much as the "sweetness of meditation." But, above all, he was an indefatigable and dedicated worker.

Viganó must have been one of those artists who cannot stop changing and polishing their work, for

Stendhal, who was invited to rehearsals, where he could see the master at work, says: "There he composes his dances and, if he feels the need for it, has, time and again, the artists repeat a few bars which do not quite satisfy him." Viganó was usually surrounded by eighty dancers on the stage, with an orchestra of ten musicians. If he could not find a musical motif which expressed what he had in mind, he himself composed it.

He never came to rehearsal with a ready-made outline of choreography and relied on his intuition. He needed to be on stage, surrounded by the dancers, for his inspiration; in this respect he seems to have his modern counterpart in George Balanchine. Viganó choreographed in a seemingly unorganized fashion. After hours of work it appeared that he had achieved very little, simply explored this or that, simply explained a movement sequence to a few dancers, when suddenly, with the help of his incredible memory, he would fuse all the loose ends into coherent action and dramatic poses, completing his huge mosaic of movement in a measured, form-fulfilled manner. He was particularly admired for his inventiveness in arranging the *corps de ballet* in endlessly varying patterns and his ability to shade the facial, pantomimic expressions of his dancers. We learn from Stendhal that, for instance, Viganó spent on his ballet *Daedalus and Icarus* almost five months rehearsing daily from ten a.m. to six p.m., and resuming at ten in the evening and working until four the next morning.

The ballets were presented with the operas, and Stendhal gave an example of an Italian opera performance in those days:

> On February 1, 1818, the show at La Scala contained the first act of *The Thieving Magpie* played from 7:00 to 8:15, followed by Viganó's ballet, *The Vestal*, from 8:30 to 10:10; then came the second act of *The Thieving Magpie* from 10:45 to 11:15 and finally Viganó's little ballet buffoonery, *The Shoemaker's Wife*, which was booed by the public as though it felt it had to uphold its own dignity. But the same public saw its second performance with great pleasure, for it had meanwhile found out that there was something new in it. The play closed with this little ballet, which reached its end between midnight and one o'clock. Each week, these little ballets show a new *pas*.

Viganó's *choréodrame* mainly combined emotional expression through pantomime with pictorial movement of groups and solo dancers. He was never interested in mere *tableaux vivants;* he aimed for the total orchestration of a movement idea, with each dancer expressing individually the inner experience of the music. He reduced solos and *pas de deux* to a minimum in order to avoid any artificial interruption in the natural flow of the dramatic action. Viganó also demanded from his miming dancers the then unconventional, "natural" gesture and movement, laden with intent, full of meaning. The great advance of archeological research at that time furnished him with the image of many wonderful Greek and Roman sculptures on which he could base some movements for classical themes.

Viganó must have realized how empty all ballet can be when it does not strive for some kind of theme and emotional expressiveness. He must have recognized the danger to which ballet, as a basically romantic art form, will always be exposed: succumbing to the playful and insipid, accepting sweetness for beauty. Speaking of a ballet, *Jucundus,* by Vestris III, Stendhal points out these dangers: "How wanting is this ballet! Nothing but garlands, flowers, sashes with which beautiful ladies adorn their cavaliers or which shepherdesses exchange with their lovers—and dance in honor of these sashes." He contrasted such feeble attempts at artistic creation with a ballet by Viganó which had a strong story line and dealt with the problem of jealousy.

Another illustration is Viganó's ballet *Othello*, which Stendhal thought better motivated than Rossini's opera based on the tragedy:

> Viganó was clever enough to insert in the second act a great scene of noble and gentle conception: it was a nocturnal festival arranged by Othello in his gardens. In the midst of the feast his jealousy is awakened. It then happens that, at the beginning of the last act, we do not feel surfeited with terror and violence, and soon there are tears in everybody's eyes. Rarely have I seen anyone cry at Rossini's *Othello*.

Viganó's *Othello* and *The Vestal* may be singled out as the best of his works—or at least as the ones that made the strongest impression on his contemporaries. He carried Noverre's concept of the action ballet one step further and was the first choreographer to understand fully the importance of the dramatic synthesis of dance, mime and music.

## The Highlights of the Romantic Ballet

Viganó's death in 1821 marks the end of a period. He was the beginning of the romantic spirit, but even more an afterthought to the eighteenth century in the ballet, a reminder of Noverre's greatness.

After him, the curtain rose on a completely new scene, another world. A new era had started with the Industrial Revolution which became the golden age of ballet. In the early 1820's gas light was introduced in the theaters. At that time the ballerinas began to rise on their toes. Although we know of much earlier attempts to dance *sur les pointes*—a contemporary critic described the German ballerina Anne Heinel as entering the stage "on stilt-like tip-toe," when she appeared in London in the 1770's—Marie Taglioni is usually identified as the first ballerina on point, probably because she perfected toe dancing in *La Sylphide* in 1832. But she already danced on toes when she made her Paris debut in 1827. Taglioni was then compared to Genevieve Adelaide Gosselin, who was *première danseuse* at the Paris Opéra until 1818: "Mlle. Taglioni holds herself on the point of the foot with truly remarkable balance. Not since Mlle. Gosselin has any nymph of Terpsichore been able to hold such a position so long."

Born in the early years of the nineteenth century, romanticism found many forms of expression: from emotional exaltation to mysticism, from the unrestricted flight of imagination to the negation of civilization, from the fantastic and weird to the idealization of primitivism and nature. But whatever it included, it certainly was a flight from reality, and nothing could have symbolized it better than a ballerina wrapped in diaphanous muslin, rising on her toes, pirouetting, floating through the air in defiance of gravity.

There was a decisive shift in all spheres of social activity. The middle class moved in, still led by remnants of the nobility. A broader layer of society became the patrons and the connoisseurs of the arts. In the theater the balconies, not the boxes began to set the standard. Tastes changed, but the dance became even more popular. Romanticism gave rise to the balletomane. And the classic ballet of the romantic era became middle-class entertainment.

Another change must be stressed. During the eighteenth century the ballerina was still fighting the male dancer for equal recognition. In the nineteenth century she dominated completely and the male dancer was degraded to the role of *porteur*. Women had become an essential part of romantic idealism. It was no longer woman as mother or earth figure, it was woman as the unattainable, the ideal, the dream. And man, the dreamer, was ready to sacrifice his life for his dream. But sometimes woman could be a spirit of the night leading man astray. In closing his *Faust*, Goethe wrote in 1832: "The Eternal Feminine leads us on!" In the same year, Marie Taglioni danced *La Sylphide* at the Paris Opéra for the first time.

*La Sylphide* and Marie Taglioni are synonymous with romanticism in ballet. Only a handful of dancers in the world have so captured the popular imagination that their names have come to symbolize the dance: Fanny Elssler, Anna Pavlova, Vaslav Nijinsky and Isadora Duncan. Marie Taglioni was the first such name. Her father, Philippe Taglioni, choreographed *La Sylphide* for his daughter's unique abilities. The story of the dance has all the romantic ingredients. On his wedding day, James, a young Scotsman, is awakened by the kiss of a sylphide, who then disappears. She returns and Gurn, his friend and in love with James's bride-to-be, catches a glimpse of the unearthly creature. While he calls the others to witness James's infidelity, the sylphide vanishes. During the wedding ceremony she reappears and snatches the ring that James is about to put on Effie's finger. She lures him into the forest, where we see the witch, Madge, preparing a poisonous brew in which she soaks a filmy scarf. In a lovely glen they dance happily, but whenever he tries to hold the sylph in his arms, she slips away. Finally, the witch, once slighted by James, takes her revenge by giving him the magic scarf. He promises the sylphide the scarf if she will be his. She agrees, and he puts it around her shoulders. Her wings seem to melt away; she dies and is carried up above the tree tops, while at the same time the wedding procession of Gurn and Effie enters.

Taglioni and *La Sylphide* became the rage of Paris, the craze of the age. Throughout her life she was identified with this part, which revolutionized the ballet concept, with its fairy-tale background in a realistic setting, its clash of the natural with the supernatural, its mingling of dream and actuality. It was the romantic ballet which sanctioned this fusing of two extremes. It is still accepted in all its variations.

What was the magic in Taglioni's dancing? The rhapsodies of the critics emphasize her perfect body control. She gave the dance world virtuosity and created a tradition. All acclaimed her long horizontal leaps, the *jetés*, her glides, and the lightness of all her movements. It was said that she crossed the Opéra stage in three leaps and only then, and with

*The celebrated Fanny Elssler dances to castanets in the* cachucha *from* Le Diable Boiteux, *Paris, 1836. (Collection George Chaffee)*

apparent reluctance, did she return to the ground.

In his writings, Théophile Gautier, a poet turned journalist, became the voice of the silent ecstasy on stage. He wrote of Taglioni: "She is just as much a genius as Lord Byron or M. de Lamartine. She has shown us ronds de jambe and ports de bras which are the equal of long poems." Although he felt that she brought a mystical quality to the dance, he is chiefly impressed by the sculptural form, the visual delight, the sensual excitement.

The Romantic ballet is clearly defined by Gautier's aesthetic principles. The exaltation with which he embraced what was holy to him was characteristic of the genuine romantic. He went through life searching for beauty, which, to him, was truth. He discarded the ideals of Noverre and Viganó, who believed in expressiveness, in giving meaning to each gesture. Gautier's concept of the dance was based on visual stimulation, and he even said that if he were the director of the Opéra, he would have ballets composed by painters. To him the sole object of the dance was to show beautiful forms in graceful attitudes. "The true, the unique, the eternal subject of a ballet is dancing." He denied ballet any deeper meaning, and the only expression of passion he granted it was love. In its final triumph of being like a living painting or a moving sculpture, dancing meant to him "physical pleasure and feminine beauty." He helped establish the prominent position of the ballerina when, in shaping the romantic ideal of the dancer, Gautier at best tolerated men in ballet. "For us a male dancer is something monstrous and indecent which we cannot conceive... Strength is the only grace permissible to men." This attitude was emphasized when he could not help praising Jules Perrot, one of the great dancers of his time and a true descendant of eighteenth-century ballet tradition. He admitted in his review: "This praise is all the less suspect from us because we do not in the least care for male dancing. Perrot has made us lose our prejudice."

In his aesthetic appraisal, Gautier was guided mainly by sensual enjoyment, by a disguised eroticism, by a flesh-created beauty. And no one else

*Fanny Elssler as Marguerite with Carey in Jules Perrot's* Faust. *She chose to revive this role for her farewell performance in Vienna in 1851. (Collection George Chaffee)*

could have made a more telling distinction between the two great rivals, Taglioni and Elssler:

> Fanny Elssler's dancing is quite different from the academic idea, it has a particular character which sets her apart from all other dancers; it is not the aerial and virginal grace of Taglioni, it is something more human, more appealing to the senses. Mlle. Taglioni is a Christian dancer... she flies like a spirit in the midst of the transparent clouds of white muslin... she resembles a happy angel.... Fanny is a rather pagan dancer; she reminds one of the muse Terpsichore, tambourine in hand, her tunic, exposing her thigh, caught up with a golden clasp; when she bends freely from her hips, throwing back her swooning, voluptuous arms, we seem to see one of those beautiful figures from Herculaneum or Pompeii which stand out in white relief against a black background, marking their steps with resounding cymbals.

Elssler reminded him of a thousand joyful things. She was the dancer for men, he felt, as Taglioni was for women. Fanny was unrivaled as a mime and had more drive, rhythm and sparkle than Taglioni. She used a great many ethnic sources, and one result was that Gautier proclaimed the glories of the Spanish dance. Elssler's *cachucha, cracovienne, gitana* and *tarantella* carried her fame all over the world. She only once dared to follow Taglioni in the role of Sylphide, but she had neither the lightness nor the brilliant leaps of her rival. Both ballerinas represented the two sides of the romanticism that Gautier thought he saw united in Carlotta Grisi, an Italian dancer and Jules Perrot's pupil; for her he wrote his first ballet *Giselle,* which has become *the* classic of the romantic age. Gautier felt that there was too much ethereal flight, too much whiteness on stage, too many *ballets-blancs,* as he termed the deluge of Taglioni imitations patterned on *La Sylphide.* He saw Grisi's debut in Paris, fell in love with her and began looking for a part that would make the world forget Taglioni's *La Sylphide.* He tried to create a

*Carlotta Grisi is caught by Lucien Petipa in her sensational leap from a high platform in* La Péri. *(Collection George Chaffee)*

composite of what Taglioni and Elssler symbolized. The sylphide was only a creature in the hero's mind, a dreamlike being with whom one can never identify. There should be a real creature which, through dramatic events, would become the unreal creature that was the romantic ideal.

*Giselle* was first performed at the Paris Opéra—at that time still called Théâtre de l'Académie Royale de Musique—on June 28, 1841, with Grisi in the title role. It was billed as a "Fantastic ballet in two acts. Music by Adolphe Adam. Choreography by Jules Perrot and Jean Coralli, Book by Vernoy de Saint-Georges, Théophile Gautier, and Jean Coralli." Some have referred to *Giselle* as the *Hamlet* of ballet. This is silly but deserves discussion as a ballet that was an immediate hit and has remained the most popular of all ballets. It has remained a favorite because it contains the ideal role for most ballerinas, one that permits the dancer to show her powers of interpretation and of pantomime as well as her technical finesse.

A week after the first performance of *Giselle*, Théophile Gautier wrote to Heinrich Heine:

My dear Heinrich Heine, when reviewing, a few weeks ago, your fine book, *De L'Allemagne*,

I came across a charming passage... where you speak of elves in white dresses whose hems are always damp, of nixes who display their little satin feet on the ceiling of the nuptial chamber; of snow-colored *Wilis* who waltz pitilessly, and of all those delicious apparitions you have encountered in the Harz Mountains and on the bank of the Ilse, in a mist softened by German moonlight; and I involuntarily said to myself: "Wouldn't this make a pretty ballet?"

In a moment of enthusiasm, I even took a fine large sheet of white paper, and headed it in superb capitals: *Les Wilis,* a ballet. Then I laughed and threw the sheet aside without giving it another thought, saying to myself that it was impossible to translate that misty and nocturnal poetry into terms of the theater... Three days later, the ballet *Giselle* was accepted....

It is the second act which is lifted from Heine's work. The *Wilis,* those fearful nocturnal dancers, wait for their male victims and dance them to death. A man named Albrecht comes to visit the grave of his beloved Giselle, when the *Wilis* appear, and among them is Giselle. She wants to protect him, but "the fatal madness takes hold of him and he pirouettes, bounds, follows Giselle in her most hazardous leaps; the frenzy to which he gives way reveals a secret desire to die with his mistress." Four o'clock strikes, and the dawn brings delivery: the *Wilis* disappear and with them Giselle.

This second act—close in its conception to *La Sylphide,* with its phantom who has an overpowering fascination for the male—needed a realistic dramatic counterpoint in act one. Gautier first thought of a beautiful ballroom belonging to some prince as the setting. But the final result was the simple story of a naive country girl who falls in love with a prince disguised as a hunter and, on discovering his deceit, goes mad and dies.

Carlotta Grisi became identified with Giselle as Taglioni had been with the sylphide. Gautier, who was responsible for Grisi's phenomenal success and for her separation from Perrot, was said to have died with her name on his lips. That was in 1872, when the Romantic ballet had outlived its climactic achievement and the year in which Serge Diaghilev, ballet's first man of the twentieth century, was born.

*Jules Perrot, the greatest male dancer of the Romantic ballet, in* La Esmeralde, *which he also choreographed. (Collection George Chaffee)*

*The 1851 debut of Lola Montez in America. She performed at the Broadway Theater "for an audience composed largely of gentlemen." (Collection George Chaffee)*

*Exercises from* The Art of Dancing *by Carlo Blasis.*
*(Courtesy Dance Collection, New York Public Library:*
*Cia Fornaroli Collection)*

## Carlo Blasis

With Blasis' second book, *Code of Terpsichore*, the
fundamentals of the classical dance were firmly
established. Blasis gave the ballet technique its final
code. Born in 1803, in Naples, of a noble family with
strong artistic leanings, he studied music, mathematics and anatomy. He was also well versed in
painting and sculpture. He grew up with the concepts of Noverre and Viganó, whose ideas can still
be traced in an earlier essay of his, *Elementary
Treatise on the Theory and Practice of the Art of Dancing.*
Blasis began his career as a dancer and was seen in
a successful series of *pas de deux* in Paris, London and
other cities. A mysterious leg injury cut short his
dancing career. He then accepted a post at La
Scala where he choreographed many ballets, but it
was as a theoretician that he made his mark.

More and more he found Noverre and Viganó too
experimental, revolutionary and even in bad taste.
In his book, Blasis explains that Terpsichore means
to him "delight in dance," precisely what his contemporary, Gautier, felt. Methodical and academic
in approach, he was rigid about consistency and a
structure with a beginning, a middle and an end.
Wherever he could, he leaned on antiquity and
borrowed from sculptures and paintings. Thus, he
modelled the "attitude," the basic pose of the classic
dance after Giovanni di Bologna's statue, *Flying
Mercury,* the dancer standing on one leg and bringing the other leg, with the knee bent, up behind him
at a ninety-degree angle.

"It is in the best productions of painting and
sculpture," he wrote, "that the dancer may study
with profit how to display his figure with taste and
elegance. They are a fountain of beauties to which
all those should repair, who wish to distinguish
themselves for the correctness and purity of their
performances." It was by means of geometric figures
that he emphasized the importance of beautiful line
for his students.

Blasis was the first to understand that only by
training each part of the body can the dancer

achieve the necessary precision. His aim was elegance without affectation. He developed the "turning-out" of feet and hips as established by Beauchamps. Above all, he realized that each body is different, and his goal of making the best of each dancer's physique has become a basic principle in teaching classical ballet. Here are some of his rules:

> Keep your body equally poised upon your thighs. Throw your breast out and hold your waist in as much as you can. In your performance, preserve continually a slight bend and much firmness about your loins. Let your shoulders be low, your head high. The head should be slightly inclined to left in order to avoid a wooden or stiff expression.

He discusses the dancer's center of gravity and his counterpoise, describes the pirouette in great detail as a multiple twirl, executed as high as possible on the half-toe—as it is today. Eighteenth-century simplicity has made way for technical precision and bravura, and elevation has come into its own. But Blasis does not encourage technique as a trick to dazzle the eye and beg applause. To him, a pirouette is utter plasticity; the body, shown from all sides, achieves the ultimate triumph of three-dimensionality.

In his book, Blasis speaks of three distinct types of dancers—each endowed by nature for a particular genre. The serious dancer is the master of the adagio, of the slow, sustained movement. The *demi-caractère* should be of middle height; his work is a mixture of all styles. Finally, there is the comic dancer, who is of small, vigorous and stocky stature; he should be used for rural, pastoral subjects.

An entire chapter is devoted to pantomime, which Blasis calls the "very soul and support of ballet." In his eyes, pantomime has a grammar and idioms like dance itself. He discriminates between the "natural" and the "artificial" gesture, and it is characteristic of the Romantic ballet that he should stress the highly stylized artificial gesture which, in his opinion, could carry best across the footlights.

Blasis detested the experiments of Noverre and Viganó, seeing too much abruptness, violence, excess in them. Every theme, every plot, he feels, must rise to a climax and unravel its drama in an atmosphere of logic and calm. He accepts the exuberant spirit of his time only on a purely technical level. When his influence was greatest, the dance of elevation became most important, the extension of legs and arms achieved maximum possibilities. The ballerina, dominating the stage, pushed the male dancer more and more into the background and degraded him to a *premier porteur*.

Blasis tried to avoid the traps of academic rigidity but failed to give the ballet at this crucial point a new perspective. His measured method, as Lincoln Kirstein called it, his fear of excess and his striving for a purity of style brought the classical ballet to tremendous technical heights, but by the same token endangered the art itself. His influence on the Russian ballet schools was especially great, and it was in St. Petersburg and Moscow that ballet history was made during the second half of the last century.

## The Reign of Petipa

In 1841, at the age of nineteen, Marius Petipa made his debut at the Paris Opéra opposite Fanny Elssler in *Le Diable Boiteux (The Devil on Two Sticks)*. He had studied with his father, Jean Petipa, and had already made a name for himself as an excellent partner, a fair dancer, an exemplary actor and pantomimist. After his debut he danced in smaller French cities and went to Spain for some time before he returned to Paris, where he danced a *pas de quatre* with his brother Lucien and Fanny and Therese Elssler. A few days later he received a terse note from the Maryinsky Theater in St. Petersburg, in which M. Gedeonov, the Director of the Imperial Theaters, offered him the position of *premier danseur* at a salary of 10,000 francs a year.

Petipa arrived in Russia in 1847; he remained there all his life. During the first fifteen years he worked under Jules Perrot. When Perrot withdrew as ballet master in 1862, Petipa accepted the post and served under four czars in the course of almost sixty years. He inherited the riches of the Romantic ballet and gave Anna Pavlova her first role as prima ballerina. Under his artistic direction Russia became the leading country of the ballet. He himself created no fewer than sixty-odd ballets, introduced the concept of the full-length ballet and built up the repertoire of the Russian ballet, still in use to this day.

Petipa's forte was not only his productivity; he also knew how to surround himself with first-rate artists. Without Lev Ivanov, he could not have achieved half of what he did. It is probable that if Ivanov had not been a Russian he would have achieved world fame, for while Russian dancers triumphed, foreigners retained the artistic leadership in nineteenth-century Russia.

A case in point is *Swan Lake*. Tchaikovsky wrote the score for the Bolshoi Theater in 1875. He had great hopes for it, but the choreography was assigned to a hack ballet master by the name of Julius Reisinger. The ballet was a failure. In 1894, after Tchaikovsky's death, the Maryinsky Theater arranged an evening to honor his memory for which Ivanov choreographed what is now the famous second act of *Swan Lake*. The role of the Swan Queen was danced by the famous Italian ballerina Pierina Legnani and the ballet was an immediate success. Realizing its potentialities, Petipa scheduled a second performance, but listed himself as choreographer, with Ivanov reduced to the role of collaborator. Deciding to do a full-length version of the ballet, Petipa staged the numbers for the ballroom scene, which contains the famous *Pas de Deux Classique* of the Black Swan, and Act One, while the other two acts were choreographed by Ivanov.

Ivanov actually helped stage almost all of Petipa's works and his name does occasionally appear as co-

*Rudolf Nureyev in* Laurentia *(Photograph Anthony Crickmay) assumes the* attitude, *a basic pose of the classical dance, first described by Carlo Blasis and modeled after the sixteenth-century Mercury by Giovanni da Bologna. (National Gallery of Art, Washington, D.C.)*

choreographer, but the only ballet for which he received sole credit is *The Nutcracker*. Originally Petipa intended to choreograph it and even discussed the score with Tchaikovsky, but he fell ill, and this gave Ivanov the opportunity to prove that he was more than a collaborator. Since there was an understanding that the name of the ballet-master-in-chief should appear on the program, Petipa often made changes in Ivanov's choreography in order to establish his right to be listed as choreographer.

Arthur Saint-Léon, the dancer-violinist, who went to Russia in 1859 after his separation from the famous ballerina Fanny Cerrito, was far less dependent on Petipa. He had staged his ballets, including his most famous ballet, *Coppélia,* in all the great European cities. He choreographed about a dozen ballets in St. Petersburg and (in *The Humpbacked Horse*) was the first to use a Russian theme. He liked to experiment, introducing such novelties to his ballets as singers and instrumentalists. The twentieth-century ballet would accept such innovations wholeheartedly, but in his own time they clashed with romantic and classical concepts and most of his ideas did not pass the director's desk in St. Petersburg. They certainly were out of keeping with Petipa's harmonious and systematized approach. But during the first two years of Saint-Léon's eight-year stay in Russia Petipa was making a tour of European cities with Maria Sourovshchikova, his wife and his pupil at the Imperial School of Ballet. After that Petipa was able to utilize Saint-Léon's abilities without clashing with him.

As instructor of the Imperial School, Petipa raised the standards of dance technique and choreography in Russia to new heights. In this work he was assisted mainly by the Swedish dancer Christian Johannsen, who had joined the St. Petersburg Imperial Ballet in 1841 and was a celebrated *premier danseur* when Petipa arrived there six years later. Johannsen became one of the most important teachers in the history of the Imperial School; Pavlova and Nijinsky were among his students. Another strong personality who helped shape the Russian ballet under Petipa's reign was Enrico Cecchetti, an Italian who came to Russia as second ballet master in 1890 and stayed for twelve years. His method differed greatly from Johannsen's, whose style was cleaner and less inclined to sacrifice aesthetic values to effect. However much Cecchetti's method was modified by the Russian dancers, his influence as a teacher remained invaluable. He also tried his hand at several choreographies—he shared responsibility for *Cinderella* with Petipa and Ivanov—but his creative attempts were failures.

Petipa had reached his peak as a choreographer at the time Cecchetti arrived. *The Sleeping Beauty* had just proved a resounding success. He had first scored in 1862 with *The Daughter of Pharaoh,* which had brought him the appointment as choreographer-in-chief. It was followed by such great works as *Don Quixote, La Bayadère, Mlada, Zoraya,* and *The Talisman.* Then came *The Sleeping Beauty* which was succeeded by *Cinderella,* the full-length *Swan Lake, The Pearl, Bluebeard, Raymonda,* and *Harlequinade. The Sleeping Beauty* remained the high point of the collaboration between Tchaikovsky and Petipa and the epitome of Russian classical ballet. Whether produced in the full-length version or in one act as *Aurora's Wedding,* it represents the essence of ballet in the second half of the last century, the end result of the decades during which the Romantic ideals had become classical spectacles with romantic overtones.

How shall we sum up Petipa as a choreographer? He was prolific, methodical, and, in spite of working within a certain pattern, very inventive. Although his basic standard was that of order and symmetry, his sense of the theater led him to stage effects that were, however conventional in presentation, theatrically convincing. He believed in dancing for the sake of dancing and in virtuosity heightened into a spectacle. He was a master of the *pas de deux,* but more skilful in choreographing for the ballerina than for the male dancer, who often had to go to Johannsen for help. Petipa made the most detailed research for every ballet he choreographed, outlined the most minute plans, and came to rehearsal fully prepared. The scenic designers were given clear instructions and a composer had to write the music to order, even if he happened to be Tchaikovsky.

For instance, when they worked together on *The Sleeping Beauty,* Petipa thus defined the climax of Act One for Tchaikovsky:

> Suddenly Aurora notices the old woman who beats on her knitting needles a 2/4 measure. Gradually she changes to a very melodious waltz in 3/4, but then, suddenly, a rest. Aurora pricks her finger. Screams, pain. Blood streams —give eight measures in 4/4, wide. She begins to dance—dizziness.... Complete horror—this is not a dance any longer. It is frenzy. As if bitten by a tarantula she keeps turning and then falls unexpectedly, out of breath. This must last from 24 to 32 measures. At the end there should be a tremolo of a few measures, as if shouts of pain and sobs: 'Father! Mother!' And later, when everybody notices the old woman, she throws off her clothes. For this moment it is necessary that a chromatic scale sound in the entire orchestra.

Tchaikovsky studied the problems posed by the moving bodies, restricted as they were by the rules of the *danse d'école* and its set vocabulary. Only because he understood gesture, pantomime, and the rhythm of the dancing body so well, could he write music which beautifully served both choreographer and dancer.

When Michel Fokine later criticized stereotyped and doctrinaire choreography, it was the natural reaction of a new generation rebelling against calculated beauty, the repetition of form, technique for technique's sake, a conventional approach. We know it was all this, and we may call it old-fashioned; yet the Rose adagio of *The Sleeping Beauty* remains with us as the epitome of the dream of love, of the beauty of lightness, of that capacity to float in midair, to demonstrate the bravura of balance by holding a position in breath-taking equilibrium.

It is difficult to believe that dancers will not always want to make those magic passages of *The Nutcracker pas de deux* come alive in all their sustained grace—or the cygnets' *pas de quatre* in *Swan Lake* with its clockwork precision. Did not this *pas*

*M. Mazurier in the character of Punchinello, London,
1825. (Collection George Chaffee)*

de quatre anticipate the dancing in many music
hall shows of the twentieth century with their
machine-age coordination? The ballet of the nineteenth century plainly offered the best escape from
reality.

The themes of the ballets of Petipa's period are

the summation of romanticism: the exotic mixed
with the weird, the escape from reality through
fairy tale and legend leading subtly back to life.
What is *Swan Lake* if not a later version of *La Sylphide*
with a touch of *Giselle?* In the more familiar one-act
version, the graceful swan is man's dream image of
woman, evanescent and eternally unrealized. The
fairy-tale element of the full-length version with its
white and black swan, the Odette-Odile dualism,
has much of the conflict in the female between the

dreamlike Sylphide and the devouring Lilith. By the same token, Odette is the ultimate glorification of womanhood, beauty made noble.

We will never completely outgrow the child-in-man stage because we cannot exist without illusions, without the poetry—however psychoanalytically interpreted—in the dream. While Jerome Robbins' *Afternoon of a Faun,* a ballet of typical mid-twentieth-century romanticism, is tinged with cynicism and a tongue-in-cheek attitude, George Balanchine's *Serenade* has all the earmarks of last century. This only goes to show how inherently romantic the ballet is and that it is at its best, truest to itself, when treated romantically. However abstractly the *pas de deux* that Petipa perfected is choreographed, its romantic nature and the interplay of the sexes is obvious. As strongly as Petipa believed in the *pas de deux* as a display of technical bravura, he did not overlook its romantic appeal, with the male dancer tenderly

lifting and admiringly supporting the ballerina while she, relying on his strength and assurance unfolds her brilliance as a virtuoso and her beauty as a woman.

The classical ballet in Petipa's day had reached the saturation point and was fated to deteriorate into a stereotype because of its total reliance on technique and virtuosity. When, in 1903, Pepita's last ballet, *The Magic Mirror,* was a complete failure, he blamed everyone but himself. He did not realize that he had outlived his own greatness, and that a new age had begun.

# 9  Cancanization

Toward the end of the nineteenth century two theatrical entertainments were the favorites of the bourgeoisie: ballet and opera. They offered not only escape for the man of the *fin de siècle,* but also possibilities for lavish display, for demonstrating that all is luxuriously well in the best of all worlds.

The hedonism of the nineties, the epidemic feeling of romantic resignation and the desire to escape at any price was, of course, little else than a thinly veiled, new romantic trend. Dandyism, above all, meant fastidious elegance, but it also involved an astounding enthusiasm for the stylized arts of opera and ballet, and this accounts for the many balletomanes of the period. At the same time an extravagant bourgeois leisure class was determined to assert itself, and there was no better symbol of this than the *cancan.* A strong desire drove the people not only to the opera house to see ballet but into the dancehalls of which the Moulin Rouge became the epitome.

The painters Edgar Degas and Henri Toulouse-Lautrec captured the spirit of this period on their canvasses better than did any chronicler. They made their immortal contribution to the dance by giving visual expression to the fascination of the age with a ballet which was then on its way to artistic decline and with cabaret and dancehall performances embodying a gay despair.

*Above: Figure from* Conservatoire de Danse Modern *by Quillenbois. (Collection George Chaffee) Right: Toulouse-Lautrec's* Mlle. Lender Dancing the Bolero. *(Courtesy John Hay Whitney)*

The fundamental differences between the approach of the two painters are reflected in their subject matter. Degas had a strong distaste for the bohemian life in which Lautrec flourished. Degas seems little concerned about people; there is never any probing of personality in his canvasses, while Lautrec sees the frailty rather than the eccentricity of his subjects. The latter's paintings and drawings stripped a fake glamor from reality, whereas Degas, the conservative recluse, desired to retain this quality.

Degas was a master in capturing the atmosphere of the world of ballet rather than ballet itself. "They call me the painter of dancers," he once said. "They don't know that for me the dance has been a pretext for painting pretty materials and delineating movement." His was a clinical study of movement, of the flawless function of limbs, the perfect posture, the synchronized motion of groups. He liked to draw two or three ballerinas at the same time in an arrested movement suggestive of the flow of ballet. He painted them on stage, in rehearsal and in the dancing class. They emerge like the shadows of a graceful dream, waiting in the wings, touching their costumes or tying their shoes. The images of his dancers are so familiar that they have become the picture postcard idealization of romantic ballet.

The sterile repetition, the stereotyped ballet images so characteristic toward the end of the last century in all centers of the dance, and particularly in Russia, found in Degas' pictures their best representation and a glimpse of past greatness. Degas saw no forceful personality dancing at the Opéra; he saw only those little girls who all looked alike in their endeavor to create the illusion of a dream world. Degas kept away from the dancers at the Moulin Rouge even though they were truer to the spirit of the time. Nor did he recognize the coming revolution embodied in Isadora Duncan, Loie Fuller or Michel Fokine.

Many painters and draughtsmen—among them Georges Pierre Seurat—tried to give expression to the spirit of the *fin de siècle,* the age of the *cancan.* But no one was as successful at it as Toulouse-Lautrec. He saw people moving, dancing, gesturing, living. He was interested in them as human beings and caught them on paper, on posters or on canvas in their most expressive attitudes. Doomed by nature to a dwarfish existence, he raged with desire for beauty and saw in sex its supreme manifestation. He was deliriously in love with life which gave him such a hard time, in love with women who made fun of his grotesque ugliness, and in love with alcohol which killed him at thirty-seven.

About the middle of the eighties, when Lautrec appeared on the scene of the Montmartre, the Elysée-Montmartre was the center of cheap dance-hall entertainment. Lautrec was fascinated by its noise and gaiety, the feverish music and lively dancing. In those days the *quadrille réaliste,* a variation of the *chahut* or *cancan,* enjoyed the greatest popularity. A kind of square dance usually done by two couples, it was faster than the *cancan,* with

*Two illustrations from an 1845 book by Quillenbois,* Conservatoire de Danse Modern. *(Collection George Chaffée)*

In the fall of 1892, the Folies-Bergère announced the debut of an American dancer, Loie Fuller. At the age of thirteen, she had begun her public career as a temperance lecturer. Later, she was a not very successful actress. Performing in a play in which she wore a voluminous skirt, she discovered the startling effects possible by the combination of lights and undulating materials; so she evolved her *Skirt Dance* and later the *Serpentine Dance*.

She went to France, and "La Belle Américaine" became the idol of Paris, almost transforming the Folies-Bergère into an artistic shrine. She even asked Madame Curie whether she could not help her to "butterfly wings of radium." She knew that radium created a pale, magical light, and light fascinated her. She usually worked on the stage with a score or more of electricians.

Loie Fuller had had only a few dance lessons in her youth. But, even if we deny her the rank of a great dancer, she remains important as the discoverer of a new aspect of the stage dance. She was a true child of her time in her search for the "new" and in her effort to throw off the fetters of a doctrinaire and sterile ballet dictatorship. Before Isadora Duncan freed the dance from ballet and Michel Fokine gave ballet a badly needed new image, Loie Fuller experimented with costumes in the new miracle of electric light.

She was often called a woman of genius. Typical is the following impression of her dancing in the *London Sketch* in 1900:

> The orgy of color was so wonderful as to leave objection mute. Light came from every side. La Loie danced upon glass, from which the vivid splendor of the headlights was reflected, while from the wings, stage and orchestra, wonderful luminous streams seemed to flow toward her. With the rhythm of the music the colors changed, and where white ruled before, there was a kaleidoscopic vision. Violet, orange, purple and mauve movements succeeded in rapid succession until a rich deep red dominated the dancer, and she became, for one brief moment, a living rose, with palpitating heart and flying leaves. Then the hues of the rainbow came from all sides, and ranged themselves upon the

dramatic accents, and it was climaxed by the rivalry of the women to see who could kick the highest and display the most leg. Even for Montmartre taste, the female dancers went too far, and a censor was appointed, but he succeeded only in making himself the target of public ridicule.

One of Lautrec's paintings of that period, *Le Quadrille de la Chaise Louis XIII à l'Elysée-Montmartre,* shows two dancing women with their skirts raised and with their right legs coming out of a cloud of petticoats. One of the women was the famous La Goulue whom Lautrec painted over and over again.

But the Elysée-Montmartre soon lost its appeal, mostly because the quadrille, for which this dance-hall was famous, was becoming too intricate for the amateur and was therefore becoming less popular. As a result, the professional performer took over, and the quadrille became an artistic feat. And when the Moulin Rouge opened, the best performers moved to this new place of amusement and with them, Lautrec. His posters helped establish the fame of dancers and singers of the Moulin Rouge.

*In this study for* La Chahut, *Seurat records his impression of* fin de siècle *night-life in Montmartre. (Albright-Knox Art Gallery, Buffalo)*

called *Au Moulin Rouge: La Danse,* we see Valentin de Désossé in a quadrille. Because of his incredible agility Valentin was called the Boneless. He could twist his joints and turn and jump with astounding ease. He was very inventive and could create the most complicated steps and intricate figures for his quadrille and waltzes. He came from a respectable bourgeois family but at night he turned dance performer.

His partner was La Goulue. A laundress at sixteen, she was a famous night-club dancer a year later. Valentin discovered her and she became one of the best-known dancers in the Paris of that time. Lautrec was attracted by her enigmatic mixture of dancing goddess and coarse fishwife and he made fifteen or more portraits of her, alone and with her partner, dancing and in repose.

Later, between 1893 and 1896, Lautrec was particularly fond of an operetta star, Marcelle Lender, who was famous for her dancing as well as acting, for her wardrobe as well as her décolleté. He made more sketches, drawings, lithographs and paintings of her in that period than of any other dancer. One of his most elaborate paintings is called: *Lender Dansant le Pas du Boléro dans Chilpéric.*

Lautrec was also fascinated by the dreamlike grace and pale delicacy of Jane Avril of whom it was said that she had "the beauty of a fallen angel." When she arrived in Paris, a penniless girl of seventeen, she went to one of the gay night spots in the Latin Quarter. Lost to the lively music, she suddenly found herself dancing all by herself, with other people standing around her. She had never learned to dance but, carried away by the music and almost in a trancelike state, she invented steps and movements. That night decided her life: she wanted to become a dancer. She had a fine sense of rhythm and an innate grace, and throughout her entire career she continued to rely on improvisation.

She also had great success in the legitimate theater, appearing as Anitra in Ibsen's *Peer Gynt* and in such musical comedies as in the world success of *La Belle de New York.* At the Folies-Bergère she performed in the ballet *L'Arc-en-Ciel* in which she

ever moving draperies... the colors disappeared, there was a flash of appalling brilliancy, and La Loïe faded under diaphanous drapery.

In her repertoire were the *Butterfly Dance,* the *White Dance* and the *Violet Dance,* but none of them was as successful as her *Fire Dance.* And Toulouse-Lautrec's portrait of her in this dance turned out to be one of his best lithographs, a whirling image of flames somewhat veiled by gauzy smoke.

On one of Lautrec's earlier paintings (1890),

*Edgar Degas portrays the backstage weariness of ballet dancers. (Permission* S.P.A.D.E.M. *1966 by* F.R.R. *Inc.)*

danced the part of Pierrot with inimitable delicacy.

Paying tribute to Lautrec in her memoirs she wrote: "It is undoubtedly to him that I owe the celebrity I have enjoyed, which dates from the appearance of his first poster of me." Lautrec had paid tribute to Jane Avril not only by drawing her portrait for the Moulin Rouge and Jardin de Paris, but also by using her as a model in many more paintings and lithographs not concerned with the dance.

A period of beginning unease had passed and the world carried the seed for many revolutions with it into the twentieth century. The world of the dance also was waiting for new great beginnings. No one could then foresee that the few "eccentric" attempts at something new would lead to a great renaissance of the dance.

# 10 The Revolt Against Renaissance Man

While the twentieth century began long before January 1, 1900, in the fields of literature, the sciences and psychology, the dance as the ultimate expression of nineteenth-century romanticism could only slowly free itself from its romantic ties. Isadora Duncan's revolutionary deed on the threshold of the new age, her blow against all sham approaches to the dance happened in an atmosphere of neo-romanticism. And the great innovator Michel Fo-

*Isadora Duncan, here seen in* La Marseillaise, *fought for an artistic freedom which opened the way to twentieth-century experimentation. (Collection of the Library of Congress) Above: Self-portrait of Jean Cocteau during a rehearsal of his ballet* Parade. *(Permission* S.P.A.D.E.M. *1966 by* F.R.R. *Inc.)*

kine saved the twentieth-century ballet from drowning in its own virtuoso sweetness by starting his career with a *Dying Swan* and a *ballet-blanc* reverie to Chopin's mellifluous tunes.

Not unlike the Renaissance man who had thrown off the fetters of medievalism, twentieth-century man is trying to get rid of the four-hundred-year-old Renaissance domination. He is still at it, wiping out all traces of a development that has run its course. As the child of the Renaissance, the theater dance developed to heights of splendor, to technical achievement and the realization of its promise; it cast off its feudal origins and flourished in the hands of the bourgeoisie; from Jupiters, Circes and Turks as well as fauns, satyrs and shepherds it turned to sylphs, swans and disembodied spirits luring mortal men to romantic doom. But all the ballet had left

157

at the end of nineteenth century was the glorification of the ballerina, virtuoso technique, the empty gesture of standardized beauty.

But a new beginning was in the making. Taking its cue from the other arts, ballet groped for a new image. It needed help and received it from composers, painters and poets. But the ballet's strongest influence came from a force in its own house: the modern expressionistic dance.

America and Germany were the two countries in which the ballet had not yet taken root during the first two decades of this century. Therefore the modern dance found a fertile soil in these areas. It was an American, Isadora Duncan, who created the image of a new form of expression at the turn of the century. No doubt, Michel Fokine would have revolted against the slavish way ballerinas pirouetted through conventional inanities and stylistic inconsistencies. But Isadora's appearance in Russia triggered his courage. In Germany, where she was best understood and where she triumphed as nowhere else, she prepared the coming of Mary Wigman. Mary Wigman would add direction and body to Isadora's burning spirit and self-devouring fire, to an art that relied more or less on the inspiration of the moment.

The modern dance is essentially self-expressive and has at times been closer to autobiographic revelation than any other theater form. In the chaos after World War I, the German *Ausdruckstanz* grew into an impressive art, trying to probe man's relation to the universe. The German dancer's preoccupation with death at that time has often been referred to as a Teutonic characteristic when, in fact, it was simply a reflection of the war and its aftermath. When in the late Twenties the American version of the modern dance appeared, the dancers there were also trying to express themselves and their time. But their experiences were different from those of their German counterparts and so was their self-reflection. Mary Wigman and Kurt Jooss did not serve directly as a model in America, but their revolutionary work that had found the idiom of its time inspired the young dancers in the New World.

By 1930, the modern dance was gaining recognition as a new art form. It mirrored the needs and feelings of the twentieth century as the artificially stylized form of ballet had expressed the needs and feelings of feudal society. But the ballet has also learned to speak to us in more idiomatic terms and with contemporary themes and yet it has done so without giving up its romantic heritage.

The modern dance became deeply involved in the complexities of self-reflection. And while reaching high points in dramatic expression, it gave birth to a non-literal dance which turned its back on all self-expressive representation. The artists had begun to discover their spiritual isolation.

The floodgates to the torrents of newness had been opened by Jean Cocteau with his ballet *Parade* in 1917 which heightened the banality of reality to an artistic revelation. From then on "isms" overwhelmed man in his anxiety to find himself. Expressionism, dadaism and surrealism knocked out all aesthetic vestiges of the past. Finally in the Fifties and Sixties came the dance of the absurd—first restricted to New York, but gradually exerting its influence everywhere—with a mixture of dadaism and surrealism filtered through the anguish of existentialism. The desperate communication of non-communicativeness, the non sequitur and seemingly forced contortions are plainly the death agonies of the past and the birth pangs of a new age.

*Contemporary choreographers use both traditional and modern idioms in their work. Above left: In George Balanchine's* Serenade, *a classical arabesque is accompanied by a floor-bound effort at expressiveness. Below: Gerald Arpino's* Sea Shadow *shows the influence of modern dance on ballet. (Both, Martha Swope) Right: Modern dance may borrow traditional elements, as the lift in Norman Walker's* Nightchanter. *(Jack Mitchell)*

# *II Three Phases of Diaghilev*

I am, firstly, a charlatan, though rather a brilliant one; secondly, a great charmer; thirdly, frightened of nobody; fourthly, a man with plenty of logic and very few scruples; fifthly, I seem to have no real talent. None the less, I believe that I have found my true vocation—to be a Maecenas, I have everything necessary except money—but that will come!

No one could have described Serge Diaghilev more scathingly than he himself did in a letter written to his stepmother in 1895. An aesthete and an accomplished amateur of the arts, he joined a circle of young artists in which the painters Léon Bakst and Alexandre Benois were leading figures. In 1899 he founded the magazine *Mir Iskusstva* ("The World of Art") in which he wrote: "Man does not depend on exterior circumstances but on himself alone. One of the greatest merits of our times is to recognize individuality under every guise in every epoch."

He edited the annual of the Imperial Theaters and supervised several productions for a season, but finding that bureaucracy was inimical to art, he resigned. For a while he occupied himself with putting on art exhibitions in St. Petersburg and Paris. In 1908 he decided to become a theatrical impresario, and that year he presented *Boris Godounov* at the Paris Opéra with the famed basso Feodor Chaliapin in the title role. The success of this

*Left: Pavlova and Nijinsky in* Pavillon d'Armide.
*(Courtesy Dance Collection, New York Public Library)*
*Above: Leonide Massine in* Aleko. *(Maurice Seymore)*

venture encouraged Diaghilev to bring the Russian ballet to Paris, but an important factor was his break with Teliakovsky, director of the Imperial Theater, which enabled him to take the best dancers with him. What followed was decisive in the history of the dance.

## The Concept of Total Theater

Diaghilev saw theater in all of its forms as a challenge. He admired the new, the fresh, the vital and he wanted his ballet theater to reflect a life that was constantly changing. His inner conflict was between his love of the classicism and romanticism of his youth and his desire to be an innovator, always in the vanguard, helping to create the excitement of the new.

When the Ballets Russes opened on May 19, 1909, at the Théâtre du Châtelet, the era of modern ballet began. The dancers—Anna Pavlova, Tamara Karsavina, Vaslav Nijinsky, Ida Rubinstein, Adolf Bolm, Mikhail Mordkin—were the products of the nineteenth century, of the traditional training at the Imperial ballet schools and the Maryinsky Theater. The scenic designers—Benois, Bakst and Nicholas Roerich—came from the circle of the *Mir Iskusstva.* With the exception of Chopin, the composers were Russian. In essence, the first period of the Diaghilev ballet, from 1909 to 1914, was marked by impressionistic, romantic and exotic trends. It was still in transition to twentieth-century ballet. By the end

*Pablo Picasso designed curtain, setting (shown above), and costumes for* Le Tricorne, *first given in London in 1919. Left: For* Le Chant du Rossignol, *which had its première in Paris in 1920, Henri Matisse designed the curtain (illustrated), setting, and costumes. Below right:* Petrouchka *was first presented in Paris in 1911, with setting and costumes by Alexandre Benois. (All, Courtesy Wadsworth Atheneum, Hartford: Permission* S.P.A.D.E.M. *1966 by* F.R.R. *Inc.)*

of this period it was undertaking many daring experiments.

What Diaghilev did from the very beginning was synthesize all the theater arts. He knew how to make the most diverse artists work together—even though he lost Pavlova after the first year—and he aimed at one thing only: a dazzling theater. To this end he sought to combine the color provided by great painters; music that was startlingly original; a choreography that did not deny the classical school but could create exciting dancing to match the ideas of great writers. Stravinsky, Ravel, Debussy, Satie, de Falla, Poulenc and Auric worked with him during his reign of twenty years. Some of the best writers—Jean Cocteau, Marcel Proust, Paul Claudel—helped spread his gospel. From Bakst and Benois to Rouault and Picasso, the painters served his cause. In fusing these creative minds, Diaghilev achieved artistic unity and realized the dreams of Lully, Rameau and Noverre: the ballet as a living art.

He was not the first to aim at a total theater. Richard Wagner tried to achieve a similar synthesis in music drama. The French poet Stéphane Mallarmé criticized Wagner for not having gone the whole way and for having minimized the role of poetry and dancing, which he saw as the nucleus of any total theater. The bold scenic designer Gordon Craig deplored the fact that the theater was "split up into departments; it has imprisoned all the arts each in its own cell.... I know of but one art." Diaghilev was not alone in believing in the creative power and effectiveness of theatrical synthesis, but he was also able to put it into practice. He wrote:

The more I thought of that problem of the composition of ballet, the more plainly I understood that perfect ballet can only be created by the very closest fusion of three elements—dancing, painting and music. When I mount a ballet, I always keep these three elements in mind. That is why almost daily I go into the artists' studios, watch their work and the actual execution of the costumes, examine the scores and listen to the orchestra with close attention, and then visit the practice rooms where all the dancers practice and rehearse daily.

The strength of Diaghilev's influence on his collaborators varied, of course, but he had a close relationship with Nijinsky, Cocteau, Massine and Lifar. Lifar admits that "at the beginning" Diaghilev educated and molded him. And he quotes Diaghilev as saying: "...in the days of Fokine as producer and Nijinsky as dancer, both decided to carry out my artistic ideas." But Fokine protested emphatically: "No one has ever molded me. I formed myself, realized my own dream of a new ballet, and only then did Diaghilev invite me and take my already completed works." It is fair to say that without Fokine, Diaghilev's dream could easily have turned into a nightmare, or at least would not have achieved immediate acclaim.

Of course, the Ballets Russes had its critics, and André Levinson, the staunch defender of classicism, opposed Diaghilev's basic concept. He condemned him for using a dramatic emotion instead of letting considerations of pure form serve as the *raison d'être* of each step. "Diaghilev consistently seeks his inspiration outside the dance itself," he declared. Another critic, Camille Mauclair, however, appreciated the high standards of Diaghilev's theatrical spectacles. "The Bakst décor," he said, "gives us a feeling of escape into the realms of dream and fantasy. Everything is true, but nothing is real. An aesthetic truth of four arts combined in one." And he saw another truth in these ballets—emotional truth.

With Fokine's help, Diaghilev succeeded in returning to the Aristotelian conception of dancing as the representation of passions, actions and manners. Instead of realism, Diaghilev offered genuine emotions in a setting of unreality, of legend and fantasy, in a flood of color, a symphony of gestures and sound. His sense of theater led him to introduce three or four one-act ballets at each performance instead of one long ballet, as had been customary in Petipa's time. He also rescued the male dancer from his pitiful position as a *porteur* and made the *corps de ballet* significant. The Ballets Russes be-

came a repertory group, but Diaghilev can be criticized for having failed to establish a training school to perpetuate his ideas, to build the dancer of the future.

He failed in it as much as Isadora Duncan did—although she, at least, tried. Perhaps their every day was too dazzling to give them time to think of tomorrow.

## Michel Fokine

Fokine did think of the future, although his roots as dancer and teacher were in the past. He had performed important roles under Petipa and was Pavlova's first partner. Pavlova loved to work with him. He had grown up in the great classical tradition and, as Karsavina said in her book, *Theater Street*, "Fokine used classical dance as the basis of his choreography. He embroidered new patterns on it; he invested it with the style of any given epoch into which he made excursions; but his starting point was always the virtuosity of the classical ballet...."

Although he was enormously successful, Fokine's intelligence rebelled against what he saw happening around him. He was twenty-four years old when he began to embarrass his teachers and choreographers with such questions as: "Why is the style of a dance seldom in harmony with its theme, costumes and period? Why does a dancer execute difficult steps if they do not express anything? Why is ballet technique limited to the movements of the lower limbs and a few conventional positions of the arms, when the whole body should be expressive?" The answer was as stereotyped as the dancing: "Because that is the tradition."

Already in 1904 Fokine wrote a letter to the Director of the Imperial Theaters in which he said:

Dancing should be interpretive. It should not degenerate into mere gymnastics.... The ballet must no longer be made up of numbers, entries and so on. It must show artistic unity of conception. The action of the ballet must never be interrupted to allow the danseuse to respond to the applause of the public.

Ballet must have complete unity of expression, a unity which is made up of a harmonious blending of the three elements—music, painting and plastic art.

His suggestions were rejected, and the letter filed for posterity. These ideas of the young Fokine came close to what Diaghilev was to transform into a reality five years later.

In 1905, Isadora Duncan, the "barefoot" dancer, came to Russia and caused an aesthetic explosion. She wanted to bury all tradition and erase the memory of the immediate past by going back to the simplicity of the ancient Greeks. She startled the dancers at the Ballet School of the Maryinsky Theater. When he saw her, Fokine felt he was not alone in his fight for reform, but having been raised in the spirit of tradition, he wanted only to give the classical school a twentieth-century look.

In April of that same year Fokine made his first attempt at choreography in *Acis and Galateau,* expressing the mythological theme with movements and poses suggested by Greek art. The same year he was asked to compose a *pas seul* of not more than three or four minutes in length for Pavlova. *The Dying Swan,* one of the immortal post-romantic dances, was the result. Fokine said that it "was proof that the dance could not and should not satisfy only the eye, but through the medium of the eye should penetrate into the soul." And like all innovators since the days of Lully, he strove to combine new groups and forms of movement, and to integrate dance, music, decor, lighting, and costuming with theme and action.

He excelled in all styles. After the strongly Duncanesque *Eunice,* created in 1907, in which the ballet dancers appeared barefoot he composed several ballets which were to become the backbone of Diaghilev's repertoire: *Les Sylphides, The Firebird, Scheherazade, Le Spectre de la Rose* and *Petrouchka.*

Fokine had a few failures, among them *Le Dieu Bleu* and *Thamar.* He felt Diaghilev's growing indifference and when he found out that Diaghilev had secretly asked Nijinsky to choreograph *The*

*Afternoon of a Faun,* he left the company and only returned in 1914 to stage his successful ballet, *Le Coq d'Or.* In this year he formulated the fundamental ideas of his reform in a letter to the London *Times:*

> 1. To create in each case a new form of movement corresponding to the subject matter, period and character of the music, instead of merely giving combinations of ready-made and established steps.
>
> 2. Dancing and mimetic gesture have no meaning in ballet unless they serve as an expression of dramatic action.
>
> 3. To admit the use of conventional gesture only when it is required by the style of the ballet, and in all other cases to replace the gesture of the hands by movements of the whole body. Man can and should be expressive from head to foot.
>
> 4. The group is not only an ornament. The new ballet advances from the expressiveness of the face and the hands to that of the whole body to groups of bodies and the expressiveness of the combined dancing of a crowd.
>
> 5. The alliance of dancing with other arts. The new ballet, refusing to be slave either of music or of scenic decoration, and recognizing the alliance of arts only on the condition of complete equality, allows perfect freedom both to the scenic artist and to the musician.

## Igor Stravinsky

It is usually difficult to assess the importance of a composer's contribution to the growth of a ballet company, but Stravinsky's influence on the theater dance cannot be overstated. If Diaghilev's venture might have failed without the body and form that Fokine provided, it also needed the direction in which Stravinsky's music turned it. He set his own standards and forced them on his collaborators.

Stravinsky's music creates the excitement of nowness, the sound of immediacy, the sound rippling in cascades of surprises but always pure, denuded, unexpectedly earthy. He is never the same, but always recognizable. His innovations derive from an all-

*Michel Fokine as Perseus in* Medusa. *(Goodwin: Courtesy Dance Collection, New York Public Library)*

embracing awareness and his rhythms are insistent because they reach far back into ritual, into unashamed primitivism.

His compositions are of such theatrical intensity that they become an extension of the imagery of ballet movement giving the dancing bodies a fourth dimension and heightening the visual excitement. His dissonances are a propelling force for the moving body, but at the same time his tempo demands self-discipline, perfect control on the part of the dancer. Stravinsky came to understand the dance better

than any other composer, and more often than not he wrote the scenarios for his scores. Of the origin of *Petrouchka* he says:

> I had in mind ... a puppet, suddenly endowed with life, exasperating the patience of the orchestra with diabolic cascades of arpeggios. The orchestra in turn retaliates with menacing trumpet blasts. The outcome is a terrific noise which reaches its climax and ends in the sorrowful and querulous collapse of the poor puppet. Soon afterwards Diaghilev came to visit me ... I played him the piece ... which later became the second scene of *Petrouchka*. He was so much pleased with it that he ... began persuading me to develop the theme of the puppet's sufferings and make it into a whole ballet....

His eight scores for the Ballets Russes did more to identify the company with a new era than most of the choreography, décors and themes of its early years.

Lully, Rameau and Tchaikovsky all served the dance. Their music was pliant, suggestive, helpful in its rhythmic and melodic richness. But Stravinsky's music is compelling, demanding, leading. If the choreographer is unable to follow the flight of Stravinsky's inventiveness or cannot yield to the complexities of his rhythms, the result is chaos—at least, from Stravinsky's viewpoint. Nijinsky is a case in point. Stravinsky admired him as a dancer and a mime, but was appalled by Nijinsky's utter lack of musical understanding. In 1912 Diaghilev insisted on Nijinsky's staging *The Rite of Spring* ("Le Sacre du Printemps"). Stravinsky felt that it "was a very labored and barren effort rather than a plastic realization flowing simply and naturally from what the music demanded ... although he had grasped the dramatic significane of the dance, Nijinsky was incapable of giving intelligible form to its essence." Stravinsky was far more satisfied with Leonide Massine's choreography in 1920, which "flowed out of the music and was not, as the first had been, imposed on it."

George Balanchine has fared best with Stravinsky because he recognized the classical austerity of his style and found the most convincing bodily move-

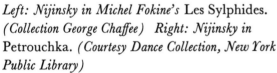
*Left: Nijinsky in Michel Fokine's* Les Sylphides. *(Collection George Chaffee) Right: Nijinsky in* Petrouchka. *(Courtesy Dance Collection, New York Public Library)*

ments for his always surprising and often perplexing atonality. Balanchine claims that working on Stravinsky's *Apollon Musagète*—which took place at the very end of the Diaghilev era—became the turning point of his life. And Stravinsky had great admiration for Balanchine's inventiveness and craftsmanship, his ability to grasp and express the meaning of the music. Balanchine responded to the vitality in the music; he learned to be guided by Stravinsky's

dynamic use of silence; he accepted the constant surprise of his new approaches. Their collaboration is unique in the history of ballet.

If Stravinsky helped the Ballets Russes become what it was, Diaghilev's merit was in having believed in the young composer. By encouraging Stravinsky, he gave the twentieth-century ballet its most important composer.

## Vaslav Nijinsky

No artist has ever captured the imagination of the public as Nijinsky did: his one leap in Fokine's *The Spectre of the Rose* became legendary. But it takes

more than training and technical ability to achieve perfection. One must have certain other qualities: personality, stage presence, magnetism. Nijinsky had them all.

Diaghilev sensed in this unusual, silent, sad peasant a gift for choreography. And what Nijinsky tried to express in *The Afternoon of a Faun* was close to the hidden primitive in man. His faun had jerky, angular movements that evoked the satyrs on Greek vases, but he also gave his faun a dynamic quality that was a denial of pure classicism. Diaghilev thought that he had found a new choreographer whose work was cerebral; in fact, it was the volcanic expression of a tortured soul haunted by strange images.

At this point Diaghilev needed someone who could prevent a successful formula from becoming rigid and shake his dancers and the public out of their complacency. Nijinsky seemed to be the right man for this task. To give his protégé a sounder foundation for his next choreographic essay, which was to be *The Rite of Spring,* Diaghilev took him to Emile Jaques-Dalcroze in Hellerau, whose influence on many creative dancers had been invaluable. Dalcroze had found that his principles of "eurhythmics"—that is, good rhythm—could help improve the rhythm of dancers. Diaghilev also engaged Miriam Rambach—later known as Marie Rambert—to tutor Nijinsky. Both were Poles, and in her Nijinsky found someone who understood him. If Diaghilev was a kind of father to him, Rambach was the friend who guided him and remedied his lack of a musical education.

Nijinsky's choreography for *The Rite of Spring* may have displeased Stravinsky and shocked the audience—the première caused a furor—but it anticipated a modern mood, a sophisticated approach to archaic movements, a naiveté rooted in primi-

*Leonide Massine and Tamara Toumanova in* Symphonie Fantastique, *choreographed by Massine and first presented in London in 1936. (Gordon Anthony: Courtesy Dance Collection, New York Public Library)*

tivism. Nijinsky envisioned a circular dance in unbroken, endless motion, visually exciting, theactrically conceived. Of this choreography his wife says:

> Nijinsky contradicts the classical position by making all steps and gestures turn inward.... It is through rhythm, and rhythm only, that the dance identified itself with the music. The rhythmical counterpoint is employed in the choral movements. When the orchestra plays a trill on the flutes, movements thin out, and so do the dancers. Then the tune begins on woodwinds two octaves apart, and on the stage two groups of three dancers each detach themselves from the lines and dance corresponding to the tune.... At the end of the first tableau great circles (women dressed in scarlet) run wildly, while shifting masses within are ceaselessly splitting up into tiny groups revolving on eccentric axes.

In 1913, the year in which *The Rite of Spring* had its première, Nijinsky also choreographed a lighter ballet in which he intended to show athletic movements expressed lyrically. *Jeux* was to be a divertissement only but turned out to be revolutionary in the treatment of its subject. The background of the story was a garden party, while the subject was love as revealed through a tennis game. For the first time a choreographer dared introduce the theme of sport and dancers in sport clothes. Moreover, the mood of the dance was conveyed with angular movements and through abstractions rather than conventionally expressed sentiments. A tennis ball bouncing onto the stage started the love game between a boy and two girls, and another ball, which the boy tried to retrieve, ended it. As the boy, Nijinsky, following the balls with two leaps that covered the stage, triumphed with his air-borne movement and grace. But the many innovations in *Jeux* made the first-night audience uneasy. Nijinsky enthralled his public with his leaps. It was "the victory of breath over weight ... the utilization of the animal by the soul," Paul Claudel said. But the people could not accept his choreography. For he was years ahead of them. His two choreographic failures in 1913 opened the way for more daring experiments to come.

*Pavel Tchelitchew's drawing of Serge Lifar dancing. (Courtesy Wadsworth Atheneum, Hartford)*

Nijinsky was a genius, but one step removed from the madness that finally overtook him.

## Jean Cocteau

Jean Cocteau said: "... dancing is the language in which I would prefer to express myself, and my favorite theatrical formula." Like most artists of the day, he was dazzled by the fireworks of the Ballets Russes and drawn to that maker of magic Diaghilev, who wielded his wand like a scepter. Cocteau designed some early posters for the company, wrote about its productions and talked ecstatically of Diaghilev and Nijinsky in Parisian salons. In May 1912, he contributed the scenario for the exotic but unsuccessful Hindu ballet, *Le Dieu Bleu.*

One day Diaghilev startled Cocteau by simply saying, "Surprise me." This was the turning point in Cocteau's life. It was with *Parade,* produced in 1917, that Cocteau eventually surprised Diaghilev and stunned Paris. According to Cocteau, Erik Satie, whose music was sparse, said modestly, "I composed a background for certain noises (dynamos, sirens, trains, planes) which Cocteau considered indispensable in order to establish the mood of his characters." Who were these characters? A Chinese who "pulls out an egg from his pigtail, eats and digests it, finds it again in the toe of his shoe, spits fire, burns himself, stamps to put out the sparks, etc..." A little girl who "mounts a race horse, rides a bicycle, quivers like pictures on the screen, imitates Charlie Chaplin, chases a thief with a revolver, dances to ragtime, goes to sleep, is shipwrecked, rolls on the grass, buys a Kodak, etc..." And then: "As for the acrobats—the poor, stupid, agile acrobats—we tried to invest them with the melancholy of a Sunday evening after the circus has ended and the children leave, casting a last glance at the ring."

*Parade* also introduced Pablo Picasso to the theater as a stage designer. *Parade* had the atmosphere of the street, the music hall, the circus, without their vulgarities. It had an ecstatic quality of the ordered chaos of life, the intense, nostalgic, lyric feeling of childhood memories, with a touch of the disintegration of society after World War I. It was new, different, a scandal.

Cocteau was convinced that "reality alone, even when well concealed, has the power to arouse emotion." He wanted to strip things bare, to see with the imagination of a child. He felt that in an age of subtlety and sophistication it was essential to return to simplicity—but without being banal.

He sought to "rehabilitate the commonplace" with the element of surprise. To understand his daring and his zest for anticipating artistic fashion, one must consider some of the influences that shaped him.

Four men were to give Cocteau the confidence he needed. Satie taught him to avoid adornment and to seek a simplicity that attains richness by a refining process. Picasso taught him "to run faster than beauty." ("If you keep step with her, your product will be photographic 'kitsch.' If you run behind her, you accomplish only the mediocre.") Stravinsky taught him to "insult habit," for only in that way can art be kept from becoming sterile. And from his poet friend Raymond Radiguet Cocteau learned to accept no premise and to distrust novelty for its own sake.

*Parade* was followed by *Le Bœuf sur le Toit ou The Do Nothing Bar,* which Cocteau conceived and staged as a mime show for the famous Fratellini clowns. While the "realistic" *Parade* did not satisfy him completely because, he said, "theater corrupts everything," he derived greater satisfaction from his next ballet. This was *Les Mariés de la Tour Eiffel,* which he did for Rolf de Maré's Ballets Suédois, and which he described as "the first work in which I owe nothing to anyone, which is unlike any other work." He called *Les Mariés* a comedy-ballet and mixed ancient tragedy (the actors wore masks) with music hall numbers.

Bronislava Nijinska's *Les Biches,* on which he collaborated in 1924, was one of the first ballets which, he said, combined classic steps with new gestures. About then Cocteau also devised *Le Train Bleu,* a ballet based on beach games, swimming, tennis and golf movements. The idea emerged from his predilection for clowns and acrobats and seemed very novel at the time.

When, in 1946, he returned to the ballet, he had left behind the idea of any composite spectacle. Experimentation did not stop. *Le Jeune Homme et la Mort* was a great success when the Ballets des Champs-Elysées produced it in Paris with Jean Babilée and Nathalie Philippart in leading roles.

*Lifar in* David Triomphant *which had its première in Paris in 1939. (Lipnitzki)*

Two years later he designed the sets and costumes for *L'Amour et son Amour* ("Cupid and His Love"), which the Ballet Theater later presented at the Metropolitan Opera House in New York in 1951. It carried the motto by Cocteau: "Love has no explanation—do not seek a meaning in love's gestures." *La Dame à la Licorne,* his last ballet scenario, was choreographed by Heinz Rosen for the Munich Opera Ballet in 1953, later produced by the Paris Opéra and by the Ballet Russe de Monte Carlo in New York in 1955. In that year Jean

171

Cocteau, the "enfant terrible" of art was elected to the Académie Française and became an "immortal."

In Cocteau's sentence: "To be reborn one must burn oneself alive," lies the key to the understanding of his genius. This thought of rising like a phoenix from one's own ashes was echoed in a later statement: "My discipline consists in not letting myself be enslaved by obsolete formulae."

Jean Cocteau was a pioneer in transferring the reflection of everyday life onto the dance stage. Instead of the spectacular sequence of heightened unreality, the fairy-tale atmosphere on which ballet had fed for so long, he offered a heightened reality. What was accepted as avant-garde in dance in the 1950's and 1960's was built in large part on Cocteau's daring and imagination.

## The Second and Third Phase

In 1913, after his marriage, Nijinsky left the Ballets Russes. Diaghilev had already commissioned Richard Strauss to write the score for a ballet based on the legend of Joseph; Nijinsky was to have been Joseph. Now the impressario had to find a replacement.

At that time Leonide Massine was a handsome young supernumerary in the ballet *Don Quixote* at the Theater Marny in Moscow. When Diaghilev saw him cross the stage, he felt at once that there was his Joseph. If ever a dancer-choreographer was completely a creation of Diaghilev, it was Massine. Ballet master Enrico Cecchetti had to train the boy for his difficult part; Diaghilev educated him and exposed him to the influence of the avant-garde circle of Cocteau, Picasso and Stravinsky. Diaghilev was certain that Massine would be able to translate the new ideas in the arts into the ballet idiom.

Massine was brilliant in the title role of *The Legend of Joseph* and a year later, in 1915, he choreographed his first ballet, *The Midnight Sun*, a suite of Russian folk dances. As a dancer he possessed more expressive talent than technique

and his choreography was strongest in its dramatic and pantomimic aspects. This became obvious in his second ballet, *The Good-Humored Ladies,* which he staged in the style of the *commedia dell'arte* and in which the pantomime was far more brilliant than the dancing. By 1917 he had mastered all styles and non-styles, as he proved when he choreographed Cocteau's *Parade.* In this ballet he made the *non sequitur* effective on stage and transformed the banal into ecstatic reality.

Massine left Diaghilev in 1921, but worked for the Ballets Russes intermittently from 1924 to 1928. Later he was associated with the Ballet Russe de Monte Carlo and other companies on two continents. In 1928 he came to America and accepted the taxing position of ballet master at the Roxy Theater in New York where he staged and appeared in four shows a day. To counteract what must have been an unsympathetic job, he produced in 1930 for the League of Composers *The Rite of Spring,* with Martha Graham in the role of the Chosen Virgin.

When Massine left the Ballets Russes in 1921 Diaghilev had to look for a new choreographer and he chose Bronislava Nijinska, Nijinsky's sister, who had assisted him in mounting *The Sleeping Beauty* in London.

She was more traditional than her brother and gave his harsh, archaic lines a softness. She tried for a "neo-realistic" approach and, probably inspired by her brother's ballet *Jeux,* she included sport, jazz and satire in her works. All this made her appear to vacillate between styles. She fared best when she was under the influence of Stravinsky or Cocteau. Stravinsky characterized her as "an excellent dancer endowed with a profoundly artistic nature, and... gifted with a real talent for choreographic creation." However, when she staged Stravinsky's *Les Noces* in 1923, the composer felt that she had listened to Diaghilev but had not followed his intentions. Nevertheless, this ballet of a Russian peasant wedding ceremony was one of her great successes. It was followed by the gently witty sketches of high society, *Les Biches,* some amusing glimpses of the smart set of the 1920's. Next came Cocteau's *Le Train Bleu,* which was full of acrobatics but little dancing.

Diaghilev did not fully appreciate Nijinska's work, for he was seeking the youthful replenishment he more and more required as he grew older. He was impressed by George Balanchine's talent when he saw the work of Balanchine's small Russian company touring Europe in the mid-1920's. Balanchine's approach, though basically classic, was gymnastic, plastic, expressionistically modern. Diaghilev recognized that Balanchine's talent, inventiveness and tongue-in-cheek humor would enrich the Ballets Russes, and in 1925 he asked him to restage Stravinsky's *Le Rossignol*. During the next four years Balanchine created ten more ballets for Diaghilev, of which *Barabau* was the most vital and daring in its theatrical devices, while in *La Chatte,* based on the Aesop fable, he revived the pure classical style. In *Apollon Musagète* he seemed to have found himself.

Balanchine's last work of choreography for Diaghilev was *The Prodigal Son,* in 1929. The title role in this ballet was danced by young Serge Lifar who was another creation and hope of Diaghilev. Balanchine taught Lifar the movements that fitted his gifts and concealed his weaknesses. Lifar was the Nijinsky of the late Diaghilev period: his grace, radiance, and commanding stage presence made him the image of eternal youth of which Diaghilev always dreamed.

For twenty years Diaghilev had sought the new, the contemporaneous expression through the ballet, but he never forgot his first love: the romantic-classical ballet. It may not have been mere coincidence that the last work staged by the Ballets Russes—two weeks before Serge Diaghilev died—was *Swan Lake.*

## A Mission for Anna Pavlova

No chapter on the origins of modern ballet would be complete without paying homage to Anna Pavlova who has long signified the ballerina *sublimis.*

The theater dance has never had a more striking

*Sketch of Diaghilev and Nijinsky by Jean Cocteau. (Permission* s.p.a.d.e.m. *1966 by* f.r.r. *Inc.)*

representative, a more important pioneer for the idea of ballet itself. And yet so little is left of so much greatness: a few photographs, a short film and the fading memory of those who once saw the "sublime Pavlova."

Diaghilev knew what he wanted from a dancer: a fusion of precision and lightness, of technique and expression. "She is the greatest ballerina in the world," he said, "excelling both in classicism and in

character." And he engaged her for the historic Paris opening of the Ballets Russes in 1909. But she left at the end of the first season and went to England to form her own company. What had happened? Nijinsky was, no doubt, favored by Diaghilev—male dancers of such stature are always rarities—and he also received better notices than Pavlova did. Even Ida Rubenstein had a somewhat better press. Moreover, both Diaghilev and Pavlova were despots. They both believed in art *per se*, but Diaghilev thought he summed it up and Pavlova thought that she did.

Some time later, Diaghilev—no doubt, hurt that she had left him—thundered, "Pavlova was never really interested in art as such. The only thing that mattered to her was virtuosity"—but he did add, "and she is a virtuoso without equal." Pavlova realized the gulf between them when she asked the critics, "Are you on my side or Diaghilev's?" and she replied to his charge in an autobiographical sketch saying, "I was essentially a lyric dancer ... never interested in purposeless virtuosity."

Technical skill alone was not the secret of her greatness, for many a dancer today is better trained than Pavlova ever was. In fact, she rarely turned more than two or three pirouettes, but she executed them with such brio that they had the effect of half a dozen. It was the spirit far more than the body itself which created the illusion of lightness. As a dancer with whom she performed, André Oliveroff, put it: "I knew ... she would be easy to lift—but I had not divined the uncanny lightness of her. When I caught and supported her in mid-air, I was scarcely conscious of her weight; her elevation seemed to continue—she seemed always to be reaching up, giving you the illusion that she was very much lighter than she really was."

Anna Pavlova was born in St. Petersburg on January 31, 1882, a frail premature baby. At the

*Figurine of Pavlova done by Lavroff, at one time her sculpture teacher. (Jerry Darvin: Collection George Chaffee)*

age of eight she was taken to the Maryinsky Theater, where she saw a performance of *The Sleeping Beauty*. Then and there she decided to become a ballerina. At sixteen she was a *première danseuse,* and her ambition was to be seen as a dancer by the whole world. Taglioni was still the most popular ballerina of the past, and Pavlova conceived the idea of surpassing Taglioni. Theodore Stier, Pavlova's musical director for sixteen years, tells us that he traveled 300,000 miles with her, conducted 3,650 performances and more than 2,000 rehearsals.

She sold ballet to the world and with it her name. She danced before audiences who had never seen dancing "on toe," she appeared in regions where people either disliked or didn't understand ballet. In Java and Mexico, in Japan and India, her name was magic, and ballet schools opened wherever she went. The people needed her. "Everywhere," she said, "our dancing was hailed as the revelation of an undreamed-of art."

Except for a few divertissements and one ballet we have no proof of her choreographic ability, although many critics maintained that she was able to wipe out the difference between "creative" and "interpretative" art by making her interpretation as personal as if it had been her own creation.

The ballet is *Autumn Leaves,* a "choreographic poem" in one act, which she created in 1928 and first produced in Rio de Janeiro. In it she tried to express the inevitability of all that is passing and the tragedy of final rejection. For the poet's tenderness is only caused by a fleeting feeling for the flower's beauty and its fading fragrance, by pity for the doomed. The moment when his betrothed appears, the flower is forgotten.

She was a romantic at heart who saw nature through a poetic prism and translated her dreams into the stage images she loved to dance: *The Snowflake, The Dragonfly, The Butterfly,* or the *Fleur de Lys*.

The question of what it was that made her such a very great dancer has often been asked, and there are almost as many answers as there are experts. Perhaps it was simply her personality. As Anatole Chujoy has said, "She was great, because she was Pavlova." But if any young dancer should dream of becoming a "second Pavlova" she should remember that she only became what she was because she did not want to be a second Taglioni.

# *12  A New Beginning*

Isadora Duncan was the soul of spontaneity, essence of the extemporaneous in her life as in her art. She left no work that could be performed again, no school of technique, no pupil of distinction. What she did leave was the notion that dance can be life, can be a religion. Her major achievement was to oppose and utterly negate her time. She was the torchbearer of the dance of the twentieth century.

Isadora gave the dance the broadest of possible goals. "To express what is most moral, healthful and beautiful in art—this is the mission of the dancer, and to this I dedicate my life," she said.

*Watercolor sketch, "Homage to Isadora," by Angna Enters. (Museum of the City of New York)  Above: Sketch of Isadora Duncan by Gordon Craig. (Collection George Chaffee)*

And her entire life was a fight for her ideals, a fight which she often thought herself to be losing. In 1911, she wrote to an American friend:

> Do you wonder I am tired and discouraged? I know you will put up a monument to me fifty years after my death, but what good will that be?... In London when I danced they said my dances were taken from the Greek. It is not true. They are American. I am an American, born in California. My ancestors have lived in America for two hundred years. My dances are of the woods, the lakes, the rivers, the mountains and the prairies of my native land—aren't they?

They were truly American in their spontaneity, in their pioneer daring, in their opening of new vistas, and their dependence on the individual. To dance is to live, she felt; and it is the highest and

*Doris Humphrey in a Burmese dance performed while she was a member of the Denishawn company. (Courtesy Dance Collection, New York Public Library)*

oldest form of living when the body expresses one's thoughts and feelings. Isadora Duncan's dancing was not of the body, which only obeyed the orders of her "soul." The exact location of her soul was where an impulse led to a motor reaction. Then, a key movement would be followed by organically related movements. She never interpreted music, but music was the Great Prompter, the inspiration that moved her. She danced to Beethoven, Wagner, Gluck, and Chopin.

As a Dionysian dancer recreating her innermost feelings, she could never repeat any dance in the very same way. This is why Stanislavsky said of her that she did not know how to make a logical explanation of her art and that whatever ideas came to her came accidentally. But like him she wanted to get rid of mere characterization, reach essentials and give the soul freedom to move. When this freedom was attained, the right movement would be there. Wanting to be her natural self, she came to worship nature. Her first dancing masters were "wind and wave and the winged flight of bird and bee." She freed the body from the constriction of whalebones, the stuffiness of tulle ruffles and the gaudiness of jewels. The nude is the noblest form in art, she said, echoing the Greeks.

She went back to the ancient Greeks and to Botticelli, and to the instinctive movement of child and animal. Move according to your frame and form, she said, forget all artificiality. She detested angularity. In nature, she felt, there are only undulating lines which never come to a stop. Herein she again proved to be imbued with the neo-romantic spirit of those days. Hers were solo performances, highly lyrical, undramatic and, in spite of their stage effectiveness, non-theatrical. Thus she created the concept of the dance recital which has become a major form of modern dance presentation.

In 1912 the sculptor Antoine Bourdelle saw her and Nijinsky dance at a soirée and said in his diary: "It seemed to me, as I watched Madame Isadora Duncan sitting or reclining, that with each of her pauses she was offering me an antique marble throbbing with eternity...."

The Germans called her *die göttliche, heilige Isadora,* and Auguste Rodin who often sketched her, wrote:

> … she has attained sculpture and emotion effortlessly. She has borrowed from Nature that force which cannot be called Talent but which is Genius. Miss Duncan has properly unified Life and the Dance. She is natural on the stage where people rarely are so. She makes her dance sensitive to line and is as simple as the Antiquity synonymous with Beauty. Suppleness, emotion, these high qualities which are the soul of the dance, are her complete and sovereign art.

She gave the human body its natural rights. She delivered the dance from the fetters of mere entertainment and recreated the art in its oldest form: as a means of self-expression. She gave the twentieth-century dancer his passport to complete freedom.

## Denishawn

Ruth St. Denis began her theater career in the 1890's. In the first few years of this century she appeared as an actress in several shows of David Belasco. Her career—or, actually, her mission—was decided during one of her tours with Belasco when she saw the image of the Egyptian goddess Isis on a cigarette poster. This commonplace experience led her to an interest in Eastern art and philosophy. From then on she created oriental dances which she presented in a highly theatrical and westernized form.

*Rahda* was her first dance resulting from these studies. Ruth St. Denis was a beautiful dancer who, in exotic costume and setting, delighted the eyes of spectators. As the goddess Rahda she rises from deep contemplation and abandons herself to the *Dance of the Five Senses,* expressing the sensual joys of human existence. Then overcome by the realization of how futile are the delights of the flesh, the goddess returns to her mystic stage of contemplation. Audiences everywhere applauded the sensual pleasure evoked by the exotic images, poses and slow-motion patterns; they seldom understood or cared about the message and religious connotation.

But for Ruth St. Denis dancing was only a means to a much more important end. She always referred to herself as a self-appointed prophetess. Feeling that our civilization was growing decadent because "too many of us take from without instead of giving from within," she became a crusader for the sacred dance, creating what she called a "rhythmic choir."

*Rahda,* shown for the first time in New York in 1906, was so successful that it led her to give many solo recitals in London, Paris, Vienna and several cities in Germany. One Oriental dance followed another: *The Nautch, The Yogi, The Cobras* and *The Incense.* While Isadora stressed simplicity and an ascetic expression of feelings, Ruth St. Denis used every conceivable theatrical device to dazzle and enchant. Her visualizations of "within-ness" were wrapped in a splendor of light and color, fancy costuming and elaborate sets. Every dance was a skilful wedding of a serious background of religious ritual and spectacular pictorialization on stage.

When she met Ted Shawn, a former divinity student, who shared her belief in the religious message of dancing, they married and founded the Denishawn school and company, which was destined to produce the rebels of the modern dance in the Twenties. Ted Shawn was more interested than Ruth St. Denis in achieving a sound technical method; she relied on her beauty, her gift for expressive poses, her capacity for improvisation and colorful theatrical effects. None of her students and dancers could escape her strong and radiant personality which did not know defeat or doubt.* With the Bible in her head and a philosophy in her

* Doris Humphrey said in a speech at the Juilliard School of Music in 1956: "There were the magnetic and stimulating personalities of two leaders, Ruth St. Denis and Ted Shawn. I think everybody who has ever been with Ruth St. Denis has come away with a little of her vitality and her spark. She was and is a magnificent person. I think that we didn't learn from her too much about dancing, because none of us who were with her has really gone on as she did. She was at her greatest in oriental dancing and also in religious dance…. What we did gain from her was vision. Here was a woman who saw the dance whole, complete. She was not interested in a little segment but in all of it and was a major influence in inspiring the future leaders of the American modern dance."

heart, she has roamed far and wide in one-night stands with her orientalized dances and her faith in the holiness of the unity of body and soul.

The Denishawn school became more and more eclectic, added Spanish and American Indian material to its varied oriental themes. Its simplified ballet technique on bare feet was gradually strengthened under the influence of the modern dance of Germany and the eurhythmics of Dalcroze. One of the Denishawn dancers, Doris Humphrey, succeeded in giving the symphonic visualizations of Dalcroze artistic meaning. Technically, Denishawn was the very beginning of the modern dance in America. But the spiritual rebellion that followed was more important. The young dancers wanted to do more than impersonate Aztec princes and Indian goddesses. In the Twenties they rebelled against Denishawn. They wanted to dance about matters that moved and concerned them. They wanted to be of their time. First, Martha Graham left with her mentor, Louis Horst; then Doris Humphrey and Charles Weidman broke away. The pioneers were ready to explore the wonders of the wilderness they had conquered.

Soon after, the partnership of St. Denis and Shawn broke up. Ted Shawn must be credited with having helped the male dancer gain recognition. He established a dance technique primarily built upon masculine actions and he choreographed many works solely for male dancers, among them *The Kinetic Molpai* and *Dance of the Ages*. In 1933 he founded the Jacob's Pillow Dance Festival, held annually through the summer months. There he gave many young dancers a chance to be seen for the first time.

Ruth St. Denis continued on her crusade, preaching and dancing, and was the main inspiration for a "sacred dance" movement in America after the second World War. When in her mid-eighties, she

*"The Green Table" by Kurt Jooss*
*utilizes dance as a powerful instrument of satiric drama.*
*(Herbert Migdoll)*

made one of her increasingly rare appearances on stage and was asked how she thought of her dancing, she replied: "Let us say I move with remembered beauty."

## Rudolf Laban's Quest

Hardly any single person, with the exception of Diaghilev, put the stamp of his genius on the development of the dance during the first half of this century as distinctly as did Rudolf Laban. He was born in Bratislava, then a small town in the Austro-Hungarian monarchy, in 1880, of a family in the lower ranks of the aristocracy. In his studies he was imbued with Asiatic and Byzantine as well as European culture. He was a serious student, a scholar fascinated by the possibilities of movement.

Before the first World War he choreographed ballets which were essentially an exploration of movement. But his genius was felt mainly as a theorist and teacher. In the beginning, Laban was chiefly concerned with plastic rhythm, with motion for its own sake. He was interested in the coordination of mind, nerves and muscles and tried to find the right physical expression for this totality. The quality of a movement had to have its psychological motivation. In the course of his investigations he also developed his ideas of space patterns and harmonies, all of which led to expressionism in the modern dance.

He believed in a dynamic urge in man. But human beings are built differently and react kinetically according to their physiological and psychological make-up. He divided all people into three groups. Tall and slender persons he called "high dancers"; those of a short and square frame were "low dancers"; and those between them the "middle dancers." He found that a certain style of movement corresponds to each type, and that dancers belonging to a type will always move in more or less the same way. It was also Laban who made clear the importance of "*Anspannung und Abspannung*"—the range of dance movement between the extremes of utter tension and complete relaxation.

His experiments with space were largely intellectual and prepared the way for the practical exploitation by his student Mary Wigman. Laban was interested in the movements of actors as well as dancers, and in his *Mastery of Movement on the Stage* he dealt with the actor's problems. During World War II in England, where he sought sanctuary with some of his students, he worked on a new approach to the time-motion concept in industry. He first studied the motions and the work of operators in factories. Then he developed aptitude tests based on his findings concerning muscular reactions. "Laban Centers" were established for artisans seeking advice about their own work problems—the strains and stresses involved in their occupations. In these centers they learned bodily awareness and found relief in courses of movement devised to meet their special needs. He also, of course, became famous for the so-called Labanotation, a system used all over the world for notating choreographic movement.

Movement and dance were not only a means of artistic expression for him. They were a philosophy of life.

## Kurt Jooss: Magician of "The Green Table"

Artistically, Laban's ideas were best fulfilled by his two outstanding disciples, Kurt Jooss and Mary Wigman.

Jooss felt that dance must be theatrical and must reflect the age: that the expressionistic modern dance was the dance form of our time. All it needed were a few fundamental steps and positions from the classical ballet, but none of its tricks. The twentieth-century dance, he believed, demanded a form that would eschew the anachronistic virtuosity of entrechats, pirouettes and dancing on toe.

By combining the principles of expressionistic dance and classical ballet, Jooss achieved a system

*Harald Kreutzberg in his solo dance* Hallelujah. *(S. Enkelmann)*

of movement which made possible a tremendous range of expression. He paved the way for an acceptance of certain ideas by both dance forms. At the time, the balletomanes chided him for mixing modern with classic dance, and the modern dancer considered him a traitor to the cause. But Jooss was really trying to achieve only a twentieth-century version of Noverre's *ballet d'action*.

His major works proved that he desired to create theater using the dance as the means of expression. For him, every movement had to have meaning and further the action. He used miming, or a poetically expressive gesture language, wherever possible to underline plot and characterization. He spoke to his audience mostly in allegorical and dramatic terms, employing a minimum of décor and two pianos as accompaniment. The bareness of the stage made the dramatic immediacy of his images all the more striking.

Not all of his works were equally successful. *The Mirror* dealt with postwar adjustments; *The Big City* displayed a cross section of metropolitan life; *Chronica* depicted a Renaissance dictator with implications for today. All these topics reflected his concern with man and the world. Situation and characters, drama and message were apparently more important to Jooss than dance itself. His work was that of a dramatist who felt closer to movement than to words.

His masterpiece was the dramatic ballet, *The Green Table*, produced with sensational success in 1932. To this day this work has lost none of the savage power of its satire on the futility of war, Janus-faced politicians and war profiteers. It has also lost none of its artistic values, because as a theater piece without words it still speaks to us with the fury of its indignation. The simplicity of the conception and the allegorical power of this Dance of Death is unique.

## The Art of Mary Wigman

A new generation of Central European dancers emerged during and immediately after World War I. The enthusiasm generated by Isadora Duncan played its part, and the impact of Jaques-Dalcroze on the dancers created a new set of values. Dalcroze's Hellerau became the Mecca of dancers. And, for a short time, the Bauhaus in Weimar—which after the first World War revolutionized art training by combining the teaching of the pure arts with the study of crafts—became a center of dance.

The Bauhaus approached the dance from the

*Rosalie Chladek in characteristic movement studies.*
*(Both, Collection Rosalie Chladek)*

*Mary Wigman rehearsing
the chorus in her work* The Temple.
*(Orgel Koehne)*

painter's viewpoint. There cubism was of greater influence than expressionism and, as Oscar Schlemmer's *Triadic Ballet* showed, the attempt at absolute abstraction led to the depersonalization of the dancer. Here his entire body was covered and was used only to create plastic images and motion within a geometrical pattern. This *Neue Sachlichkeit,* the new functionalism of the mid-Twenties, resulted in beautiful shapes in motion, but this choreography was the child of a nondancer's fantastic notions. It was not before the early Fifties that Alwin Nikolais

took up this idea again and gave it the exciting effect of total theater.

Dalcroze, however, had a far-reaching influence on many dancers; their lyricism would be both a strength and a weakness. Grete Wiesenthal and Pola Nirenska were prominent in this school, but they were overshadowed by Rosalie Chladek; the latter's musical feeling was embodied in every movement, and she knew how to create lyric images both with large linear gestures or sparse movement. Far more theatrical and indeed almost spectacular, was Harald Kreutzberg, whose visual sense underlined the pictorial aspects. He, too, was limited by lyricism and pictorialized moods.

Only Mary Wigman emerged from this background as a giant. On the one hand she said, "Without ecstasy there is no dance," and on the other she said: "Without form there is no dance." She gave form to ecstasy and wedded the Dionysian to the Apollonian. The need for form made her conscious of space. For Isadora Duncan space was still limitless. For Mary Wigman space became a challenge and partner in her movement. She felt that the dancer's awareness of space creates conflicts similar to those caused by man's awareness of his environment. It stimulates and frustrates, it is a force to be mastered and utilized.

Mary Wigman began to create in the era of expressionism, at a time of struggle when all old values were being re-evaluated. What she danced about was man in relation to man and to his environment. "Man needs man," she said. "Art is communication spoken by man for humanity in a language raised above the everyday happening." Most of her dances have a somber mood. She tries to deal with the ultimate things in life: visions, fate, sacrifice, death. But she was so deeply rooted in life, and so strong and positive a person, that she saw the vision of death only as a counterbalance to the dynamic energies of life.

She created dances without music because she felt that the dancer has his own music, with a percussive accompaniment in his body's rhythms. She freed herself from musical enslavement and, like a primitive dancer, relied on her own pulse of the simple melodic line played on a flute supported by percussion instruments. Also like primitive man, she often made use of masks to underline the symbol behind the reality of the dancing figure.

Movement must be evocative, she feels, regard-

*Mary Wigman in her solo* Dances to Hungarian Songs. *(S. Enkelmann)*

less of beauty. Her movements are low-keyed; she kneels, crouches, creeps, and falls. Many of her dances end on the floor as a natural place to return to, a going back to Mother Earth. Her dances move from tender moods to the grotesque and demonic as well as to man's tragic struggle with himself and his world. However introspective her work was, it has always been vibrant and vital. Perhaps because she created only when she could not help but create, she expressed her delight and her torment.

# 13 Pioneers of Modern Dance in America

When Hanya Holm entered the dance scene in America in 1931, it was in a formative stage. There was a restlessness, a reappraisal of old values, a searching for new form and content. As Mary Wigman's assistant in Germany she came to the United States to direct a Mary Wigman School in New York. She soon sensed the undercurrent of vitality, a dynamic force about to assert itself, and she became part of it.

In Europe she had participated in one of the first productions of Max Reinhardt's *The Miracle,* danced the solo in an early staging of Stravinsky's *L'Histoire du Soldat* and assisted Mary Wigman in

*Martha Graham in* Lamentation. *Above: Merce Cunningham. (Both, Barbara Morgan)*

her gigantic antiwar memorial pageant, *Totenmal.* In America she did not rush into creative work at once but tried to absorb what was going on around her, gradually adjusting to her new environment. In 1937 she presented her first work of major stature, *Trend.*

*Trend* was a large group composition and Hanya Holm was one of its few soloists. Her great sense of form, her musical sensitivity and her urge to make a comment became immediately obvious. Her ability to work with large groups paved the way from *Trend* to her famous choreography for *My Fair Lady.* It was a long and sometimes difficult path, but her indefatigable interest in people and closeness to the pulse beat of life helps to explain her extraordinary Americanization. Her willingness to experiment was also part of it. Already in *Trend* the music used

*Hanya Holm in* Trend, *presented in 1937. (Both, Thomas Bouchard)*

was the new and radical all-percussion *Ionization* and *Octandre* by Edgar Varèse. Holm worked with designer Arch Lauterer, whose sets were functional but fascinating in conception. With surrealist paint-er Kurt Seligmann she later experimented in the use of masks in her concert work, *Golden Fleece.* In another work, *They Too Are Exiled,* she used the spoken word. *Metropolitan Daily,* a newspaper satire, in 1938, was the first dance composition to be televised, a daring act. She was the first to use Labanotation, employing it to duplicate the New York production of the musical, *Kiss Me, Kate,* in London. She also set a precedent when the same choreographic score was photographed on micro-film and accepted for copyright.

After *Kiss Me, Kate* came the choreography of several musicals: *Out Of This World, The Golden Apple,* and her most brilliant contribution to the joyful art of the musical, *My Fair Lady.* When she was assigned to choreograph the latter, she first went to London to get the authentic atmosphere, to absorb the spirit of what went on outside of Covent Garden. "I like to watch people in their daily role," she said, "in life apart from the stage. Their emo-tions, actions and reactions, at ease and under fire, all are noted. I absorb, then translate into dance."

No medium is alien to her. Besides plays and television she has staged operas and worked in films. She has created modern dance works for the concert stage every summer at her summer school in Colo-rado Springs. But she has always expressed herself best in the lyric theater that fuses music, drama and dance.

## Louis Horst

In 1915, Ruth St. Denis engaged Louis Horst as accompanist for a two-week tour with her company.

They liked his understanding of the dancer's musical needs; he liked to play for them, and the two weeks turned into ten years of close collaboration.

But things changed in 1925. Louis Horst recognized the potential genius in Martha Graham, he encouraged Doris Humphrey and Charles Weidman—the most outstanding members of the Denishawn company—to break away from Denishawn to find their own personalities and what they wanted to dance about. He went with them. He was ready to compose for them, to play for them, to help them to their self-fulfillment. They went out into a wilderness that meant artistic freedom, or into a freedom which was an artistic wilderness. They had to establish their own rules and their own technique. In the beginning, each new dance was a new experiment in discovering and revealing themselves. With greater freedom the dancers had to make greater demands on their artistry.

But Louis Horst was always there to help, to inspire, to guide. He saw that all the other arts were undergoing a transformation, and he felt that in order to build anew, one had first to go back to primitive and archaic forms. He was determined to give the new dance the same freedom and originality that the other arts were enjoying. He also was determined to give it structure and discipline, choreographic principles that could be taught. He wanted the modern dance to recapture the relation that the primitive has to his body, an intimacy with the muscle tensions of daily movements lost by modern man.

The natural posture or gesture was used as a point of departure for a poetic metaphor. This was in sharp contrast to the ballet principle of a secure powerful center of gravity in an upright back from which the stylized movements of arms and legs emerge. Modern dancers began to talk of movements based on the principles of tension and relaxation—not unlike those that Laban had explored. The flexibility and shift of movement to various parts of the body gave it a range of expression as wide as life itself.

In his lectures Horst would say: "The new dance

Tragic Exodus, *with Hanya Holm and her company.* (*Nina Leen: Pix, Inc.*)

does not depend on beautiful line, unearthly balance, or sexual titillation. The movement is abstracted to express in esthetic form the drives, desires, and reactions of alive human beings." In his teachings, Horst began with the pre-classic dance forms, the music of the sixteenth and seventeenth centuries. He used the form of the *pavan, galliard, courante, saraband, gavotte,* and *minuet* as a basis from which the student could develop a mood that fit the music, and fill it with emotion and a theme. Contrasting structure was strictly adhered to. The student learned to think choreographically. Then he showed the growing dancer how modern artists used space, texture and time in contrast to artists of the past. He analyzed such attitudes, styles

*Erick Hawkins in Martha Graham's* El Penitente, *1940. (Barbara Morgan)*

*their* identity in their time. When he was asked where he thought the modern expressive dancer was going, his answer was: "When Petipa was called to Russia, when Diaghilev asked Fokine to choreograph for him, did they know where they were going? Did we know it in the late Twenties when we felt we had to find a new way of expressing ourselves? What difference does it make where the new dancer is going as long as he is going!"

## Martha Graham

In 1930, Martha Graham said: "Like the modern painters and architects, we have stripped our medium of decorative unessentials. Just as fancy trimmings are no longer seen on buildings, so dancing is no longer padded. It is not pretty, but it is much more real."

Martha Graham was the most controversial dancer at that time, chided for her obscurity and angularity. Today her name is synonymous with the modern dance in America. She undoubtedly became the most successful exponent of the new dance form in the late Twenties. She was a magnificent performer and developed a very personal vocabulary of tensions, of percussive movements which would take hold of the entire body in the form of a beat, of contraction and release. She evolved suspensions and falls from different positions and in various accents and speeds, applying them to the expression of emotions. The concepts of the Graham technique are now accepted from New York to San Francisco, from Stockholm to Tel Aviv. "I never wanted to destroy the ballet," she said. "I only went my own way."

Her roots were in the American cultural climate: "Nothing is more revealing than movement. What

and idioms as introspection, cerebralism, impressionism or jazz, and the student learned to express in dance terms the forces which had molded the world around him.

He taught in many schools for many decades. There is hardly an American dancer who has not gone through Louis Horst's classes and many famous actors refer to him as the man who made them conscious of their bodies. He showed the pioneers the way through the wilderness in the late Twenties and Thirties, yet lived to see the new dancers in the 1960's again trying to experiment, searching for

*Martha Graham in* The Witch of Endor. *(Herbert Migdoll) Overleaf:* Night Journey, *1960, with Paul Taylor as Tiresias, Martha Graham as Jocasta, Bertram Ross as Oedipus. (Martha Swope)*

*Left: Doris Humphrey and Charles Weidman in* Duo Drama, *1931. (Museum of Modern Art)   Right: Charles Weidman's* Bargain Counter. *(Barbara Morgan)*

you are finds expression in what you do. The dance reveals the spirit of the country in which it takes root. No sooner does it fail to do this than the dance begins to lose its indispensable integrity and significance." Most of her earlier dances reflect this mood. From the solo, *Frontier* (1935), which she created with astounding economy of gesture, evoking the image of the vast American plains and the indomitable will of the people to conquer them, to *Appalachian Spring* (1944), the most fulfilled of her

dances, she recreated the story of her country with a warmth and exuberance that expressed the hope of a great tomorrow. She wanted to liberate the American soul from the prison of Puritanism, to free the spirit from industrial enslavement.

The characteristics of her entire work can be found in her very beginnings. In 1931 she created *Primitive Mysteries* which, based on American Indian themes, had the air of a miracle play, the ascetic feeling of the early Christians. It was a tryptich of pagan origin executed with a fascinating simplicity and earthy strength in its movements. Two decades later she choreographed her final version of Saint Joan, *Seraphic Dialogue,* with the same inner simplicity. But how different here was the concept of the ritual! The adoration of the Virgin, the Virgin's grief and the final exaltation in *Primitive Mysteries* have their three counterparts in *Seraphic Dialogue* in the initiation of the Maid, the inner struggle of Saint Joan the Warrior, and the glorification of the Martyr.

In many of her works Martha Graham used this device of splitting the main character into complementary parts to illustrate the various aspects of a character. It permitted her to penetrate psychological motivations and provide illuminating insights. The duality of Emily Dickinson in Graham's *Letter to the World,* the threefold images or phases of one and the same person in Saint Joan and in *Samson Agonistes,* are examples of this device. In *Herodiade* the figure of the woman attendant is her alter ego, the beast in *Errand into the Maze* is the destructive power in the self. Basically, most of these dances remain rituals—*Alcestis* a rite of winter and spring, *Phaedra* a rite of sexual obsession.

In her many portraits of mythological and Biblical heroines, her increasingly analytical approach to the psyche, to the complexities of motive and deed, became a striking and dramatic element. Knowing her limitations, she shaped these classic stories from the viewpoint of the woman in them. The Oedipus story was recreated as the experience of the mother of Oedipus, Jocasta, and the tragedy of Orestes became the tragedy of Clytemnestra. Martha Graham once said of her female figures that she feels ready to choreograph them only when she is certain what they had for breakfast, when she can, in short, create from an intimate knowledge of her characters.

As a change of pace she choreographed *Diversion of Angels* which has a truly angelic lyric quality. *In Canticle For Innocent Comedians,* she again expressed a poetic joyfulness, singing "the praise of the world as it turns." Her gift for lightness and humor is especially demonstrated in some of her storyless works and in a few comedy dances. She played the "Empress of the Arena" in the 1939 dance comedy *Every Soul Is a Circus,* and returned with mellow humor and self-irony to the circus theme as the "ringmistress" in *Acrobats of God,* a danced paean to the world of the artist.

She introduced symbolic sets and mobile props. She even used costumes dramatically, doing so in one of her first solos, *Lamentation* (1930). In this piece a shrouded woman seated on a bench communicates grief; she uses her costume creatively by making it her antagonist, symbol of the confining world, of the fate against which she revolts.

Her work is essentially dramatic, it never becomes overly theatrical, because her observations and interpretations are filtered through a poetic experience whose symbolic expression is inescapably vivid. An inner restraint peels movement to its bareness. Her technical discipline creates a taut structure which she fills with lovely lyricism, with the tragedy of human failure as well as the laughter of satire. She always returns to the same themes on a different level and in another form. She always searches for the totality of artistic expression. She knows how to evoke the revelation of a mystery, how to reach from the particular to the universal. She is the most unique and prolific dance creator America has brought forth so far. She made the dream of Isadora Duncan come true.

## Doris Humphrey

Doris Humphrey was a less glamorous personality than Martha Graham. But her work was no less important. While still dancing with Denishawn, she experimented with music visualizations. The process of dance composition itself fascinated her. She was not concerned with the relationship of emotional impulses to the creation of movement. That was part of the creative process. She wanted to achieve a sound foundation on which the creative will could operate freely.

She found a direction for her thinking in the juxtaposition of man's search and his saturation, of

*Lester Horton with Joyce Trisler. (Collection Joyce Trisler)*

*Helen Tamiris with Daniel Nagrin in* When the Saints Come Marchin' In, *choreographed by Tamiris. (Barbara Morgan)*

partly in keeping an effortless state of balance while challenging unbalance. But Doris Humphrey was the first dancer to explore equilibrium analytically and to base her choreography on her analysis. In the sphere of danger, in which the dancer's body defies its fall, lies the strongest dramatic effect, tension and dynamic force. These principles seem clear today, because Doris Humphrey clarified them; and they are fundamental and functionally effective.

*Water Study* was Doris Humphrey's first step in experimental choreography. We still note the influence of Isadora Duncan in its reliance on the rhythms of nature, a reliance extended in her *Life of the Bee*, which was inspired by Maurice Maeterlinck's classic and in which she used continuous humming sounds to accompany the dramatic death duel between the old and new queen. This work was followed by *The Shakers* in which she made use of the ritual of "dancing one's sins away" for a theatrical presentation, accompanied by speech, song and accordion.

But it was only in *New Dance* trilogy, a longer work, that Doris Humphrey mastered a major subject. *Theater Piece,* the first section, dramatized human selfishness through a figure protesting competition in a world gone mad; *With My Red Fires* dealt with romantic love and the destructiveness of possessive love; finally, *New Dance* was a strong affirmation of faith in the world and in man.

It was as a dancer and theorist that she made her greatest contribution to the development of the modern dance at its very beginning. Her works of profound choreographic conceptions were still to come, although her *Passacaglia in C Minor* (1938) translated the architectural beauty and the spirit of religious ecstasy into movement as pure and simple as Bach's music. Arthritis forced her to retire as a dancer in 1945, but she continued to teach and choreograph. For years she conquered constant pain and remained a dynamic force in the development of the art. As artistic director of the José Limón company she created a series of enduring works. In *Lament for Ignacio Sanchez Meijas* she took a few lines

movement and stability. She would stand before the mirror and study her body in its struggle with gravity, in its attempt to maintain equilibrium. And her observations resulted in her theory of "fall and recovery," based on the idea of the complete balance of the human body and its contest with the power of gravity. For her, the excitement of movement lay between these two poles.

It was all a matter of balance. The wider the sway, the more dramatic and stronger would be the movement which restored the balance. This theory of "the arc between two deaths" has, in a way, been the problem of ballet, whose visual excitement lies

of a Garcia Lorca poem and painted the bullfighter's doomed life and fear of death in sombre colors. Then there is the incomparable pastoral, *Day on Earth,* proclaiming the blessedness of family life and the sustaining power of work, with the epitome of hope seen in the growing child; or *Ruins and Visions* in which the poetic imagery of the dance communicates the greatness of the human spirit. *Night Spell* which shows a tortured man wrestling with his nightmares and then trying to hold on to the image of love while his wakening face is still marred by the fears of the night; or the intoxicating rhythm based on Iberian peasant songs, in *Ritmo Jondo,* a tense and ironic story of the meeting and parting of men and women.

Finally there was another attempt at Bach, using his fourth *Brandenburg Concerto,* whose first section she was still able to choreograph with joyfulness and sweeping grandeur. But she could not finish it. In the last few months of her life, bedridden, she wrote her testament in the form of an invaluable book, *The Art of Making Dances.*

## Charles Weidman

Charles Weidman was closely associated as partner and teacher with Doris Humphrey in the 1930's. His practice was to stage a scene for himself in most of her early group works. And when she had to retire as a performer, he founded his own company.

He created a few serious works such as *Lynch Town* which was described as exciting and terrifying; when revived thirty years later it still had dramatic impact. His portrait of Abe Lincoln in *A House Divided* was one of the earliest character studies in the modern dance. But it soon became evident that Weidman's strength was in humor and pantomime.

He developed an uncanny sense of timing and achieved his greatest success with broadly comic or gently satirical dance works. He loved to comment on the simple, senseless things in life. He made fun of the silent movies in *Flickers,* or of "old times" in *And Daddy Was a Fireman.* A more ambitious work

was his full-length ballet *Candide.* Later, he became particularly known for bringing James Thurber's sophisticated fables to the dance stage. Through pantomime, posing and clowning he achieved comic visualizations with the character of cartoons. As a partner to Doris Humphrey he helped the expressionistic dance get over its first difficult years. But essentially, he is to the modern dance in America what Ogden Nash is to American poetry.

## Lester Horton

Lester Horton was a unique, spectacular personality possessed of a rage to create. His early training was that of a designer and stage manager; then he took up ballet under Adolph Bolm, the famous Diaghilev dancer. He adventured into North American Indian reservations and, while still in his early twenties, became an authority on the Indian dance. He was commissioned to stage an open-air Indian spectacle in Los Angeles and there he began to study with Michio Ito, whose orientalized Dalcroze system greatly influenced him. Horton learned from him the Japanese way of using props and he extended this knowledge to the dynamic realization of his dances. He gathered a group of dancers around him and began to work feverishly. In 1946 he founded his Dance Theater, and two years later showed his productions for the first time. From 1942 to 1953 he did the choreography for seventeen Hollywood films. In that year he died of a heart attack at the age of forty-seven. He crossed the dance horizon like a meteor flashing briefly and brightly, and then vanishing.

Horton had a flair for theatrical dance. In 1937 he staged Stravinsky's *The Rite of Spring* for the Hollywood Bowl. He was met by a storm of applause and violent criticism. He decided to go on, evolving his own technique and style. He saw to it that the dancer's body was constantly stretched to keep muscles long and to give easiness of movement to all parts. There were exercises for each part of the body, including the eye, the eyebrows, the mouth and even the tongue. But it was not a technique of subtleties, it was broad, it did not belong to any one level or dimension. It was often called acrobatic or gymnastic; and it was certainly "free."

Combined with his technical studies were exercises with dramatic motivation. There was, for instance, the Guernica study, based on Picasso's images, of a person in shock. This required a great deal of technical control. With the help of such exercises Lester Horton made his students dance in class long before they set foot on a stage. When the time came to perform, they were truly ready.

One of his first works was *Totem Incantation,* a long piece that dealt with Indian puberty and marriage rites. *The Beloved,* one of his most powerful creations, was a dramatic *pas de deux* on bigotry in New England. Visual caprices inspired by Paul Klee came alive in *Another Touch of Klee,* to a jazz score. Duke Ellington's music was used for *Liberian Suite,* ethnic in flavor, with hips held at odd angles and pelvises rotating in all directions. He turned Lorca's "Yerma" into *Prado de Pena* (Field of Pain) and, employing three dancers as Greek chorus, treated it like a *choréodrame.* He did his own version of *Medea* and, fascinated by *Salome,* reworked this theme five times.

He created seventeen dance compositions for his group within a short span of time. For most of them he designed the décor and costumes, and for some of them he wrote the music. He was not afraid of color and mixed it boldly. He choreographed and designed in long, broad, sure strokes. He was bold, full of vitality and creative energy—a near-genius that death prevented from becoming perhaps the most vital force in the American dance.

## Helen Tamiris

Helen Tamiris belongs with the other pioneers of the late Twenties, even though her artistic background was different from theirs. She studied with Fokine and danced with the Metropolitan Opera Ballet for three years. She toured South America as

Helen Tamiris. (*Thomas Bouchard*)

a ballerina, appeared in revues although she already knew that she did not want a ballet career. The dance she visualized would have to be a part of herself, expressing what she thought and felt. She took a look at the Duncan school, but found its posed lyricism of little interest to her.

When she began to experiment, she worked out a few principles which she published in the program bill of one of her first recitals. Indicative of the revolutionary spirit of this period was her thought that there were no general rules and that each work had to create its own code; that each age creates its own art which, however international it may be, must carry the stamp of its environment. She felt that "the dance of today must have a dynamic tempo and be vital, precise, spontaneous, free, normal, natural and human." She saw dancing as movement with a personal rhythm, a rhythm so innate that the motion could become theatrical without music. Tamiris experimented with several dances without accompaniment (as did Mary Wigman), or she used as music a siren or the patterned beating of piano strings. She felt very strongly that the body should be able to communicate without the aid of costumes. So she experimented with dancing in the nude.

In 1929 Tamiris began to attract attention to her abilities after the performance of a few striking dance moods and, even more, with her *Negro Spirituals*. As seen on film today, its vigorous, beautiful movements testify to the sincerity and simplicity of her approach. Later, she became a well-known choreographer for American musicals and was responsible for various Broadway shows: *Up In Central Park*; *Annie, Get Your Gun*; *Inside U.S.A.*; *Show Boat*; *Touch and Go* and others. But neither her artistic conscience, nor her agile mind could be satisfied by shows. She returned to choreographing for the modern dance toward the end of the Fifties and tried to continue where she had left off, the result often appearing close to the early style of the modern dance.

One of her important creations in the later period was her *Dance For Walt Whitman*. With its spacious designs and powerful movement patterns it successfully suggests Walt Whitman's love for America. In such works as *Arrows of Desire* and *Memoir*, the emotional statement is rich in meaning, and such meaning is one of the prime reasons that makes her do choreography. Even when she ventured into non sequitur dances, she retained a sensitive and poetic quality. Through many of her dance scenes her social conscience speaks with unmistakable intensity. In such moments she became very eloquent.

As early as 1928 she set forth her principles in a "Manifest." Some of them were:

*Art is international, but the artist is a product of a nationality and his principle duty to himself is to express the spirit of his race.*
*A new civilization always creates new forms in art.*
*There are no general rules. Each original work of art creates its own code.*
*Sincerity is based on simplicity. A sincere approach to art is always done through simple forms.*
*Toe dancing... Why not dance on the palms of the hands?*

It is characteristic of Tamiris that over the years she never gave up the struggle to organize repertory theaters for the modern dance. In May 1960 her *Call to Action* appeared in Louis Horst's magazine, *Dance Observer:*

The modern dance has matured to the point where it can count its masterpieces. But sadly, they exist now only in the minds of those who saw them. We have no stage and no company to perform them.
These masterpieces were produced in a field deplored as chaotic and individualistic. Each choreographer felt his way to be the one true path to the creation of the modern dance. Each cultivated his own group and his own audience. However, in looking back, I find it startling that what seemed to be a great weakness emerges, by virtue of its individualism and diversity, as its strength.... We have produced a rich, creative, new Dance-Art. The masterpieces of the past must cease to be treasured memories and re-emerge as performed, living realities. New works should be commissioned. Our skilled dancers, performing in the works of a variety of choreographers, will grow and flourish.
We must consolidate efforts of the last thirty years. In this way we will move into the future of modern dance as a genuine expression of America.

# *14  Heirs and Seekers*

In the wake of the great pioneers of the American modern dance we find a host of choreographers who have continued the tradition established in the Thirties or have extended its symbols and themes. Some of them started their own rebellion against the rebels of the Twenties.

The majority of those rebels were trained by Martha Graham and were her partners. Her strong personality and her highly disciplined technique, which leaves the dancer little freedom for his personal expression, may well account for her influence. But there were some who tried to find their own language while still holding on to the vocabulary they had been taught.

Pearl Lang is a dancer-choreographer of stature who is drawn, like Martha Graham, toward subject matter from the past. Mythology, as in her colorful ballet on the Persephone theme, and the Bible are among the main sources of her inspiration. Her *Apasionada*, on the theme of death, demonstrates how she uses a dramatic idea in a theatrically effective manner. Fear and daring, outbursts of joy and brooding moods are here woven into a colorful tapestry of images; it has, like many of her other works, a rich, dark beauty. The device of scenery being moved by the dancers is Grahamesque. Her *Shirah* is an ecstatic song in movement, a parable of love and faith, singing the praise of eternal renewal.

*Valerie Bettis in her dance-drama* As I Lay Dying, *based on the William Faulkner story. (Courtesy Isadora Bennett)  Above: Ruth Currier in* For a Fervent One. *(Radford Bascome)*

203

Poem, *choreographed by Sophie Maslow. (Irwin M. Schor)*

In one section of this dance she uses the mechanical device of "shimmering strands that stretch between still points of tension," suggesting a vibrating stream of light. This device is handled imaginatively and dramatically, becoming a living part of her creation.

Her works are organically conceived and apply intellect and emotions with equal intensity. She said about herself: "The technique I employ is Graham modern as I have personalized it and expanded upon it for my creative purposes. I look to my own interior for the 'material in Turmoil,' so to speak."

Sophie Maslow, once a member of the Graham company, is an exciting choreographic talent, one who moved more sharply away from her apprentice years than Pearl Lang. She has a striking sense of theater, and one of her great gifts is the use of the spoken word as much as music to paint a stunning background for her movement patterns. Such works as *Folksay*, a piece of Americana, or the much later *Poem*, choreographed to Duke Ellington's jazz and the verses of the avant-garde poet Lawrence Ferlinghetti, one of the strong indictments of our time, testify to her special talent. Her strong feeling for folklore and her own past has also found expression in *The Village I Knew*. Whether she uses contemporary material, as in *Manhattan Suite,* or weaves a haunting tapestry of medieval man's love-making and mourning during the Plague in *Prologue,* her comments show how concerned she is for man and his fate. Her choreographic designs have the clarity and impact of well-constructed theater pieces.

Coming from the same background as Maslow and Lang, Anna Sokolow has become a rebel without having gone to extremes. She has adhered to the principle that content creates its own structure. She is to the modern dance what Jerome Robbins is to ballet: an unruly spirit that wants to be of its time and express bitterness and distress over man's desperate flight from himself, a spirit always in the throes of agony over the miseries and frustrations of our time. Like Robbins she found jazz the rhythm for what she has to say. Even in such a rhapsodic work as *Lyric Suite,* an awareness of man's relation to man dominates. *Dreams* depicts a descent into the unconscious, and one cannot watch it without a frightful realization that we are of such stuff as nightmares are made.

Anna Sokolow's works throb with life: *Rooms* is one of the masterpieces of the American modern dance. With sure craftsmanship and invention she catches the pulse beat of our time. *Rooms* is devastating in its realization of man's inability to cope with his sense of the futility of life. In scene after scene, with existentialist conviction, it presents man's struggles, fears and helplessness. When John Martin, then The New York *Times'* dance critic, left the theater after the première of *Rooms,* he was heard to say: "I'm ready to jump into the river." Anna Sokolow's aims are similar to those Bertolt Brecht uses in his epic theater: to disquiet and shock the audience into awareness.

Jean Erdman, born in Honolulu, was introduced first to the Isadora Duncan style and then became a leading soloist in Martha Graham's company. She founded her own group in 1944. From her first work, *The Transformations of Medusa,* to *The Coach With the Six Insides,* a dance play based on James Joyce's *Finnegan's Wake,* Jean Erdman created about fifty dances, revealing a remarkable versatility.

Her method is to let each dance evolve and dictate its own style. This permits her to treat a variety of topics, mainly inspired by literary works and images. She is well known for her dances to E. E. Cumming's poems; for *Ophelia,* a solo in which she probed the agonies of the rejected woman; for her group work, *The Perilous Chapel,* and her humorous study of Shakespearean ladies in *Four Portraits from Duke Ellington's Shakespeare Album.* Even in such a work as *Changing Woman,* in which the development of human feeling is suggested through a series of nature images, her intellectual approach is manifest. Her poetic presence is most evident in *The Coach With the Six Insides,* in which the acting is based on a rhythmic pattern subtly in harmony with Joyce's intoxicating flow of words.

Among Hanya Holm's artistic heirs are Mary Anthony, Valerie Bettis and Glen Tetley; they have carried with them her idea of strict discipline and of understanding the purpose and meaning of movement, as well as her conviction that artistic growth involves the power to explore and to expand. This has brought Glen Tetley closer to balletic principles, while Mary Anthony and Valerie Bettis have turned to more literary material. The latter have fused the spoken word and the dance idiom into a theater experience. They could achieve total theater if the modern dance ever had the esthetic inclination and financial means to add décor and costume to its artistic equipment. Among the literary works with which they were most successful were plays by Garcia Lorca and Tennessee Williams, both used by Mary Anthony, and William Faulkner's novel *As I Lay Dying,* staged by Valerie Bettis.

The influence of Doris Humphrey was very wide. She acquired the greatest number of disciples and had a strong impact on many dancers outside her orbit. This must be ascribed to her solidly grounded esthetic principles and her relentless efforts as a teacher. Unlike Martha Graham, whose self-centered approach made no allowance for the individuality of students, she did not isolate herself. Doris Humphrey recognized artistic potentialities in many young dancers and helped them to find themselves and make their own artistic statements.

When Pauline Koner was studying with Fokine, he said: "In her the soul dances." At the age of fourteen, she joined Fokine's company. Always restless and eager to learn, she embraced the Spanish and Oriental dance. She also became one of the pioneer dancers on television. She was a well-known dancer when, in 1946, she asked Doris Humphrey to direct her in a solo, *Voice in the Wilderness*. In the same year, she joined the Limón company, which was under the artistic direction of

Doris Humphrey. For the next fifteen years she appeared as a featured artist in almost all dance works created by Doris Humphrey or José Limón for this company. Two years after Humphrey's death, she left the company to concentrate on her solo work.

Pauline Koner is a unique artist with a rare sense of responsibility for her work. Almost everything she created seemed inspired and inspiring. In one of her later solo dances, *The Farewell*, a tribute to Doris Humphrey, she mastered the subject matter with the most sparing means, creating a monumental effect through utmost simplicity. Most sensitive to music, she also has a sense of form so tight that she does not make a single superfluous gesture. She is a dramatic dancer who knows how to combine dynamic intensity with sustained movement.

Pauline Koner has given the modern dance a few works of substantial merit. Who will dance her works when she is no longer able to perform? Must the creative work of such an artist die with the memory of those who saw her? Classical works such as Pavlova's *Dying Swan* have not vanished from the ballet repertoire. In the modern dance, however, solo works seem utterly dependent on the individuality of their creators; none of them is likely to be danced so widely as *The Dying Swan*.

José Limón is the most impressive representative of the dance as conceived by Doris Humphrey. Although faithful to her essential concepts, he gave her works as well as his own the unmistakable stamp of his personality. A Mexican by birth, he came to the United States with his family when he was seven years old. Early exposed to music—his father was conductor of a military band—he learned to play the organ and to love Bach, whose music gave him the sense of order and stately rhythm which most of his dances possess. As a young man he felt he was destined to become a painter, and his dance cre-

*Left: Pauline Koner. (Peter Basch)*
*Right: Pearl Lang in* Windsung.
*(Courtesy Pearl Lang)*

ations have always shown a predilection for colorful pictorial images.

When he was twenty years old, he came to New York where, dissatisfied with his progress as a painter, he turned to dancing. He entered the Humphrey-Weidman school. Happy in his new environment, he knew this was what he wanted: to be a dancer and choreographer. After a few years of intense training he became the leading dancer of the Humphrey-Weidman company and stayed with it until 1940. The war interrupted his career but in 1947, he formed his own company under the artistic direction of Doris Humphrey. He danced the leading parts in her works and choreographed some of his own outstanding dances.

The way he dances and choreographs is due profoundly to his background and personality. His face has the cut of a Mexican Indian, with its deep-set eyes, hollow cheeks and intensity of expression. There is great nobility in José Limón's bearing in life as well as on the stage—a mixture of spiritual nobility and worldly nobility. Doris Humphrey once described him as an anachronistic, baroque personality. His movements are dynamic, tense, angular, his elbows are hyper-extended, in a moment of heightened emotion his head is turned to one side and thrown back, his arm thrust out straight with the hand held facing him like a mirror.

In his choreography the flow of the dancing is marked by the contrasts between lyric and dramatic experiences. Whatever he does is finished in form and has an almost classic structure. He loves order and formality. And within the measured form his content develops. He has much to say and says it in a plastic, representational manner. His works are humanly meaningful, as in his *The Moor's Pavane* where the stately rhythms of a pavane embody the tragedy of Othello. While violence rages in their hearts, the dancers glide about to the dignified

*Jean Erdman in* Duet for Flute and Dancer.
*(Walter Daran)*
*Overleaf: José Limón. (Martha Swope)*

*The American Ballet Dance Theatre production of*
*Limón's* Choreographic Offering: A Tribute to
Doris Humphrey. *(Herbert Migdoll)*

strains of Purcell. It is his best work and belongs with
the best of the American modern dance.

José Limón turned O'Neill's *The Emperor Jones*
into a haunting ballet. The image of two men locked
in mortal conflict occurs frequently in Limón's
creations, as in *The Traitor,* his Judas tragedy, or in
*La Malinche,* in which an Indian peasant turns
against the figure of Cortes, the conquistador. He
did a few abstract dances; of these, *Concerto Grosso*
has clearly woven patterns of movement and noble
gestures. He has retained the essential teachings of
his Catholic faith. His belief is reflected in *There Is
A Time* which tells in a circular pattern, the story
of man: the cycle of birth and planting, of sorrow
and laughter, of love and hate. His second masterpiece *Missa Brevis,* is an expression of pure religious

ecstasy and oneness with God. Danced to Zoltan
Kodaly's music, it affirms enduring values. In it
an observer, a passerby stops to watch a cluster of
people at worship in a bombed-out church. He is
the tourist through history who becomes involved
in the ordeals of man. The people, drably dressed,
seem a mass of misery seeking understanding
through closeness and warmth. They circle in a
kyrie and gloria. The group melts away, the observer dances abjectly expressing his helplessness.
Then the people reappear and he mingles with
them, sharing their hopes and concerns without
losing his identity as an observer. This work has a
touch of greatness. As is characteristic of Limón's
composition, the dancing of the ensemble is juxta-
posed to that of the observer, who walks with the
off-balance movements, the intensity and nobility
typical of José Limón's style.

Among the many dancers who came under Doris
Humphrey's spell, two more ought to be mentioned.
One is Ruth Currier: ethereal in appearance, fair,

a natural beauty who can move with remarkable speed and vigor. She created a number of dances that have dramatic impact, such as *The Antagonists,* depicting enmity and fear, and others that are essentially lyrical, such as *Quartet, A Tender Portrait,* and *Toccata.* Her work has a subtlety and delicate phrasing, and is often a kind of pastel of lyricism. Another dancer, Lucas Hoving, tall, slim, long-legged, came from Holland to join the Limon company. His *Icarus* and *Strange, To Wish Wishes No Longer* are like haunting dreams and reveal a penchant for creating theatrically effective images out of unfulfillment and lost desires. Relying on humor with ironic overtones, he presents his images as though they were merely passing thoughts. *Has the Last Train Left?* is such a dance creation—a charming piece verging on vaudeville. Out of the aloneness of three people waiting for a train, he shapes a few vignettes into an artistic entity.

The Canadian-born Sybil Shearer, who studied in France and England, was a leading member of the Humphrey-Weidman company for some time before she made her headquarters in Chicago. She is a dancer of surprising technique who very early broke away from the established concepts of narrative and representational dance. She is a highly intuitive artist of extraordinary originality, and is eloquent with a minimum of movements. Because of her uncompromising attitude, her audience remained limited. But as a dancer's dancer, her influence on the new generation, searching for its artistic identity in the 1950's and 1960's, was very strong.

Young dancers who worked with earlier or later pioneers often show the influence of their teachers. In his association with Helen Tamiris, Daniel Nagrin developed a faculty for creating character studies. His *Strange Hero, Man of Action* and *Indeterminate Figure* are trenchant portrayals of man's foolish obsession with illusions and the unrealities of modern life. Jeff Duncan, who danced with Anna Sokolow, has inherited her social consciousness, as is evident in his *Statement;* but he finds his own identity in such experiments as *Canticles,* an orientalized ritual using percussive effects. Dancing with

the Alwin Nikolais group, Murray Louis displays the influence of his master, but in his creative work reveals a very personal style distinguished by poetic imagination and theatrical effectiveness. His *Entr'acte* is among the best works achieved by the third generation of modern dancers.

These are only a few of the host of dancer-choreographers—Merce Cunningham, Paul Taylor, Alvin Ailey, and John Butler are discussed in other chapters—who have followed the trails blazed by their teachers and then made paths of their own.

*Ruth Currier in* Threshold. *(Radford Bascome)*

# 15  After Diaghilev

The development of ballet has generally coincided with a shift in its geographical center. It moved from Italy to France and, from there, after more than two hundred years, to Russia where it reached a climax and then returned, as the Ballets Russes, to Paris in the beginning of this century. After the first World War, economic difficulties in Europe and a cultural awakening in the United States, made the New World and in particular New York the new focal point of ballet activity.

Pavlova had everywhere sown the seeds of dance consciousness during her transcontinental tours.

*Arthur Mitchell and Diana Adams in George Balanchine's 1958* Agon. *(Martha Swope)  Above: Anthony Dowell as Oberon. (Anthony Crickmay)*

Diaghilev's company made its first American tour in 1916 and Fokine settled in New York in 1923. During Diaghilev's second American tour Adolph Bolm, one of his principal dancers, decided to choreograph and teach in the United States. Soon Leonide Massine followed. Mikhail Mordkin, who had danced with Pavlova at the Metropolitan Opera House in 1910 and returned to America several times, finally left Russia and came to live in America in 1923.

Meanwhile the American dancers were revealing a restlessness. Ruth Page worked for the Chicago Opera and created some of the first ballets of American folklore, such as her remarkable *Frankie and Johnny*. The Ballet Russe de Monte Carlo which, under various leaderships and with varying success, was trying to keep the memory of Diaghilev's great

days alive, made a place for this purely American piece in its repertory.

In Philadelphia, Catherine Littlefield created American genre works for her company, and in New York, in the 1930's, Lincoln Kirstein sponsored many young talents; among the latter was Lew Christensen who became famous for his dance creation *Filling Station.* Kirstein's greatest discovery was Eugene Loring, whose *Billy the Kid,* now in the repertory of the American Ballet Theater, became the first modern classic in the New World. This work had great influence on another choreographer, Agnes de Mille, most of whose ballets utilize characteristic features of American folklore.

Miss de Mille created the ballet *Rodeo* for the Ballet Russe de Monte Carlo in 1942. It was a mixture of vigorous cowboy steps and riding and roping movements, it introduced tap dancing and realistic comedy to the ballet for the first time. Six years later came *Fall River Legend,* which also dealt with an American theme, the famous case of Lizzie Borden's murder of her father and stepmother. The world of puritanical New England is the ballet's background. The importance of de Mille's work lies in her deep ties with American culture and modes. Even if she chooses a medieval theme, as in *Three Virgins and a Devil,* it remains a truly American ballet in structure and movement. She continued to work for the American Ballet Theater, a group founded by Lucia Chase and Richard Pleasant in 1939.

Originally an offshoot of the Mikhail Mordkin company, the American Ballet Theater was destined to play a major role in the theatrical dance of

*Above left: Ruth Page and Bentley Stone in* Frankie and Johnny. *(Serge Lido) Below left: Agnes de Mille's* Fall River Legend, *produced by the American Ballet Theater. (Jack Mitchell) Above right: Eugene Loring's* Billy the Kid, *now in the repertory of the American Ballet Theater, was one of the first ballets to use American folklore. (Jack Mitchell: Courtesy American Ballet Theater) Below right: Agnes de Mille's* Rodeo. *(Fred Fehl)*

the United States. Its policy has been to revise classic works (Fokine restaged *Les Sylphides*), to present new works of established choreographers such as Antony Tudor, Anton Dolin, Kenneth MacMillan and George Balanchine, and to experiment under the guidance of newcomers such as Herbert Ross, Glen Tetley, and Michael Kidd.

Ballet Theater has tried to balance its American creations with others of foreign origin. If it had done nothing else but invite one of its young dancers, Jerome Robbins, to stage his ballet *Fancy Free* in 1944, it would have justified its existence.

As a dancer, Robbins had worked his way up from *corps de ballet* to soloist. *Fancy Free* was a triumphant snapshot of three sailors on shoreleave in wartime America. Robbins' accomplishment has been to catch the human quality in man's little comedies and tragedies in balletic terms. He captured the spirit of the time in his themes and style more subtlely and intensely than any other twentieth-century ballet choreographer. From his *Age of Anxiety* to his *Events,* a ballet done almost a decade later, he portrayed man's desperate desire to communicate, to understand and to be understood.

As a child of his age, he tried to redo older ballet themes in terms of today. He did so with Nijinsky's *Afternoon of a Faun,* giving the romantic, narcissistic encounter between two dancers and the mirrors in a studio a tongue-in-cheek treatment. His *West Side Story* is *Romeo and Juliet* vividly translated into the terms of New York street gangs. Robbins created a *ballet d'action* in which the dance is supported by the spoken and sung word; it is total theater with emphasis on movement. Essentially, his ballet *The Cage* is a modern version of the second act of *Giselle* in which the Wilis, taking revenge on the male by dancing him to death, are represented by devouring female insects. In these works he proved to be the master of the most lyrical of styles as well as of the most explosive drama.

The humor that characterized the unheroic heroes in *Fancy Free* reappears in his work time and again. It is a zany, often biting humor, but one that has a liberating quality. Whatever Robbins choreo-

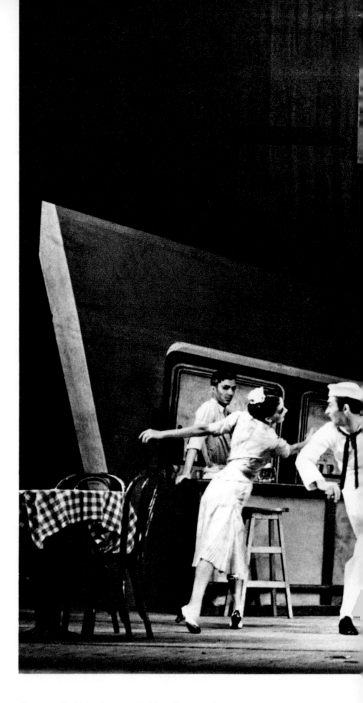

*Jerome Robbins' early ballet,* Fancy Free. *In the original production, Robbins danced the role of one of the sailors. ( Jack Mitchell: American Ballet Theater)*

graphs, from his hilarious *The Concert* to the electrifying rhythms of *N. Y. Export, op. Jazz* to the rich peasant imagery of his *Les Noces* he wants the spectator to experience the movement; the ritual of the dance itself thus becomes revelation. Acutely conscious of all the forces in contemporary life, he boldly extended his ballet language by using the

jazz idiom. Concerned, aware, intensely alive, Jerome Robbins is one of the great artists of our time.

And, in a very different way, so is George Balanchine. He still has one foot in the nineteenth century, upholding the classical ballet tradition, as is plain in many of his works. And he considers himself the heir to Petipa's legacy. But, strangely enough, he also is attuned to the angularity and dissonance of our time.

He is one of the most prolific choreographers. The experience of turning out three or four ballets every season has given him a facility and assurance in creating any kind of dance image on "union time," as he once said. He combines the attitude of a *grand seigneur* with that of a strict disciplinarian. The fact that the New York City Ballet is his creation and artistically dominated by him illustrates his strength as an artist and his weakness as a man.

When Lincoln Kirstein went to Paris in 1933 to invite George Balanchine to America, he had a vague dream of creating an American ballet. That Balanchine was able to fulfill this dream was due not only to his artistic genius, but also to his ability to respond quickly to the special gifts of American dancers and to the special cultural climate he found in the New World. He had foresight and insisted on having a school. In this School of American Ballet the teacher Balanchine has fashioned the dancers with whom the choreographer Balanchine has worked. Almost all of his ballerinas came to his school when they were between nine and fourteen years old. He wants them to dazzle the audiences with technical proficiency, with expressiveness of face and body, with remarkable speed and accuracy. The "Balanchine dancer" has become a trade mark in the ballet world.

Balanchine recognized the potentialities of the long-legged, sturdy American girls, in their natural musicality. He has also often pointed to a "kind of angelic unconcern toward emotion as a special charm of the American dancer." They do not carry their emotion on their sleeves; whatever feeling they have seems to become part of the drama of the dancing body itself. Balanchine was attracted by these qualities because they corresponded so very much to his own approach to pure ballet in which the moving body alone must create artistic excitement and evoke images of fantasy and human relationships.

He developed the physical qualities, the stamina and intensity of the dancers as elements of style. He made his dancers look natural even in the most classical attitude. He has been accused of being both cold and romantic, modern and old-fashioned, athletic and mechanical, intricate and abstract. He is probably all of these because he is too impatient to repeat himself or a theme. He has a way of surprising his most ardent admirers with the unexpected. He is master of the spectacular story ballet, sumptuously costumed against a rich setting, to which such ballets as *A Midsummer Night's Dream* and *Figure in the Carpet* testify. But in these ballets he is doing little more than continue the tradition he learned in Leningrad.

His strength lies in the ballet that has no story, in which movement is self-explanatory. Of this kind is his ballet *Serenade* which belongs with the most enduring dance creations. Here, the lyricism has a timeless quality. In his hour-long *Liebeslieder Walzer* ballet he achieved a synthesis of all his many aspects. He captured all the romanticism of the nineteenth century, of a waltz-intoxicated world that found forgetfulness in the gyrations of this dance, of long-forgotten forms of courtship and longing and of gentle but significant pressures.

His *Ivesiana*, based on the music of Charles Ives, lies between such lyricism and a modern mood distinguished by visual sparseness and taut, clipped movements. In this vein one can follow his creative progress from Hindemith's *Four Temperaments* to Stravinsky's *Agon* to Webern's *Episodes* and to Stravinsky's *Movements For Piano and Orchestra* and *Variations*. All these ballets have in common a perfect control of line, analytically designed poses marked by surprising wit and invention. Movements assault the spectator with their calculated precision. The sculptured bodies, meticulously manipulated, have the luminosity of Greek marbles. In spite of their clinically impersonal quality, these ballets often have emotional sweep and dramatic point.

At the age of twelve, Georgi Balanchivadze danced as a member of the *corps de ballet* in *Don Quixote* at the Maryinsky Theater. This had been in 1916, and ever since then he had dreamed of choreographing his own version of the famous knight. In 1965, George Balanchine staged *Don Quixote* for the New York City Ballet with himself in the title role. Petipa's version, still in the repertory of the Bolshoi Ballet and other companies, is a string of divertissements on the thin thread of Cervantes' story. The dramaturgic difficulty of this topic lies in the fact that its central figure cannot be danced but must be mimed.

Balanchine's pantomimic extravaganza is superior to Petipa's in every respect. He visualized the figure of the Don as the eternal dreamer, the lover of womanhood, the fighter for illusions. His Don Quixote symbolizes the artist surrounded by a world of hostile realities and has the intensity of an autobiographical confession. Balanchine tried to balance the mimed story of the knight with the

*Opus Jazz, choreographed by Jerome Robbins. (Martha Swope) Overleaf: George Balanchine's* Serenade, *one of his most lyric ballets, danced by the New York City Ballet (Herbert Migdoll)*

dance scenes and achieved a choreographic epic in which the hero is vindicated in the hour of death, with all the insults and mockeries he had to bear finally expunged. *Don Quixote* is the work of a mature artist, and to see Balanchine miming the knight is to realize that this is the work of someone who has not stopped dreaming for fifty years.

George Balanchine has written his name in large letters in the history of ballet. He brought many regional ballet companies in America under his influence. Of these the groups in Washington, San Francisco, and Boston are equipped to make a valuable contribution to the growth of American ballet and to find their own identity. But Balanchine's New York City Ballet, which is most representative of his life's work, will always remain strongly identified with the mid-century development of ballet in America.

Much is expected from two younger companies, the Robert Joffrey Ballet and the Harkness Ballet. Both have excellently trained dancers and an eclectic program. Although the Harkness Ballet mainly strives for a contemporary approach to classical ballet, it is not limited to any one style. Its artistic

director, George Skibine, created several of the ballets in the company's repertory; of these, *Daphnis and Chloe* and *Sarabande* are most characteristic of his choreographic scope, classic in technique but contemporary in mood. As proved by the impressive *pas de deux* in *Daphnis and Chloe,* his inventiveness is particularly strong in lyric passages. *Sarabande,* a rather abstract ballet, demonstrates the beauty and purity of ballet dancing in an atmosphere, in which the formality of the age of Louis XIV and its "noble dance" is blended with contemporary technique.

Many young choreographers have contributed to the repertory of the Harkness Ballet and have given it an almost kaleidoscopic image. Gian Carlo Menotti's music and scenario of *Sebastian* was choreographed by John Butler. It is a seventeenth-century story, set in Venice, about the slave Sebastian, who sacrifices himself for a courtesan he loves. Butler gave this overly theatrical idea powerful and sensual movements.

Only a few of the ballets in the repertory are plotless and mainly lyrical such as Donald Mc-Kayle's *Daughters of the Garden,* a ballet that praises the beauty of the human form, the awakening of the senses, and the joy in love. Without a story and pure dance is also Robert Scever's *Saint-Saëns Concerto,* a highly romantic ballet. Brian MacDonald's *Time Out of Mind* characterizes the reckless pace of our age through movements which are close to those of primitive rituals, vehement, frantic, and danced with reckless abandon. And in the midst of accelerated rhythm there is a moment of touching tenderness, only to be lost again in a surge of violence.

But the trend in the repertory of the Harkness Ballet is toward the dramatic ballet. Stuart Hodes' *Abyss,* based on a story by Leonid Andreyev, juxtaposes the innocence of passionate youth with brutality. The ballet story is about the love of a young couple which is suddenly attacked by three assailants, who rape the girl. Alvin Ailey contributed two dance dramas, convincing and theatrically effective: a modern treatment of the legend of Ariadne and the ballet *Feast of Ashes,* inspired by Garcia Lorca's play, *The House of Bernarda Alba.*

Artistic director George Skibine said about the aims of the Harkness Ballet, founded in 1964: "We need to exploit the span of the American dance—not just classical ballet or modern dance—but we need to build a corps like a great orchestra trained to play or perform all kinds of works."

The Robert Joffrey Ballet is as much at ease in a classical ballet as in the jazz idiom of such an avant-garde work as Anna Sokolow's *Opus '65,* a sharp and lucid comment on the restless mood of contemporary youth. Robert Joffrey's choreography is essentially lyrical and close to traditional style. His *Pas de Déesses,* based on a lithograph of 1864, successfully evokes the images of four famous ballerinas of the romantic era and echoes in a delightfully humorous way the rivalry which existed among them. In his *Gamelan* he created Oriental vignettes, which, in their tight structure, have visual beauty and poetry.

Gerald Arpino's ballets have a wide range and are dynamic in their projection. *Olympics,* danced by eleven men, is an apotheosis of the athlete whose competitive activities are vividly pictured in a highly stylized manner. *Sea Shadow* is a lyric duet which, in an underwater landscape, recreates a sensuous feeling of languor and love, somewhat reminiscent of Robbins' *Afternoon of a Faun.* Arpino's *Incubus* tells of a girl who lives through agonizing nightmares in which her fears and desires are dramatized; it is a ballet convincing in its compellingly eerie approach. In mood and technique both *Olympics* and *Incubus* are very close to the modern expressionistic dance without denying their ties to the classical ballet. His *Viva Vivaldi!* to a guitar concerto arranged from a Vivaldi score is a plotless ballet skilfully based on baroque music with a Spanish flavor. The great charm of this flawlessly conceived classical ballet lies in the sparing use of the Spanish dance idiom, which adds a touch of difference and poetry to it.

The Robert Joffrey Ballet is one of the youngest companies, able to embrace all styles and techniques. Its dancers have exuberance and élan, its choreographers, imagination. Although the aims of both the Harkness Ballet and the Robert Joffrey

Ballet are similar, their ways of approach are different. But they are both destined to develop the traditional ballet as well as the modern expressionistic dance and perhaps create the amalgam of a new style under the influence of jazz, musical theater and social dancing, a true twentieth-century American style.

A survey of the American scene would be incomplete without considering Antony Tudor although he is British-born, studied with and choreographed for the Rambert Ballet in London before he accepted an invitation from the Ballet Theater in New York in 1939 to stage four of his works. Two years later he became its chief choreographer and artistic director and has since lived in the United States.

It was said that Tudor added psychological depth to the ballet. His work shows a subtle understanding of motivations and an ability to make feelings clear through movement. He does not stage a story, a theme or a mood in terms of its idea, but in terms of human beings and often with a particular dancer in mind. He choreographs in traditional as well as in free style. But the quality of the movement and the gestures depend on the character to be projected. The action is continuous, one situation flowing into another. He deals with ordinary human beings and their commonplace problems, but presents their little hopes and disappointments, their struggle and hungers with poetic sensitivity. The movements are no longer stylized; a *jeté* is not only a leap but an expression of flight or anxiety, a human statement.

Of all classical ballet choreographers, Tudor is closest to the modern dance and its wide range of serious expressiveness. This became obvious when, in 1942, he choreographed *Pillar of Fire,* one of the masterpieces of contemporary ballet. The story of a frustrated woman, who has a sensual encounter with a young man before finally finding release, gratification and hope with the man she loved, was told with dramatic intensity. Above all, it was the understanding and revelation of the emotional struggle in the leading character that gave the ballet a new dimension. Tudor fully succeeded in charac-

terizing the heroine and her environment through different styles. He skilfully created an atmosphere of explosive tension between his characters, and every step and gesture was clear in motivation and meaning. It was recognized by all critics as a "tremendous achievement," as John Martin expressed it in his review in the New York *Times,* an achievement which was a turning point in the history of the theater dance: the psychological ballet became firmly established.

Tudor's understanding of human feelings and his ability to dramatize them in terms of movement had already found expression in one of his earlier works. *Jardin aux Lilas (Lilac Garden),* in which two couples must make the choice of their future partners. It is lyric expression at its most sensitive and, at the same time, the gripping drama of lost hope and love. The end of the plot, a marriage of convenience, is conventional. But the feelings expressed by the characters in a continuous flow of movements are revealed with poetic beauty and lucid simplicity and make us accept the ending as inescapable. Tudor came back to the exploration of intricate feelings in *Dim Lustre* in 1943. Two people conjure up memories of their past; they are more involved in their own dream images than with each other. Before they part the spectator has lived with them through their past experiences. Tudor once likened the remembered scenes to a blurred photograph. It is as if Tudor wanted to find the secret of his hero's feelings and expose them in a stream-of-consciousness technique.

*Dark Elegies* to Gustav Mahler's *Kindertotenlieder* is a ballet of mood in which mourning is expressed in various ways. There is no specific plot or action, which may explain what calamities preceded the dance scene. A man on stage sings a series of songs, which tell of his, or any parent's, feelings about the death of children. The dancers seem to be villagers of a place near the sea. Tudor could have told the drama of a tragic incident through movement. But he was far more interested in creating images of mourning, in exploring many facets of suffering. This ballet is a ritual of grief, which ends with the acceptance of whatever has happened. Its greatness lies in the scrupulously detailed image of each person's suffering, fused into epic flow and grandeur.

Tudor also has a strong sense of humor, sophisticated in its wit, sometimes with an eye toward burlesque. *Gala Performance* is a funny trifle, observing the foibles of dancers. *Offenbach in the Underworld* was Tudor's excursion into the world of the light-hearted cancan, in which the mood of wild gaiety is tinged with more serious overtones. In *Judgment of Paris* a drunken man tries to choose between three showgirls. The characterization of the girls and the environment in which the judgment takes place is a sarcastic comment and demonstrates burlesque wit.

Two of his more important works tried to fuse realism with symbolism of which he is the uncontested master. Realism is the least interesting part of any of his creations and where it dominates the work, as in *Undertow* and *Echoing of Trumpets,* it is often intrusive in its effect. In *Undertow* we follow the hero from birth and are confronted with his committing murder. *Echoing of Trumpets* evokes the horror of Lidice, a city ravished by the enemy.

However powerful these stories may be, the leading figures call forth less compassion than those of his other ballets, in which his poetic allusions create memorable images of human beings, of frustrations and conflicts, of hope and joy.

## *The Royal and English Ballet*

Tudor developed under the tutelage of Marie Rambert, who has remained a great influence in the dance world since her days with Nijinsky. In 1930 she founded the Ballet Club, which became the Rambert Ballet, a unique dance institution in that it does not have the equipment and technical facility

*Lawrence Rhodes and Brunilda Ruiz of The Harkness Ballet in Brian MacDonald's* Time Out of Mind. *(Courtesy Harkness Ballet) Overleaf: Robert Joffrey's* Contrasts. *(Herbert Migdoll)*

of any of the leading companies and does not attempt to compete with them. Basically, it is a workshop that puts its stress on creativity, on the development of choreographers and on the understanding of the dancer's needs in style. Its productions have an aura of the academy in the best sense of the word.

Besides Tudor, Marie Rambert nurtured such artists as Frederick Ashton, Andrée Howard, Walter Gore, Frank Staff and the youngest of them, Norman Morrice. The famous ballerina Karsavina ended her spectacular career with the Ballet Rambert and such a star as Alicia Markova, who became artistic director of the Metropolitan Opera Ballet in New York, was a mere beginner when she joined Rambert's company. Marie Rambert has an uncanny feeling for talent and, when she has found it, is able to awake the creative spirit in the artist. To realize fully the stylistic nature of each work is

no doubt the essence of her artistic aim. A worker of relentless drive, she sees in each season a new challenge.

Marie Rambert wanted to work experimentally, free from performance or other outside pressures. Ninette de Valois, who had also been with Diaghilev, dreamed of a royal company. And her genius made the dream come true. The Royal Ballet was the creation of de Valois and, beginning under the name of the Vic Wells Ballet Company, it took about twenty years to become one of the world's great companies. De Valois had some of Diaghilev's gifts. She knew how to attract many of the best talents and make them work creatively. It all began with a ballet, *Les Petits Riens,* which she staged successfully in London's famous Old Vic theater, then under the direction of Lilian Baylis. Out of the Vic Wells Ballet emerged the Sadler's Wells Ballet which de Valois guided, with Frederick Ashton as principal choreographer and Constant Lambert as musical director. Her great successes were: *Création du Monde* (1931), *The Haunted Ballroom* (1934), *The Rake's Progress* (1935), *Checkmate* (1937) and *The Prospect Before Us* (1940). By 1946, de Valois had choreographed thirty-one ballets for the company. Its repertoire also included Ashton's *Façade* and *Les Patineurs* and Robert Helpmann's *Hamlet* and *Miracle in the Gorbals* among many others. Margot Fonteyn and Moira Shearer were well-known ballerinas by then. In 1957 the Sadler's Wells Company officially became the *Royal Ballet* of Great Britain.

Frederick Ashton turned out to be as dependable a choreographer for the Royal Ballet as Balanchine was for The New York City Ballet, maintaining a high level of accomplishment. In 1965 he took over artistic and administrative control from de Valois and he proved in a short time to have a better under-

standing of the needs of a company than even Balanchine. Although he himself had choreographed a *Romeo and Juliet* ballet for the *Royal Danish Ballet*, he asked his younger colleague, Kenneth MacMillan, to stage his version for the company, realizing that a company dominated by the genius of one man tends to decline when he no longer can lead it.

The comparison with Balanchine is not far-fetched: both have grown artistically over the years and have been able to produce steadily for a company on whose dancers they can rely. Ashton shows more elegance and deeper feeling in his works than Balanchine, but he lacks Balanchine's curious mind and interest in experiment. In the beginning Ashton had a sparkling humor, exhibited at its best in *Les Patineurs* or *A Wedding Bouquet*. His Rimbaud ballet, *Illuminations*, was a rare work of poetic imagination in which the subliminal events of which Rimbaud

sang were projected in vivid imagery. In such longer works as *Cinderella* and *The Dream* he displayed his strength in working for groups. But, unlike Balanchine, he does not let his technical skill get in the way of creating with profound feeling. When he choreographed *Ondine* for Margot Fonteyn and *Marguerite and Armand* for Fonteyn and Rudolf Nureyev, once with the Kirov Ballet, he proved one of the most imaginative and yet disciplined choreographers of his time. His *Romeo and Juliet* makes the great love story an evening-long *pas de deux*, full of wonderfully detailed tenderness and warmth. It concentrates on the two lovers with such glowing warmth that we lose sight of their environment; for this reason Kenneth MacMillan's version seems richer in conception, and more spectacular.

Ashton has a few outstanding colleagues. Robert Helpmann is the most theatrical choreographer in

Conflicts *by Marie Rambert, in whose work experimental theater and ballet are expertly combined. (Anthony Crickmay)*

England, at his best in dramas of violence. Kenneth MacMillan has the power to probe and experiment. He learned from Tudor to let the heart speak through gesture and movement, but he can also be formal or violently dramatic. He is one of England's finest young creative dancers.

There are a few lesser ballet companies active in England. London's Festival Ballet has done a workmanlike job, the London Ballet Company under Walter Gore's guidance held brief promise. The most interesting group is the Western Theater Ballet which tries to take a fresh look at the dance and to create a repertory that reflects the mood of the time. But none of these companies compare with the remarkable *Royal Ballet.*

## German Dance in Search of a Profile

Full of vitality, ambition and talent, John Cranko worked his way up in England as one of the daring young men of the Fifties. After a few tentative attempts, his *Harlequin in April* surprised with its near-tragic theme on the uncertainties of youth, choreographed as a *commedia dell'arte* story. He considered it his best work, although *Sea Change, Pastorale,* and *Pineapple Poll* were equally rewarding. In 1957 he successfully staged a three-act ballet, *The Prince of the Pagodas,* to a score by Benjamin Britten. Cranko's special talent lies in comedy and in doing the unexpected with the classical vocabulary of the dance. His wit triumphed in the eccentric and sophisticated revue *Cranks,* which delighted audiences everywhere. As he demonstrated in works choreographed for the Royal Ballet, he can be convincingly dramatic when probing tormented souls, and very funny. He has boundless enthusiasm and a bold imagination. Even in his failures he is fascinating. Needing more scope, he accepted an invitation to head the Stuttgart State Theater ballet.

The ballet as a separate art form never took root in Germany. The various opera houses supported the ballet groups needed for a few operas. Ballet was a minor handmaiden among the arts that brought Germany to the forefront in operatic productions. Some opera houses, such as those in Vienna, Berlin and Munich, gave their dancers a chance to put on an independent ballet production from time to time, or even once a week. But ballet remained an

artistic stepchild. The Germans apparently produced too many overpowering opera composers. This was one of the reasons that Germany gave such enthusiastic reception to Isadora Duncan and, later on, Mary Wigman. Germans could easily identify with modern dance, so different from classical ballet.

After the Hitler interregnum between 1933 and 1945, Germans felt uneasy about their past. The modern dance, the German *Ausdruckstanz* had been suppressed by Hitler as "degenerate art" because its essence was an individual expression that was anathema to Hitler. The desperate attempts in the late 1940's to pick up where the modern dance had left off in 1933 failed. Trying to forget those twelve cataclysmic years, the Germans felt that the ballet was un- and non-German, alien. What could be better than to turn back to the classical ballet? And this is exactly what the Germans did.

*Igor Stravinsky's* Jeu des Cartes, *choreographed by John Cranko and produced by the Stuttgart Ballet. (German Information Center)*

But the ballet needs roots and many years to grow. The process of developing a neoclassic dance form was a slow one, requiring to be fed by choreographers such as Mary Wigman and her gifted associates Dore Hoyer and Yvonne Georgi. The latter, for instance, restaged Fokine's *Les Sylphides*. And Wigman's choreography for *Orpheus* demonstrated at its best the assimilation of the classic idiom. Moreover, there were some old-timers in Germany who had survived the holocaust. Tatjana Gsovsky had come to Germany from Russia in the early 1920's to live in Germany and had stayed on as a dancer, choreographer and teacher. Working in Berlin, Frankfurt and other cities, she had established a reputation as an avant-garde choreographer in classic terms. Her *Labyrinth of Truth (Rashomon)* was the impressive product of a new creative will. Her *Hamlet* and *Joan of Zarissa* were staged in Germany as well as by the *La Scala Ballet* and at the Teatro Colon in Buenos Aires. Gustav Blank, director of the Berlin Municipal Opera, made a successful transition from modern dance to ballet as choreographer and teacher in Hamburg and Berlin.

Marcel Luipart, tolerating Nazism and being tolerated by its leaders, was engaged as chief choreographer by the Bavarian State Opera after World War II. He was one of the most talented dancers and choreographers, who had risen to prominence in the 1930's, at a time when the theater dance had reached its lowest point in Germany.

Trained as a classical ballet dancer, he tried to achieve a modern style. He was particularly successful with the ballet *Abraxas* to music by Werner Egk in 1948. It was a new version of the Faust theme that contained a few daring passages and was, despite its success, soon withdrawn.

Luipart was followed by Victor Gsovsky, who had also worked in Paris for many years. His ballets *Castor and Pollux, Cinderella,* and *La Perle* displayed his traditional classical ballet background to which he strictly adhered. As a teacher he was well known for his lyric style, thoroughly classical with its soft, elegant lines. Together with his wife, Tatjana Gsovsky, he opened a ballet school in Berlin in the early Twenties, and some of the best German ballet dancers had been their students. One of the most gifted dancers to emerge from this school was Peter van Dijk, who, for a short period, was ballet master in Wiesbaden, where he had not enough opportunity to unfold his choreographic talents but maintained his reputation as one of the finest lyric dancers of our time. In 1953 the Swiss-born Heinz Rosen, who had done good yeoman work in Basel, triumphed in Munich with his choreography for Jean Cocteau's *La Dame à la Licorne.*

All this constitutes lively ballet activity, and in their search for a new identity the Germans have become very ballet conscious. At least a half-dozen opera houses in as many cities have partly succeeded in building up the nucleus of a trained company. Among these cities, Stuttgart ranks highest, priding itself on having John Cranko as its guiding spirit. Even though he made certain mistakes in the beginning, Cranko within a few years made Stuttgart, as in the days of Noverre, a focal point of European ballet activity. He met the test as organizer and choreographer of a large ballet company and was able at the same time to put his very personal stamp on it. In a way he kept the channels open between Stuttgart and the Royal Ballet, MacMillan and Peter Wright contributing works to his repertoire. The backbone of this repertoire is the full-length ballets *Romeo and Juliet, Swan Lake, Onegin,* as well as *Nutcracker.* But Cranko's shorter ballets, *L'Estro Armenico, Variations,* and *Firebird,* add spice to the work of a company that has become exciting and maintains a consistently high level.

Many German ballet companies—particularly those in Berlin and Munich—are struggling for a well-balanced repertory and offer, more or less, pleasant ballet fare. In Hamburg, Peter van Dijk has meanwhile been more successful than in Wiesbaden and has created an impressive repertory in which his revivals of Balanchine ballets are outstanding. Kenneth MacMillan, in close cooperation with John Cranko, begins to reorganize the Opera Ballet in Berlin. But John Cranko in Stuttgart remains the great hope of Germany. He has not only built a program that can command international respect, but also created an ensemble and school of dancers that is exemplary. Perhaps the Englishman John Cranko will one day be to Germany what the Frenchman Marius Petipa was to Russia and the Russian George Balanchine to the United States.

## From Lifar to Béjart

Serge Lifar and Boris Kochno were present at Diaghilev's death in Venice in 1929. Kochno, as his secretary and close friend, had great influence on Diaghilev during the last five years of his life. After Diaghilev died, he joined the Ballet Russe de Monte Carlo, as artistic collaborator and wrote the books for *Cotillon* and *Jeux d'Enfants.* He then helped Balanchine found his short-lived company, Ballets 1933, and later became the artistic director of Roland Petit's Ballets des Champs-Elysées in Paris.

Of all French dancer-choreographers Janine Charrat is the least typical. Although as a dancer she has never quite achieved the polish of many of her colleagues, as a choreographer she has attained true stature. Her staging of *Abraxas* in Berlin was the most successful of many versions shown in Germany, where, of course, the Faust theme in whatever form is popular. Charrat's designs have a striking quality, sometimes close to German expressionism.

Roland Petit's work, on the other hand, is probably a good example of the true spirit of French ballet. He began his career at the Paris Opéra but left it in 1945 to form his own company. He rebelled against the academic approach and dusty tradition that prevailed at the Opéra. His famous ballets *Carmen, Le Rendez-Vous,* or *Le Jeune Homme et la Mort* are characterized by emphasis on ornament and esprit, as well as a captivating liveliness, particularly when danced by such performers as Zizi Jeanmaire and Jean Babilée. In most of his works, however, he became too slick, and his startling inventions in movement did not stand the test of time. In 1966 Roland Petit returned to the Paris Opéra with a brilliantly conceived ballet. Traditionalists considered his *Notre Dame de Paris* too much of a "show," but he told the Victor Hugo classic simply and with almost no miming. Although he employed many theatrical tricks, filled the stage with exciting dance

*Serge Lifar rehearses with Tamara Toumanova at the Paris Opéra. (Serge Lido)*

action and eighty members of the *corps de ballet,* he skilfully combined his gift as a showman with that of a great choreographer.

Although the Grand Ballet du Marquis de Cuevas was financed with American capital, it had its headquarters in Monte Carlo and Paris. It presented a varied program in a flamboyant manner, produced many works in a choreographically eclectic approach and hired such illustrious dancers as Marjorie Tallchief, Rosella Hightower, and George Skibine. The company toured many countries but added little to the art since it lacked stature and identity. At the very beginning, Serge Lifar was its artistic director for a few months.

Lifar was the last dancer discovered by Diaghilev, and it is difficult to say whether the master would have been satisfied with the way the younger man developed. When Balanchine withdrew from an assignment to stage *The Creatures of Prometheus* for the Paris Opéra, he recommended Lifar as the one to complete the choreography. This was Lifar's debut as choreographer, *premier danseur* and ballet master at the Paris Opéra. He was then twenty-five years old and had little background or training, but he was determined to master the position.

His ballet *Icarus* (1935) resulted in a controversy since he danced without using any score and merely instructed the conductor to "clothe the rhythm of his dancing with music." In general, his choreography moved in theatrical rather than poetic channels. He undertook many big subjects such as *Alexander the Great,* or *The Triumphant David,* but the story appears generally to have overpowered his imagination. His creative ability was best demonstrated in *Le Chevalier et la Demoiselle,* a dance of theatrical magic in which his flair for the decorative and the use of literary images of the Middle Ages found effective expression.

His later works showed him more and more as a traditionalist and purist defending the academic approach. His influence was greatest on the French dance, which tends to rely on the idea that classical technique is meaningful in itself and generates dramatic interest.

The work of Maurice Béjart, a Frenchman whose center of activity is the Théâtre Royal de la Monnaie, the Brussels opera house, represents the complete opposite of Lifar's. In the beginning of his career in 1954 he headed a small company, Ballets d'Etoile de Paris, and soon became known for the shockingly erotic subject matter of his work. But he has come a long way from that first outburst against the establishment. Even though there is an uninhibited sexuality in his *Bolero* and in *The Rite of Spring,* it is lifted into the sphere of meaningfully ritualistic movement. His subject matter is always solid, its expression fraught with significance. His *No Exit* ballet, based on Sartre's play, is as strong a balletic statement of human despair as his version of *The Seven Deadly Sins* is of the atmosphere of the roaring Twenties.

Closely related in spirit to Jerome Robbins, Maurice Béjart is the hope of contemporary French ballet.

## Danish and Swedish Royal Companies

The Royal Danish Ballet has a tradition reaching back over almost two hundred years, and it is this tradition together with a strong sense of the present that gives this company its special character.

Vincenzo Galeotti, a famous Florentine ballet master, came to Copenhagen at the end of the eighteenth century and succeeded in producing a group of well-trained dancers. He was followed by August Bournonville, whose work, in turn, was continued by others up to Hans Beck and Harald Lander in our time. The company is especially famous for its male dancers. At a time when the male dancers were little more than *porteurs,* Bournonville saw to it that they were as well trained as the female dancers and were given good roles in all ballets.

*Roland Petit with Danielle Jossy in his ballet* Maldoror. *(Serge Lido)*

This results in an even level of performance. The Danes were able to keep the romantic ballets better intact than did any other company. Their style has remained pure, and they are masters in the production of period ballets. Lately, they have balanced their repertory by such modern works as Flemming Flindt's *The Lesson,* an exciting translation into ballet of the play by Eugene Ionesco. The scene of the homicidal professor who stabs his pupils during a mad philology lesson, was successfully transformed into a Grand Guignol scene in a ballet studio, with the pupils danced to death by a ballet master.

Dance drama has always been the forte of the

Danish dancers as much as lack of leadership and new choreographers has been its weakness. Since the last century when Bournonville established the Royal Danish Ballet as one of the leading companies in the world, it has lived on its reputation and borrowed choreographers from other countries: Ashton and MacMillan from England, Cullberg from Sweden, and Balanchine and Robbins from America. Flemming Flindt, who, at the age of twenty-nine, accepted the post of ballet master and the difficult task of guiding one of the oldest European companies, brought to it many qualifications which should enable him to provide the Danes with badly needed leadership.

In the early nineteenth century Bournonville's influence was also evident in the Swedish ballet, but Stockholm was oriented far more toward St. Petersburg than was Copenhagen. A Taglioni vogue gripped Sweden in 1841, and Taglioni herself was so impressed by her Swedish partner, Christian Johansson, that she persuaded him to return with her to Russia. Johansson became one of the greatest teachers there.

It was not until early in the twentieth century that Les Ballets Suédois was founded by Rolf de Maré (1920). The company was caught up in the new experimental spirit. Guided by its choreographer, Jean Börlin, it created a series of ballets with bold ideas. Like most opera companies in Central Europe, the Royal Swedish Opera had its ballet department, but this unit did not become important until Mary Skeaping came to it from the Sadler's Wells group in London.

The most significant choreographer in Sweden is Birgit Cullberg. Fame came to her relatively late in life. In 1950 the Stockholm Opera asked her to do

*Left: Inge Sand and Fredbjørn Bjørnsson of the Royal Danish Ballet as Blackamoors in* La Sonnambula. *(Arnold Eagle)*
*Right: Anne Borg and Palle Damm in* Eden, *choreographed by Birgit Cullberg for the Royal Danish Ballet. (Indris Lipkovskis)*

her ballet version of *Miss Julie*. It was an immediate success, and she staged it for many other companies, including an excellent production by the American Ballet Theater. She achieved further world-wide recognition with such ballets as *Medea* (which she also staged for the New York City Ballet), *Lady from the Sea* by Ibsen and *The Moon Reindeer*. In the latter she caught the spirit of a Lapp girl and dramatized her erotic dreams. Her leading figures are always women and her theme is their dreams, frustrations and loves. In *Dionysus*, the central character, the Greek God of wine and vegetation falls in love with four women who represent the elements earth, fire, water and air, but finally returns to earth. This work, first choreographed in Dortmund, Germany, in 1965 mixes ballet and modern dance idiom.

Originally a student of Kurt Jooss, Miss Cullberg believes strongly that a modern approach to ballet is essential. She finds the Martha Graham style and technique very much in the spirit of our time, and she is now fusing the classical ballet and modern dance into a stage reality. There can no longer be any doubt that both styles are compatible. With each season they merge more and more.

This has become especially evident in Holland where, after a long interval, ballet has come to the fore recently. The Het Nationale Ballet, the Dutch National ballet company, specializes in a repertory that is mainly classic and offers a great selection of familiar works. But the company does not exclude altogether the presentation of new works. Some of the ballets choreographed by Rudi van Dantzig and Henryk Tomaszewsky testify to the company's willingness and ability to include new and even controversial themes in their repertory. Van Dantzig's *Monument for a Dead Boy* and other ballets of his demonstrate his interest in themes of social conflict.

However, the Het Nationale Ballet's competitor, the Nederlands Dans Theater, is oriented more evidently toward a repertory of twentieth-century ballet. The Nederlands Dans Theater is guided by the American choreographer Benjamin Harkarvy, whose background is the classical ballet, and by the Dutch Hans van Manen, who has also gone through the training of the academic *danse d'école* but who strongly tends to embrace the neoclassic trend of our time.

The policy of this progressive company has made it possible for many American choreographers to stage their works there, among them Glen Tetley, John Butler, Joe Sanders, and Anna Sokolow. Essentially, it is a company based on classical principles, but its tendency to assimilate the American modern dance and to identify itself exclusively with the contemporary approach to ballet has become its international trademark.

*Birgit Akesson, Swedish dancer and choreographer, famous for her experimental work. (Radford Bascome: Courtesy Dance Magazine) Right: Dance and drama combine in* Polish Mime. *(Herbert Migdoll)*

## Tradition and Revolution: Russia

It is an irony of history that the most traditional ballet is danced in the home of "social realism," Russia. The Russians undoubtedly possess a gift for dancing, an incontestable vitality and exuberance in balletic expression. But social realism is basically incompatible with the romantic character of classical ballet. Ballets dealing with the problems of modern life need a freedom of invention and approach, a far cry from the rigid forms of the old style.

Ever since Peter the Great ordered his guardsmen to drag to balls those women who did not accept his invitation; ever since every aristocrat and landowner forced the daughters of his serfs to take ballet lessons to be able to entertain his guests, the Russian people have been ballet-conscious. This dates back

*The Leningrad Kirov* Sleeping Beauty. *(Wayne J.Shilkret: Hurok)  Right: Maris Liepa in the Bolshoi* Sleeping Beauty. *(Anthony Crickmay)*

to the early eighteenth century, with the most important event taking place in 1735, when the Empress Anna Ivanovna ordered all her cadets to take dancing lessons from ballet masters whom she invited from France and Italy. Thus the famous Russian Academy came into being.

Today the Russians have two great ballet companies, the Kirov Ballet in Leningrad and the Bolshoi Ballet in Moscow. But many cities in Russia, such as Gorki, Saratov, and Odessa, have their own ballet groups. The Kirov dancers are very different from their colleagues in Moscow. The city once called St. Petersburg, with its famous Mary-

insky Theater and School, was always the window with a view toward the West: toward the traditional, imperial and dignified. Leningrad's Kirov company has continued the tradition of style, and the key to its style is restraint. There is the long lyric line, the impeccable taste, the sensitivity that approaches decadent refinement. The presentations of the Kirov Ballet lack dramatic urgency. Its dancers are not so interested in what they do as in how they do it.

Moscow has always been closer to the heart of the country. The descendants of the dancing cadets and serf girls found their way more easily to Moscow than to Leningrad. Thus the Bolshoi Ballet has always been more vital, vigorous, theatrical. Its productions show the complete involvement of dancers who are not afraid to display their emotions. Intense passion and expressiveness, often to the point of flamboyance, are manifest in all their presentations, be it *Giselle, Swan Lake, Romeo and Juliet, Les Sylphides,* or *The Dying Swan.* These are brilliant productions enchanting in their lyric moments, dazzling in their technical and almost acrobatic feats. Whatever they do is always dancing at its best.

Plotless ballets are rare in their repertory, since everything must have a meaning or a message. They see social significance even in such an old romantic ballet as *Giselle,* in which the differences of the classes—the aristocratic lover of the peasant girl—are stressed. This is why they put stronger emphasis on the role of Count Albrecht than is done in any other production. The feuding families in *Romeo and Juliet* are supposed to symbolize class struggle. The production of *Swan Lake* with a happy ending was defended by the great ballerina Galina Ulanova, the spokesman for the company, on musical and ideological grounds. A great deal of poetry was thereby sacrificed for the sake of a doubtful ideological and musical interpretation. This is futile enough, but it is in their new ballets, such as *Stone Flower,* based on folklore of the Urals, and the massive and misguided *Spartacus,* and particularly in

*Galina Ulanova in* The Dying Swan. *(Martha Swope)*

the space-age visualization of the Kirov Ballet, *Distant Planet,* that they fail most of all. Sentimentality easily takes the place of sentiment, and drama labors. The imagination needs freedom to unfold and it needs training, too.

But there are certain indications that the Russians are about to find pleasure and meaning in creating plotless ballets. The most significant and impeccable of the new works to come from the Bolshoi Ballet was Asaf Messerer's *Ballet School,* which exposed the loving care that goes into the training of Soviet dancers and the exciting technical proficiency they achieve. *Ballet School* re-enacted a dancer's growth to stardom. Why should seeing one of the Bolshoi choreographers guiding a young dancer to technical greatness turn out to be such an impressive experience? The answer is that, aside from giving us an intimate glimpse behind the scenes in a great institution, it lets us share in the fulfillment of a dream, in the magic life of the theater.

The postwar era was strongly dominated by realism and a reliance on the past which stifled experiments. Until the end of the Fifties, the Bolshoi's chief choreographer, Leonid Lavrovsky, whose *Romeo and Juliet* and *Giselle* were masterpieces in their own right, created a ballet image which has since been criticized in Russia.

A new trend has emerged in the work of two young choreographers, Igor Belsky and Yuri Grigorovich. Both recall Fokine's principles of expressiveness, meaningfulness of gesture and continuity of action. Grigorovich adds a deeper psychological insight and a new lyric dimension. Although the influence of the West is becoming noticeable, Grigorovich does not borrow from modern dance as do Western ballet choreographers. Rather, he explores movements derived from sport, work and everyday life. He also does not encourage the myth of the great ballerina or the ecstasies of divertissements, preferring a unified choreographic structure.

With a new generation asserting itself, it seems likely that in the very near future Russian dancers will apply their matchless talents to the creation of modern ballets.

# _16_ _Experiment: Second Phase_

In the fall of 1962, the American composer John Cage—who once said about the arts: "We must begin from scratch!"—was invited to the Grand Shinto Shrine of Ise in Japan for a special service in his honor. At this ceremony the officiating priests blessed his avant-garde activities and all such activities throughout the world. In 1963 the London _Times_ called one of Robert Rauschenberg's retrospective shows "the most exhilarating art exhibition in London."

Cage is musical director of the Merce Cunningham Company and Rauschenberg was one of its

_Paul Taylor and Bettie de Jong in_ Scudorama.
_(Courtesy Paul Taylor Dance Company)_ _Above:_
_Sybil Shearer._ _(Helen B. Morrison)_

main designers for many years until he himself began to find pleasure in manipulating moving figures on stage. Cunningham was one of the first dancers to break away from the representational, expressionistic school of dancing, and he once said in a manifesto that if it is self-expression you are looking for, then the place for you is the analyst's couch. The trio of Cage, Cunningham and Rauschenberg has set the artistic clock ahead to an hour that some of us cannot yet read.

The forces that influenced this school of dancing include dadaism and surrealism and, in a fundamental way, existentialist philosophy. But some of the principles of Zen Buddhism and _I Ching_, the book of changes, which explains often in a mystifying way, a system of divination, also play a part. They led to the dancer's acceptance of chance and whim

*Left: In* Summerspace, *created by Merce Cunningham with costumes and set by Robert Rauschenberg, time and space are explored in a new fashion. (Richard Rutledge) Right: The Joffrey Ballet in Anna Sokolow's* Opus 65. *(Herbert Migdoll)*

to express the apparently inexpressible or indefinable, letting his body discover its own direction in "automatic movement." It is said that chance can open up vistas beyond imagining. Tradition binds the dancer to the past; and remembered sequences of movement stifle the free flow of the body's impulses. Freedom lies only in the revelation of the moment itself, which is neither now nor then, neither here nor there; it *is*. The new dance is no longer concerned with stories or experiences whether of a social or individual nature. The movement is without human quality in dramatic or theatrical terms. It expresses nothing but itself. Music and dance are no longer dependent on each other, they do not necessarily meet; they co-exist.

In minor artists, these principles can lead beyond the illogic of the Dance of the Absurd to an ultimate nothingness. James Waring, a refugee from the ballet, went so far as to say: "Dance is any aimless movement—any movement without an object in mind.... Art is anything you point your finger at and say, 'This is Art.'" It is a declaration of utter independence of the dance.

Merce Cunningham happens to be a great artist, and his presentations are a unique experience, an exploration of time and space in a new fashion. If there is such a thing as a meaningful world without conventional meaning, he creates such a world. He denies that he wants to *say* anything, and certainly he constantly uses surprising images and the most unrelated forms. Despite the lack of emotional unfolding, his dance creations are specific in their moods—lyrical, satirical, or pensive. His *Summerspace* is an abstract painting of moving color in a late August landscape as seen through half-closed eyes. He leaves the concrete and submerges in the subliminal when he probes vacillation and duality

of character in his *Changeling*. He enjoys the absurd to the fullest and in *Antic Meet* lampoons style and mannerisms of certain dancers. His is a dry, wry humor dangling from a cerebral thread. He creates a rich and varied program closely subject to his canons. But then he seems to forget himself and creates such an enticing love duet as *Night Wandering*. The five fingers of his hand against which her head rests when they both come on the stage become a radiant crown. And what a tender lullaby of love he sings to her at the end when she lies on his body which, cradlelike, bespeaks safety and sweet care! However detached they try to be, this dance remains a triumph of humaneness, full of the warmth of an eternal emotion.

Like Merce Cunningham, Paul Taylor was a

*Paul Taylor, known for his scurrilous humor, probes human behavior in* Party Mix. *( Jack Mitchell)*

member of the Graham Company. Although a rebel against the conventions of the psychological dance drama, he is ready to compromise. This does not make his work less interesting. On the contrary, its veneer of pleasantries make it acceptable to a broader public.

Taylor's dance creations are most effective on a purely kinetic-visual level. They are often reduced to images of arrested movement or blown up to the eccentricities of contortion. He is a many-faceted choreographer. In *Aureole* he created a delightful dance that is a nineteenth-century "white ballet" freely translated into modern idioms. On the other hand, *Scudorama* is a serious work, an incisive indictment of the state of our souls, a work in which the drifting of aimless spirits, the anxieties and absurdities of the age are presented in crude choreographic patterns. There is a great deal of cringing and crouching, of men hurrying along, trying to get nowhere in no time, or all huddling together in a shapeless, forlorn heap. Like drifting wraiths they form figures and patterns, scattered and erased by

250

fear, or clinging to any other wraith that passes by, fools, adventurers without purpose.

But his forte is a remarkable instinct for comedy, for a tongue-in-cheek humor. These qualities are demonstrated in the beguiling *Piece Period* and in *Party Mix,* a scurrilous facsimile of human behavior, full of pantomimic fun and the unexpectedly grotesque juxtapositions of dancing bodies. Taylor seems to see with the eyes of a painter who often creates two-dimensional images on the stage and likes the shock value of the unexpected. He is avant-garde, but also on guard not to lose himself or his audience.

Even more than Taylor, Alwin Nikolais approaches the stage as a painter and sculptor. He does not offer us dancing as we understand it, that is, in terms of expression through movement. His aim is a theatrical totality. He does not conquer weight and gravity through conventional means of ease and grace, but through a strange conglomeration of suggestive, even though not always clearly defined, images. Instead of familiar choreographic patterns, we get designs outside life and its problems.

The theater which Alwin Nikolais envisions has many links with the past. It vaguely reminds one of the experiments of the Bauhaus in the Twenties;

or of some of Rolf de Maré's ballets for his Les Ballets Suédois, where the dancers were also treated like marionettes; or, going even further back, of Stéphane Mallarmé's identification of ballet with the "plastic rendering of poetry" and his suggestion that the choreographer eliminate the human factors because they distract from the purely visual experience.

Nikolais purposely excludes the drama of man. He permits the theater to function only on some magic level where the conflict lies in objects, not in man, and in a land where inanimate things are free from their subjection to animate beings. His is

a fairy-tale atmosphere, but with the stamp of tomorrow's technology. He forces upon us a kinetic rapport through the sheer playfulness of the way he moves his objects. Baffling and abrupt tricks with light as well as mysterious but compelling sound effects are a significant part of his approach. Instead of a narrative, he offers an experience resting solely on the effect of depersonalized bodies moving in harmony with personalized props and costumes.

Alwin Nikolais found his own way in the non-literal trend in the artistic expression of our time. Waving his choreographic wand with half-closed eyes, but with all windows of his subliminal mind

*Alwin Nikolais'* Sanctum. *(Ken Kay)    Overleaf:*
Imago *by Nikolais. (Herbert Migdoll)*

open, he lets things happen. Following their own inclinations, bodies begin to move, creating an unidentifiable but self-revealing imagery. At his best, Nikolais creates movement effects that are triumphant flights from reality into the realm of theatrical magic. The titles and subtitles he uses are intended only as suggestive signposts. They are not explanatory, because there is nothing that can be explained. They are points of departure for the spectator's free association.

Erick Hawkins approaches the dance with a sculptor's vision. He tries to create movement in its most concrete and pure aspects regardless of the-atrical effects. Movement must be felt, he says; it does not express anything. His technique which cooperates with gravity rather than fights it, produces a quality of effortlessness. The choreography emerging from it is often uncommunicative as a stage experience because it is completely engrossed in the purity of its own motion. He never shocks, and his work is non-violent. Like the lines of a *haiku* poem, Hawkins' movements evoke, instant by instant, a feeling, an impression, a thought. In some of his shorter works, as in *Early Floating*, this method achieves a highly poetic effect; in such a long work as *Here and Now With Watchers* it is mesmerizing or bewildering in its ritualistic, innocent quality. But there is a madness in this method, a madness supported by the unorthodox music of Lucia Dlugoszewsky, who creates a gamelan type of music on instruments of her own invention. In contrast to avant-garde choreographers who keep the oriental influence a peripheral element, Hawkins makes it central. He thus dispenses with elements basic in the occidental theater: accents and repetition, duration and dynamics.

Yvonne Rainer, Ann Halprin and a great number of young dancers with varied artistic inclination have reduced reality to its bare bones and often covered it with a teasing veil, borrowed from the romantic era. Their art is the glorification of the banal, the ultimate in non-form. Their attitude is totally narcissistic, the act of creation being more important to them than the result. They are, so to speak, instantaneous dancers.

Such unpremeditated creations are sometimes called "Happenings" a name taken from the score, *18 Happenings in 6 Parts* (produced in 1959) by Allan Kaprow, a student of John Cage. In these Happenings, theater dance depends on spontaneity and improvisation. This "action" dancing, this on-the-spot creativity has one historic precedent: the *commedia dell'arte*. But where the actors of the *commedia*

253

*Left: Erick Hawkins. (A. John Geraci) Above: Yvonne Rainer. (Peter Moore)*

*dell'arte* were highly skilled performers, dancers and fencers, a great many of those who participate in the Happenings are non-dancers or are poorly trained. Their rudimentary calisthenics, their running, falling and jumping make the dance an antidance or at least a non-dance.

The parallel between such dancing and action painting is clear. Aesthetically, is there any difference between a work of art consisting of a car grille, billboards and boiled spaghetti, and a dance in which the performer assumes various static positions only occasionally interrupted by attempts at movement? What is supposed to be the effect of dancers, who, for the purpose of accompaniment, carry radios tuned to a wave length that one night may broadcast Mozart and another night the news?

But among all these groping and desperate attempts at achieving a fresh art form, one or two artists may perhaps elevate what appears to be a fad into the realm of enduring art. It is foolhardy to try

257

to play the prophet and single out a few from the many who have indulged in such experiments lately. But Yvonne Rainer clearly has great talent together with a fantastic and capricious wit, as when she punches and heaves mattresses, or chases her dancers through a ritual of everyday movements, or organizes a "chance" game in which balls are thrown at dancers followed by a love duet which is finally followed by a processional to the music of Bach.

An artist of apparently greater scope is Ann Halprin of San Francisco. She seems able to involve the audience in her creations, and her performers are most like those of the *commedia dell'arte* since they are well trained, whether as dancers, acrobats, whistlers, singers or speakers. Props and décor play an important part in her choreographic schemes. She starts with images from ordinary life but lets the action that follows depend on improvisation and experiment.

Ann Halprin's theater concept derives from quite different aesthetic sources than that of Nikolais. She does not depersonalize but, rather, emphasizes human relationships. She does not divorce theater from dance. The human voice is often employed together with noise effects and silences. Her Happenings fuse reality and symbolism, replacing conventional meaning with a new, if often incoherent, set of implications.

Paul Klee once said: "The more horrible the world, the more abstract our art...." There is an obviously self-destructive trend in this triumph of the non-artistic exploration of artistic expression in the Fifties and Sixties, a frightening reflection of the world around the artists. It is strange, to say the least, that artists should discover non-communicativeness in an age which has perfected communications and that their feeling of futility and alienation should be demonstrated in a world that understands more of the universe than it ever did before.

259

# 17  The Mass Media

The dance found a warm welcome in the film. In fact, the film opened up a new field of expression for the dance. But the question arose of how to synchronize their basically different rhythms. In ballet, people move; and the spectator's eyes combine the images of one moment with that of the next to form a moving totality. In film, the whole picture moves. Filmed dance must therefore be a compromise. The movement of the cameras must serve the movement of the dance, and the dance must be choreographed with an eye to the camera. The camera's technical facilities are the source of its artistic means: the

*Televising Stravinsky's* Noah and the Flood, *choreographed by Balanchine. (Martha Swope)  Above: Gene Kelly. (Universal)*

intimacy of the close-up, the dramatic effect of superimposing one image upon another, the shifts in focus, the unusual angle, dissolves, and double exposures. They are visual miracles that only motion photography can achieve. But they can also distort and destroy the natural beauty of the dance.

Whatever the theory, it is only the results that count. No other movie dancer has as yet surpassed Fred Astaire in utilizing the power of the film. Throughout his long screen career he opposed all camera tricks that would make the audience more aware of the photography than of his dancing. To convey fully the choreographic idea and the uninterrupted flow of movement, he insisted on the full view of the dancer and the dance. Astaire gave his steps his jazz-band sense of rhythm. After a few bars of music to establish the theme, Astaire would

*Gene Kelly in* Invitation to the Dance. *(Courtesy Dance Collection, New York Public Library)*

tap it out, embroidering it with his own rhythmic idiom; the music would then carry the theme until Astaire came in again with more sophisticated variations. He handled this kind of rhythmic dialogue brilliantly.

Gene Kelly, on the other hand, used all the tricks the camera offers. In the film *Cover Girl* he enchanted movie-goers using double exposure and uncanny timing to create a dance in which he stages an emotional struggle with his alter ego. His experiments continued in *Anchors Aweigh* and achieved full fruition in *Invitation to the Dance,* where he came close to a pure form of cinema dance in a gay *pas de deux* with a harem beauty in the shape of a cartoon. He thus combined Walt Disney-like animation with slow motion, soared into space with incredibly elongated leaps, and glided and turned in utter defiance of the laws of gravity. Some sections of

*Invitation to the Dance* had shortcomings, but Kelly's pioneering efforts to explore the camera's potentialities were most rewarding.

There were other pioneers of dancing in films. Who can forget the *Gold Rush* in which Charlie Chaplin made two pieces of bread on forks dance on a table while he joyfully waited for his sweetheart? Dated though he may seem now, the idol of the silent movies, Rudolph Valentino, combined suave dancing technique with dramatic intensity in his celebrated tango scene in *The Four Horsemen of the Apocalypse* (1921).

With the first sound pictures, colossal "production numbers" became the vogue. Regiments of over- and underdressed dancers were used in lavish efforts to outdo the famous Ziegfeld Follies of the Broadway stage. But earnest attempts were made to use dancing more imaginatively. Discarding the usual practice of shooting from three angles simultaneously and letting the cutter establish the choreography, Larry Ceballos planned dances for special camera angles. He insisted on simplicity and logic

sequence. His café dance scene in *The Singing Fool* (1929) and the dance sequence in *Tiptoe Through the Tulips* achieved a genuine artistic quality.

Some of the finest dances in sound films came from the Walt Disney Studios. They first came in 1929 with the imaginative choreography in the Silly Symphony of *Skeleton Dance* to the *Danse Macabre* of Saint-Saëns. Most of Disney's animations are the epitome of the dance. His *Fantasia* (1940) was rich in dance ideas and the sequence of thistles performing a Russian dance from the Nutcracker Suite was technically and artistically an unparalleled achievement.

By 1932 dancing was firmly entrenched in films. Dancing has had a part, if only a very incidental one, in countless pictures. But it was more than a decade before dancing became functionally integrated in the plot. The films of the 1930's were dominated by tap dancing. Besides Fred Astaire and Gene Kelly, Ray Bolger and the incomparable Negro tap dancer Bill Robinson captured the public and filled the movie houses. Robinson scored his first success with his performance in *The Little Colonel*, featuring a sequence in which he taught child star Shirley Temple the "stair dance." He appeared in fifteen movies, including an outstanding demonstration of his dancing and acting abilities in *Stormy Weather*, an all-Negro film.

The films made many dancers into actors and vice versa. This fusion of the two performing arts took place particularly among ballerinas and actresses: Moira Shearer, Leslie Caron, Audrey Hepburn, Zizi Jeanmaire, Jean Harlow, Marilyn Monroe, Ann Miller, Joan Crawford and Cy Charisse. The combination of talents was in demand during the 1940's and '50's when several films centered on dance themes. *The Spectre of the Rose* (1946) was the story of a psychopathic dancer who ended his life after a tortured dance in a hotel room. Written by Ben Hecht, it featured the sensitive dance-acting of the ballerina Viola Essen. It approached the achievement of Moira Shearer in the English film *The Red Shoes*, wherein a ballet sequence, choreographed by Robert Helpmann, struck a fascinating

*Ginger Rogers and Fred Astaire doing the* Carioca, *from the 1933 film,* Flying Down To Rio. *(Courtesy Dance Collection, New York Public Library) Overleaf: The exuberance of the* cancan *is recreated in a scene from the film* Moulin Rouge. *(Eliot Elisofon)*

balance between fantasy and reality. Hein Heckroth's designs contributed notably to its effectiveness, greatly influencing the choreography.

With the Broadway musical—from *Oklahoma!* to *My Fair Lady*—achieving a more mature approach to the musical dance drama, the films based on these musicals tried to stay as close to the originals as possible. An outstanding example of a movie version that excelled the original Broadway production was *The King and I;* in it Jerome Robbins' ballet, *The Small House of Uncle Thomas*, was of the highest artistic quality.

From the Bolshoi company came an ambitious full-length ballet *Romeo and Juliet* made memorable by Galina Ulanova's dancing. The Russians filmed

many ballet excerpts with divertissements that gave glimpses of the great dancers of the Bolshoi and Kirov companies, and in 1956 Paul Czinner, using very few camera tricks, made the best photographic record of the Bolshoi Ballet.

The various versions of wide-angle screens, such as Cinema Scope and VistaVision, created a number of problems for the choreographer. Michael Kidd, who staged rousing dances in the film *Seven Brides for Seven Brothers* found it difficult to fill the out-sized screen. The choreographer had to design as if for a fresco, not for a canvas. The new oversized dimension demands a new style of dancing and, as the movie version of *My Fair Lady* proved, the choreography for such dimension is almost the same as the choreography for a stage play. Perhaps it will no longer be necessary for the film choreographer to think in very different terms from his counterpart of the stage.

*Below: A scene from the musical* Mary Sunshine. *(Martha Swope) Right: Dance from the Broadway show* Kiss Me, Kate, *choreographed by Hanya Holm. (Bob Golby)*

## The American Musical

There were musicals on Broadway, and a great deal of dancing in them, long before Agnes de Mille choreographed *Oklahoma!* in 1943. The old operetta and vaudeville presented Terpsichore in her lighter moods, Broadway importing the European successes of Franz Lehár and Oscar Straus, and also concocting its own musical entertainments. Working in vaudeville and night clubs, young dancers acquired the background for their later Broadway successes. Among the dancers were Adele and Fred Astaire, who became famous in 1922 when the show *For Goodness' Sake* was written for them. Throughout the Twenties they starred in the best musicals Broadway had to offer, *The Punch and Judy, Smiles,* and *Funny Face*—a nickname Fred gave his sister Adele. Then,

for a musical comedy called *Lady Be Good* a young American composer, George Gershwin, wrote the tunes.

By the time the name of the Astaires made headlines, Ray Bolger had decided on a dancing career. He worked in vaudeville and movie houses from New York to Los Angeles for many years until he established himself as a comedy dancer of unlimited talents and eccentric styles in the Broadway show *Life Begins at 8:40*. He reached the peak of his career when George Balanchine, who had successfully choreographed the *Ziegfeld Follies* of 1935, chose him as the leading male dancer for the musical *On Your Toes* (1936). In the main dance number, *Slaughter on Tenth Avenue*, Bolger achieved a serious, tautly organized and forcefully projected work of art about

an unmistakably American subject. It was a dramatic ballet within a musical and demonstrated how an American upstart could hope to make good in a famous Russian ballet company.

These were the first indications that the musical might lend itself to the purposes of the serious dance. A great many first-rate choreographers were drawn to the musical, seeing the possibility of reaching a wide public and stimulated by the challenge of the popular light opera medium. The musical, heightened into drama as in *West Side Story* (1957), or fused with a comedy as in *My Fair Lady* (1956), proved that it can successfully surmount all limitations. In fact, choreographers found a fertile field in the musical theater in creative as well as technical respects. Because of its wide range of subjects, the musical permits the use of all kinds of techniques: ballet, tap, jazz, ethnic and modern. Very often an amalgam of various techniques are employed, so that one could almost speak of a dance form unique to American musicals. It has made the best use of the strength and vitality of most American dancers and a dramatic energy and invention equalling that in any of the world's greatest ballet companies. On the level of popular entertainment, the choreographer in America has made a vital contribution to the light opera theater: the musical.

One cannot expect all the shows produced on Broadway year after year to be equally good or worthwhile. But the tremendous stream of creation in this field has produced a few extraordinary theater experiments and experiences. A number of choreographers have left their very personal imprint on the musical. Jack Cole, Gower Champion, Robert Fosse, Peter Gennaro, Michael Kidd, and Donald Saddler have brought to it a jazzy, bouncing and exuberant quality. In the Thirties, George Balanchine adjusted his classical ballet style to the

*A scene from* West Side Story, *scored by Leonard Bernstein and choreographed by Jerome Robbins. (Fred Fehl)*

musical theater and helped shape the taste for this new art form. Helen Tamiris came from the modern dance, but, being well trained in ballet and jazz, brought to the Broadway show a distinct folklore character. But three choreographers in particular gave the musical direction and identity—Agnes de Mille, Hanya Holm and Jerome Robbins.

Agnes de Mille has excellent dancing in several shows, such as *Brigadoon, Allegro,* and *Paint Your Wagon* to her credit. But in 1943 she made history by fully integrating the dancing with the plot of *Oklahoma!,* using the dances to develop character and dramatic atmosphere. Hanya Holm followed a similar line in *Kiss Me, Kate,* and contributed an even more finished theatrical quality to dancing in *My Fair Lady.* In it Hanya Holm made dance a vital, expressive part of the play and thereby reached a peak in musical comedy achievement.

The greatest contribution to the musical came from America's choreographic genius, Jerome Robbins. He has been responsible for memorable choreography in many Broadway shows: *On the Town; The King and I; High Button Shoes; Billion Dollar Baby; Look, Ma, I'm Dancin'* and *Bells Are Ringing.* They have all had his inimitable touch of dramatic intensity and effervescent lightness. How authentic and bold he can be in handling folk traditions is seen in *Fiddler on the Roof,* a stage version of Sholem Aleichem's tales. But he will go down in theatrical history as the creator of *West Side Story,* which uses all elements of the theater—dramatic action, music, song, dialogue, décor and dance—to create a twentieth-century musical on the Romeo and Juliet theme to Leonard Bernstein's score. His greatest accomplishment was in remaining faithful to the ballet and pantomime concept in the course of the drama, in characterizing the actor-singer-dancers through gesture and movement taken from everyday life but heightened through stylization. He thus achieved a unique theatrical totality. He showed the road the lyric theater must take. He helped produce a cinematic version of *West Side Story* that was very effective—so that the whole world could see the American musical at its best.

*Thomas Hasson and George Marcy in the duel scene from West Side Story. (Fred Fehl)*

## Dance on Television

The initial hope that dance might prove as vital to television as music has been to radio has not been realized. Nevertheless, dancing has penetrated most television shows as part of the entertainment, or has been presented for its own artistic sake. Of course, television has brought to millions of viewers all kinds of authentic dance performances, from exotic Balinese troupes to celebrated ballerinas, that they would otherwise never have seen.

The basic problems the choreographer faces in television are similar to those in films with the added limitation of a tiny screen. In the 1940's, dancers swarmed to the television studios with bright ideas. Choreographers, directors and cameramen tested new ideas and effects in the new medium. The choreographer developed a new reflex, discarding composition as related to space and learning to see with the eyes of the camera. The cameramen and director had their say in this very complex new form. The stress was no longer on choreography alone; a dance composition had to be *cameragraphed*. By the early 1950's the technique had developed to such a degree that dissolves or a montage of camera shots and superimpositions no longer disturbed the rhythmic flow. On the contrary, they heightened fluidity of movement as well as the dramatic impact. The performer realized that he must always be conscious of the camera eye to be able to project in its direction—yet he must look through it, not at it. He must be aware, yet unaware, of the cameras.

Artistically, television turned out to be the most demanding and exacting medium for both dancer and choreographer. Many gifted young choreographers soon found out that in committing themselves to television they were selling their souls. Like a monster the weekly television show has a way of devouring a man and destroying his talent. But a few choreographers who made a reputation on television have managed to move on to the ballet stage or the recital hall. One of them is the talented John Butler. Another, Toni Charmoli, has held out longest as a gifted contributor to light entertainment shows in television. He has a special talent for projecting a mood and for creating an illusion of depth and distance.

Most dances on popular programs try for little more than a gay, romantic atmosphere and use acrobatics as well as camera tricks. Certain shows—

*A scene from the television ballet,* Noah and the Flood.
*( Martha Swope )   Right: Igor Stravinsky rehearses*
Noah and the Flood. *( Courtesy* CBS*)*

such as *Camera Three* and some religious Sunday shows in America or the third program of the BBC in England—have catered to a smaller, more select audience, often have attracted and often stimulated fresh and unusual choreography. The greatest choreographers have been challenged by the possibilities and demands of this tricky medium, and some of the greatest have failed to meet the challenge. The most striking example of this was Stravinsky's *Noah and the Flood* (1962) for which Balanchine provided the choreography. Both must have learned from this experience—as did an audience of millions—that television has a temper of its own that will yield its best only to those who master its special disciplines.

In the early 1960's a rebel appeared on the scene. She was the Swedish choreographer Birgit Cullberg. "The dance has been abused and violated by the cameras!" she said, "It will never be a successful marriage until only one stationary camera will embrace the dancers like a cyclopean eye!" She felt that when the camera is focused on a foot or a face in a ballet, we have hopelessly lost any impression of the whole dance. Why not move the dancers rather than the cameras, she asked. But how are we going to get close-ups of the face? Let the dancer approach the camera and make an artistic virtue of the movement. Why not create an exciting choreographic composition by showing a dancer's head in a lower corner of the screen while the other dancers fill the remaining space in the background. Why not ignore the "law" of gravity and let the dancers make their entrances from above or below the picture? And why not construct a floor with three different platforms for the dancers to move on and thus create three distinct distances from the camera's viewpoint?

Among Birgit Cullberg's television ballets are *The Lady From the Sea, The Evil Queen,* and *Cain and Abel.* She composes the movement patterns to fit the small screen as if it were a stage and achieves fascinating images with cut-off arms and bodies. Is Birgit Cullberg's method the answer to the problem this medium poses? It is only if you neglect the electronic miracles inherent in the camera eye and deny the camera the right to move about.

*Rudolf Nureyev and Svetlana Beriosova in the* Black Swan pas de deux, *for the Bell Telephone Hour. (Martha Swope)*

273

# *18   Jazz and the Negro Dance*

The Negro dance is one of the most viable and vital contributions of America to the theater dance. Its theatrical potential went unnoticed until the beginning of the present century, and it only began to assert itself as a mature art form at mid-century. Its historic roots reach back as far as the first shipment of slaves to America. They brought with them the rich heritage of their native Africa, their rituals and religious dances, their ancestral memory of free-flowing movements and steps, and above all the innate rhythms of the race. But, yielding to the environment, they began to adapt themselves to

*Bill Robinson in one of his tap dances. (Dance Collection, New York Public Library)   Above: Alvin Ailey. (Jack Mitchell)*

American society in the eighteenth and nineteenth centuries.

This process of adaptation was accelerated after the Slave Laws of 1740, which prohibited "the beating of drums, blowing horns or the like" because they might arouse the slaves to insurrection. Their dancing, however, continued. Nothing could take that away from them. Besides their spirituals, which also play a great role in modern Negro dancing, the Negroes had their natural feeling for rhythm which needed an outlet. They danced to hand-clapping and to the sound of the banjo. The sound of their own steps provided a natural accompaniment, as they shuffled and used heel and toe beats.

The Negro dance developed in this "New World" as "a dance toward freedom," as Martha Graham

275

once said. But this tendency did not prevent the Negroes from adapting the square dance and cotillion in their "sukey jumps." They also interpreted American tunes, cowboy songs, sea shanties and even hymns in their style. Seen from this viewpoint, as some experts did, one might even term jazz the result of the attempt of Negroes to sing white men's tunes. Such improvisation, subjected to an innate sense of rhythm was the link between the music of the slaves and jazz. And when the Negroes began to compose by mixing their native African with acquired American musical styles, the blues song, lamenting the oppression under which they lived, came into being. Syncopation, the spirit of jazz, is basically African. But jazz itself, hardly more than fifty years old, has been in the making for over two hundred years.

From the shuffling and tapping of feet emerged the tap dance. When Irish clog dancers came to the United States in the middle of the nineteenth century, they accepted the tap dance of the Negroes and colored it only slightly with their own rhythmic approach. But it took quite some time before tap dancing came into its own. In 1830, a wandering entertainer named Thomas D. Rice played at a theater in Louisville, Kentucky. In a stable yard he saw an old Negro perform a dance in a grotesque way to his own 'sing.' The very same night he imitated him on the stage. This was the beginning of the "minstrel show." In the first phase of its development, the Negroes were the backbone of the tap dance. The most famous of them was William Henry Lane, who was known as "Juba" and is vividly described by Charles Dickens in his *American Notes.*

A great many minstrel shows toured the United States from the 1840's to the beginning of the first World War, and many of them were all-Negro companies. The historic importance of the minstrel show lies in its influence on the concept of the

*Pearl Primus in* Speak to Me of Rivers.
*(Barbara Morgan)*

277

American musical comedy. An earlier contribution of the Negroes was the "Cake Walk" which became the craze in America at the end of the nineteenth century. It was a couple dance performed in competition, each team trying to outdo the other with higher kicks, faster steps, breath-taking leaps and intricate turns. It was the American counterpart of the European cancan craze of the same period.

Negro dancers were already typed as "entertainers," when Broadway theaters began to open their doors to them in various revues during the 1920's. In the main, they were seen in night clubs and vaudeville. Josephine Baker appeared on Broadway in *The Chocolate Dandies* before leaving for Paris and international success. Bill Robinson, America's most popular tap dancer, established his reputation in *Blackbirds of 1928.* It was seven years later before George Gershwin created the first American folk opera, *Porgy and Bess,* and made the Negro dancer and singer acceptable as a serious performer.

The 1930's brought about a change of attitude. Asadata Dafora of Sierra Leone, one of the foremost exponents of African Negro dance and culture, appeared in the African opera *Kykunkor.* In it the relationship between the original African dance and the American Negro dance became apparent. In 1940 a brilliant and beautiful young Negro dancer came from Chicago to New York to show herself and her revue, *Tropics and Le Jazz Hot,* in a one-night stand but continued to play on Broadway to full houses two more weeks. Her name was Katherine Dunham, and her ancestors had come from Madagascar. She studied ballet to achieve assurance and discipline. She studied Mary Wigman technique, but never became a concert dancer; her theatrical instinct was too strong. Although she is a scholar and holds a doctorate in anthropology, she

*Left: Katherine Dunham in the 1945/6 production,* Tropical Revue. *(Dance Collection, New York Public Library) Right: A student of Percival Borde in Liberia. (Collection Pearl Primus) Overleaf: Six vignettes of the* Alvin Ailey Company. *(Jack Mitchell)*

lost her heart to show business. Her tropical revues made her world-famous, and she has also appeared in many Broadway musicals. Katherine Dunham has helped greatly in making the Negro dancer a part of the American theater.

Pearl Primus was another dancer to establish the reputation of her race in the dance field. Having studied with Doris Humphrey and Martha Graham, she was closer to the modern concert dance

279

than to the theater, even though she was seen in Broadway musicals and night clubs. She became the most serious Negro dancer of the 1940's. Her primitive dance came out of books reinforced by racial memory and a love for the traditions of African culture. Her modern dance came out of contemporary racial problems. It was through her knowledge of modern dance technique that she was able to give her basically ritualistic dances an artistic form while retaining their native flavor. Twice she went to Africa to do research among the native tribes, and the people took her to their hearts: she was adopted by the giant Watusi dancers of the Belgian Congo and renamed "Omowale," which means "child returned home."

In Africa Pearl Primus found what she was looking for—and yet did not quite find it. White man's influence had gradually deprived Africa of its native teachers. It was an ironic twist of history that in the late 1950's the governments of Liberia and Ghana invited Pearl Primus to help them perpetuate African culture, dance and folklore. She accepted the offer from Liberia and stayed for some time to find, encourage and train native artists.

Pearl Primus was a dancer of unequalled emotional intensity and physical strength, famous in particular for her leaps. Her visualizations of spirituals belong with the strongest of the Negro's early contributions to the modern dance. *Study in Nothing, Strange Fruit, The Negro Speaks of Rivers* were among the first eloquent statements of her race on stage. Toward the end of the Fifties she shifted from the recital stage to teaching. A cultural ambassadress with headquarters in New York City, she has worked

*Donald McKayle and Carmen de Lavallade. (Courtesy Donald McKayle)*

*Jean León Destiné in his* Slave Dance. *(Arnold Eagle)*

indefatigably on two continents for the better understanding of the Negro's racial roots.

The appearance of Katherine Dunham and Pearl Primus changed thoroughly the situation of the Negro dancer. But the dance scene in general had also changed. With the exception of Helen Tamiris and Hanya Holm, a new generation of choreographers began to work on Broadway in the 1940's. Jerome Robbins, Michael Kidd, Valerie Bettis and Anna Sokolow employed Negro dancers in their shows. Even more important was the full recognition of the modern dance, because Negro dancer's improvisational and self-expressive talent is, of course, closer to the modern dance than to any other form of expression.

It is therefore not surprising that some of the greatest talents in the modern dance are Negroes. Donald McKayle decided to become a dancer-choreographer after he saw one of the early recitals of Pearl Primus. He surprised the dance world with *Games* in 1950, a work that reflected the joy and terror of poor children in big cities. *Rainbow Round My Shoulder* conjures up moods of despair and hope, of struggle and ultimate defeat; the stifled spirit in man and the yearning for freedom is pictured with bitterness and passion. His *District Storyville* recreates the legendary New Orleans of 1903, the cradle of jazz, where the "demimonde" was the whole world, where the trumpets screamed, and the sounds of life were drowned by the jazz drums. It is a hilariously satiric piece with dancing that moves at top speed—a tempo that only Negro companies can produce—but it does not let us forget

that joy is close to grief, and triumph to defeat. Beyond its theatricality, this dance work has a kinesthetic intensity of astonishing power. McKayle's is a great theater talent.

McKayle is an example of how the American dance has been enriched by the Negro dancer with his astounding vitality and the rhythms of his race. The school and company of Lester Horton in Los Angeles brought forth a few powerful talents among Negroes, dancers of great ability, such as Carmen de Lavallade and James Truitte, and a choreographic talent perhaps less disciplined than McKayle's but of explosive power: Alvin Ailey. Ailey's creations are full of excitement, wild sensuousness, and beautifully caught moments of lyricism and ecstatic feeling. Most characteristic of his choreographic talent are *Revelations* and *Roots of the Blues*.

Talley Beatty, who began as a very young dancer with Katherine Dunham, developed an equally strong talent for the vigorous treatment of material close to the heart of the race. *Come Get the Beauty of It While It's Hot* and *The Road of the Phoebe Snow* are dramatic dances that not only create familiar images of Negro life in a white world, but also depict the Negro as a human being with all his special tenderness and violence.

There are others who hail from the Caribbean islands, such as Jean León Destiné and Percival Borde. They have all immensely enriched the American dance which, in turn, has offered them a rich outlet for their talents. As artists they all excel through their native gifts. The Negro dancer proves the truism that dancing is "in one's blood."

# Afternote: Recording the Dance

Ever since man has found pleasure in the dance and wanted to teach it to others, he has faced the problem of recording or preserving it. Generally, this was left to chance, dances being handed down haphazardly from master to pupil, from one generation of dancers to the next. We will never know how much was lost, changed or distorted in the process. But many dancers and teachers have been aware of the problem and, time and again, attempts have been made to find a satisfactory system of recording movements of the dancing body and of preserving methods as well as choreographic conceptions.

## In Notation, Film and the Written Word

In the beginning dancing masters used written descriptions, but these were often vague or unsystematic and failed to transmit the spirit as well as any exact image of the movements. All kinds of symbols, from musical notes to sketches, have been

tried, but it remained for our age to combine the film with notation systems to solve the problem of putting on paper the total orchestration of the dancer's movements.

The first attempts at notation were a kind of shorthand description. A number of writers during the Renaissance used combinations of letters to indicate various steps. About the time Guglielmo wrote his treatise—the first bridge from the *ballet de cour* to the *théâtre du ballet*—we find this rudimentary form of notation in the Dance Book of Margaret of Austria. A characteristic early contribution is Jehan Tabourot's *Orchésographie,* in 1588, which was published under the pen name Thoinot Arbeau. As canon of Langres, he was one of those churchmen who freely mingled wordly interests with spiritual fervor. He was mainly interested in astronomy and mathematics, but his works on these have long been forgotten while his "scribblings to kill time," as he described his *Orchésographie,* played a significant role in the development of the art of dancing. It is a treatise on the dances of his time in the manner of

*Illustrations from Arbeau's*
Orchésographie.
*(Kamin, 1948)*

Lucian's dialogue on pantomime. He cast himself in the unlikely role of a dancing master and invented a pupil, whom he called Capriol and who was probably much like himself as a young man.

Arbeau was a highly musical man. Not only does his book contain a detailed tabulation of drum rhythms, but he also refers in it to all kinds of instruments. He stresses the musicality of the dancer and the dependence of dancing upon music. We must not forget that in this period almost all the great music was dance music and that instrumental music, the development of the musical forms known as suites and sonatas, is essentially based on the inventiveness of the dancing masters of the Renaissance and the early Baroque. An effort was made to have each dance followed by a different or even contrasting dance; and composers were inspired to follow suit. If we may say that early Greek music served the uses of poetry, the music of the Renaissance may certainly be said to have served the dance. Many orchestral suites from Lully's day to ours, carry the names of dances described in Ar-

beau's *Orchésographie*. At this time, too, the invention of printing made possible great improvements in the calligraphy of music. Whereas Guglielmo's treatise had had to be copied as a manuscript, the dissemination of Arbeau's disquisition was much easier since it appeared in book form.

We do not know how much of a dancer Arbeau himself was or how much of his interest in the dance was part of the general reawakened joy in life that characterized his time. He did note that dance is "both a pleasant and profitable art which confers and prefers health; proper to youth, agreeable to the old and suitable to all…" And seeing that his student Capriol was coming of age, he advised him: "If you desire to marry, you must realize that a mistress is won by the good temper and grace displayed while dancing."

Whether or not Arbeau was a skilful dancer, and without knowing anything of the five absolute positions that the *danse d'école* would develop—the ABC's of ballet—he hinted at them unmistakably in the drawings he inserted in his text.

285

*Left: One of the earliest attempts at dance notation, Spain, C.1450. Right: Two tracts from Feuillet. A* Chaconne *and (far right) a* Bourée. *(Courtesy Dance Notation Bureau)*

He described most of the dances known at his time in scholarly fashion, comparing the *pavan* with the *emmeleia,* the dance of the Greek drama, the *galliard* with the *kordax,* and the *branles* with the *sikinnis,* thereby vividly characterizing them. He treated the many variations of the *galliard* and other dances in detail, explaining terms and steps with surprising simplicity. In his notation, which he called "tabulations," he listed the corresponding "pas" next to the music notes for each dance.

The significance of Arbeau's contribution to dance literature is unquestionable, particularly when we compare it to the work of two other writers, Italian dancing masters, who were active about the same time in Paris. Fabritio Caroso published a book, *Il Ballarino,* in 1581, and mentioned "diuerse sorti di balli & balletti," but he lacked the ability to make clear any of the dances. Cesare Negri, a well-known choreographer and teacher, who was part of the treasure the French took back to Paris in 1554 after conquering Milan, then the center of dance activity, brought the idea of figured dancing

with him. Later he published a book, *Nuove Inventioni di Balli,* which, in the main, relied on Caroso but also included his own dance compositions. The minor contributions of these two writers mark the decline of the cultural leadership of Italy in the sixteenth century and the growing importance of France.

## Danse d'Ecole

Louis Pécourt, a dancer of whom it was said that he was "handsome and well made, and danced with all possible *noblesse,*" was a charmer and one of the many lovers of the celebrated French beauty Ninon de Lenclos. More than anyone before him, Pécourt felt the need to do something about the accurate recording of dances. He foresaw the danger of distortion, of wilful or unconscious changes in choreographic conceits. He also felt acutely that the creator of a dance loses too much of his own work because of the difficulty in keeping combinations

286

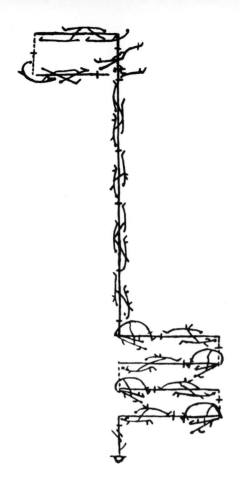

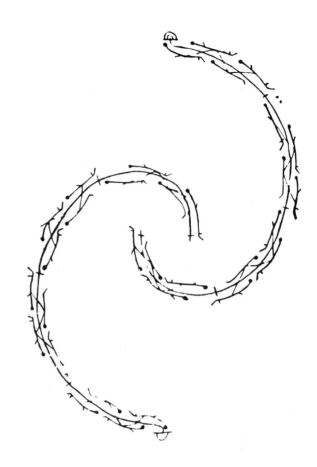

of steps in mind and in redoing a ballet after a considerable lapse of time. He was the first to think of recording dances by means of symbols. He introduced them in his book *Chorégraphie ou l'Art d'Ecrire la Danse,* which was so well edited by Raoul Ager Feuillet that there is still some question as to which of the two was the more original.

Their work was the most widely used in the eighteenth century; their success is not surprising in view of the ingenious devices Pécourt put into use. Pécourt and Feuillet still thought in terms of a floor plan and the direction in which each dancer must move, but they did help clarify matters by combining the dancer's path and his movements and by using a center line to mark off the right and left sides of the body. Basically, their system is only a pattern traced by the dancer's feet, with positions indicated by symbols resembling music notes.

A companion piece to Feuillet's *Chorégraphie* (the word originally meant the transcription of movement, not the creating of dances) is Pierre Rameau's *Maître à Danser (The Dancing Master,* 1725). Dealing mainly with social dances and illustrated with engravings of various postures, Rameau's work is an ideal guide to the most popular dances of his time. Moreover, his constant references to such great performers as Louis Pécourt, known for his "danses galantes," whose solo dances challenged the popularity of the grand ballets at the courts, and to Jean Ballon, famed for his exceptional lightness as the partner of the *première danseuse* at the Opéra, Françoise Prévost, also had a considerable effect in shaping the course of theater dance. Through Rameau's descriptions, whether of the minuet or any other dance, we get a clear image of manners and mannerisms of the period. Believing that "dancing adds graces to the gifts nature has bestowed on us," Rameau discusses correct posture and stresses the importance of the concept of the five basic positions, which he attributes to Pierre Beauchamps. From then on, the concept of the five positions is firmly established as the structural basis from which each ballet movement must come and to which it must return. In Rameau's work, we find descriptions not

only of these steps, but also of *pirouettes, jetés* and *entrechats,* even though all these steps are now executed with far greater accomplishment. But his was the time of great ballet innovations, stupendous and perplexing in the eyes of Rameau's contemporaries.

It was about the same time that John Weaver, dancer and ballet master at London's Drury Lane Theater and the translator of Feuillet's book, decided that Feuillet's method was "incapable of any farther improvement." As a forerunner of the Age of Reason, Weaver based—like many of his contemporaries who were investigating the inner workings of the arts—his ideas of dance on the "laws" of nature. As early as 1712, in his *Essay Towards an History of Dancing,* he stressed the importance of expressiveness in dancing—the role of bodily movement in conveying plot and character. He wrote:

> Stage dancing was at first design'd for Imitation; to explain Things conceiv'd in the Mind, by the *Gestures* and *Motions* of the Body, and

plainly and intelligibly representing *Actions, Manners* and *Passions;* so that the Spectator might perfectly understand the Performer by these his Motions, tho' he say not a word.

Nine years later in his *Anatomical and Mechanical Lectures upon Dancing* Weaver re-affirmed his belief that dancing is "built upon the Fundamentals of Anatomy; agreeable to the Laws of *Mechanism;* consonant to the Rules of *harmonical Proportion,* and adorn'd with the Beauty of a natural and cultivated *Gracefulness.*"

By the end of the eighteenth century, Feuillet's system was no longer adequate. Noverre found it useless for the more complicated steps and suggested in his *Lettres sur la Danse et sur les Ballets* that words and pictures be added to the notation so that every detail would be covered.

In 1796, Moreau de Saint-Méry wrote *Danse,* the first book on dancing published in the United States. In many ways, it echoes the eighteenth century, but when Moreau de Saint-Méry tells us that the principal object of the dance is like that of music, "the

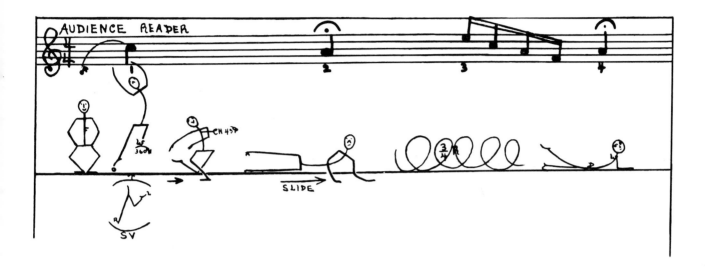

*Left: Ballet master's* Aide de mémoire, *a sketch to help reconstruct a choreographed movement pattern. (Collection George Chaffee) Above: An example of Letitia Jay's notation method. (Courtesy Dance Notation Bureau)*

expression of sentiment and passions," and that "a gesture is beautiful only when it depicts sadness, tenderness, pride—in a word, the soul," it anticipates the romantic era. Probably the greatest importance of the book lies in the fact that thirty-three years later, Carlo Blasis quoted freely from it.

During the romantic era the search for a workable notation system was continuing. The dancer and choreographer Arthur Michel Saint-Léon published a treatise, *La Sténochorégraphie ou l'art d'écrire promptement la danse* (1852) later expanded by the German dance teacher Friedrich-Albert Zorn. They used a six-line horizontal staff above the music, five lines containing the symbols for legs and feet and the top line the symbols for head, arms and body. Basically, the symbols were stick figures indicating the different positions. But the system was inadequate for the elaborate movements of Romantic ballet.

In 1892, Vladimir Stepanov went back to the use of musical symbols in his *Alphabet des Mouvements du Corps Humain* and, with the help of anatomists,

devised a rather scientific approach. Though it was helpful in the revival of some of Petipa's works, his system, like the others, remained limited. For in all these notations, the emphasis was on legs and feet with too little attention paid to the rest of the body.

## Notations Today

In the twentieth century, the search for a universally applicable notation was intensified. But most of the notators either continued to use stick figures, such as the Letitia Jay notation, or still depended too much on the musical note concept. The shortcoming of the latter approach is that there are many more movements than musical symbols can show. This fact complicated Pierre Conté's system, published in 1930; its major flaw is its lack of economy. Margaret Morris devised a system that meets every new problem with a new symbol, thus creating an impractical number of symbols.

The Benesh notation, first published in 1956, has

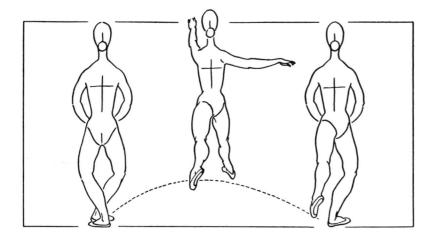

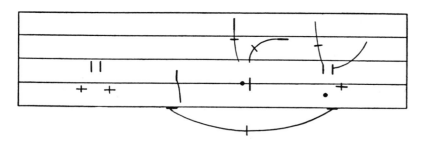

been renamed choreology. It is written horizontally on a music staff, and the five lines form a perfect base for the human figure. The bottom line represents the floor and each line above the other indicates the knee, waist, shoulders and head. In order to record a pose or position taken by a dancer it is only necessary to note the exact spots occupied by the four extremities, the arms and hands as well as the feet. Moreover, the position of a bent knee or elbow is also recorded with the position of the whole body. It is a simple method that can be applied to any form of movement. Since Rudolf and Joan Benesh, the inventors of this notation, were associated with the Royal Ballet School in London, their system was first applied to ballet and has since been used successfully by several European ballet companies.

Many other systems have been tried through the years. Among them, the Eshkol method and Labanotation seem to be the most universally useful. The Eshkol method, a highly scientific approach, concentrates on movement, disregarding stylistic or emotional elements. A vertical line represents the body line, a horizontal line, the time flow. Important is the way in which the lines show parts of the body change in relation to one another. This notation is practised mainly in Israel, while Labanotation has found its most enthusiastic followers among the modern dancers in America.

The strength of Rudolf Laban's system, first published as *Kinetographie* in 1928, lies in its effort to achieve a simple and logical basis: its applicability to any style of dance; its extreme accuracy and economy; its use of symbols having visual meaning in terms of movement; and showing the dancer's relationship to space as well as his relationship to other dancers; and its emphasis on the flow of movement.

One of the earliest experiments in Labanotation was undertaken in Germany in 1936 in preparation for the staging of a mammoth performance at a Dance Congress. The thousand dancers who were to take part in the presentation were in forty cities.

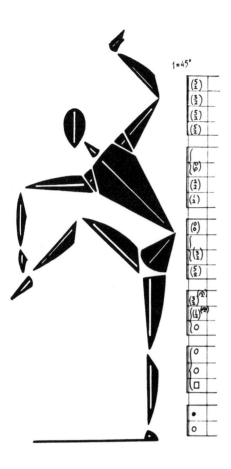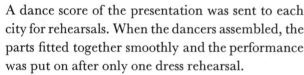

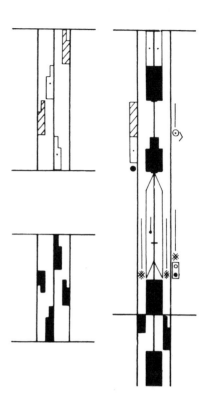

A dance score of the presentation was sent to each city for rehearsals. When the dancers assembled, the parts fitted together smoothly and the performance was put on after only one dress rehearsal.

Since then, some great choreographers have embraced the system. Many Balanchine ballets have been labanotated, Hanya Holm's choreography for *Kiss Me, Kate,* was repeated in London from the dance score, and more and more modern dance works were notated throughout the 1950's and 1960's than ever before. Labanotation has spread as far as Tibet and Japan and the notated library of ethnological dance material is growing steadily. After Kurt Jooss used the written score in restaging his ballet, *The Green Table,* with an entirely new company in Chile, he said: "If I ever entertained any doubts as to whether the notation was practical and worthwhile, they have long since been removed. The scores have proved to be invaluable on so many occasions, and have saved time, if only in settling the inevitable disputes among the dancers."

## Filming the Dance

Of all the arts, the dance is undoubtedly the most "photogenic," and the affinity between the dance and the movies seems unquestionable. Because of this, it was not surprising that cinematic documentation should seem the most logical solution to the problem of recording the dance.

Difficulties arise, however, when the camera abandons its role as the mere recorder of movement and begins to assert its own personality. When the very first dance movies were made, the film art was in its infancy and the shooting of the pictures was straightforward and direct, with the camera facing the object head-on. As early as 1897, Edison & International Photographic Films shot various dance movements ranging from a *Dance of Rejoicing* by the nations of the Fiji Islands, to a *Fantastic Toe Dance* executed by Amy Muller. Many of the dancers filmed in that early period are of little historic significance; the exceptions, however, are Loie Fuller, whose *Fire Dance,* Pathé recorded in 1906,

Left: Anna Pavlova in Hollywood.
(Courtesy Dance Collection, New York
Public Library) Right: A scene from
Doris Humphrey's The Shakers.
(Thomas Bouchard)

and the *Moulin Rouge* dancers photographed in 1902 by Biograph Studios.

Since the turn of the century such a tremendous number of dance pictures have been made that there is no way of tracking down or even cataloguing all of them. Meanwhile, there has been a huge output of commercial dance movies that in their incidental dance sequences reflect to some extent the recent development of the art form. But it is mainly the amateur photographers who in the last few decades have created a tremendous repository of dance films. The quality of these films may often be doubtful, but they have great value for the dancers themselves, who are thus able to view their own choreography and performance. Equally important, especially to other students of the art, is their recording of outstanding soloists or dance companies. The Chicago dance critic, Ann Barzel, has, for instance, taken many hundred of dance pictures during actual performances. Although she has rarely recorded a complete ballet, her films of the high points of performances are invaluable in showing choreography and the dancer's artistry.

When they can afford it, artists utilize the camera to record their work, and schools have made increasing use of films in their teaching. But it is very doubtful that the film can render the dance the same far-reaching service that the phonograph and tape have given the composers and musicians.

With the tremendous development in cinematic art, film makers have increasingly exercised the artistic freedom to photograph the dance from whatever angle they think best. In some instances this had led to the re-choreographing a ballet for the film or television camera. When, for example, Thomas Bouchard filmed Doris Humphrey's *The Shakers,* such adaptations were made for the camera that the choreographer felt that the dance was no longer hers but, at best, a cinematic version of it. A genuine dance library would preserve a choreographic conception or an outstanding performance

simply by recording the work as it is presented on stage, eschewing angle shots, close-ups, superimpositions and all camera tricks. How invaluable, for instance, would be such a cinematic record of an Isadora Duncan, a Nijinsky, or any other great dancer of the past! By chance, a few test shots of Pavlova have survived. Taken at Universal Studios in Hollywood, they show her in *The Dying Swan, Fairy Doll, Oriental Dance, Columbine, Christmas, California Poppy* and *Fading Rose*. In spite of their fragmentary form, they are priceless documents, the only visual reminders of Pavlova's great art.

But even if the integrity of the choreography is maintained, the cinematic record has shortcomings. It is extremely difficult to recreate any dance work from a film. First, right and left must be reversed since the movie is photographed from the audience side; second, when action is studied in slow motion, the beat is lost; and third, it is not easy to determine the rhythm when a film is run without sound. Moreover, a choreographer may have to rerun a film

countless times before he can restage the dance. Just as a recording can never replace a score, so a film cannot replace dance notation. But it is a blessing for the music lover as much as for a conductor to be able to hear Toscanini's interpretation of Beethoven or Bruno Walter's reading of Gustav Mahler. So it will be just as important for future choreographers to see a film showing the interpretation of a ballet by its choreographer. Since World War II, an increasing number of documentary dance films have been created solely to secure a permanent visual image of a dance and its performers. On occasion, television kinescopes also preserve a dance. Thus some of our greatest dancers will be far more than a verbal legend to tomorrow's dance enthusiasts. Such an extraordinary film as Martha Graham's *The Dancer's World* illustrates how one may make a simple record and yet give the camera creative freedom. The film illuminates Martha Graham's ideas on the art while showing her theory and technique in vivid dance terms.

*Two dances, on the left a* Minuet, *on the right a* Passacaglia *or* Chaconne, *from Tomlinson's* The Art of Dancing. *(Courtesy Library of Congress)*

## Writing on the Dance

The written word was the first means of recording the dance. It is a great help to us in following the development of the theater dance from its very beginning in the early Renaissance. Before the eighteenth century, descriptions of dance movements were the only way a teacher could assist his memory of a dance or other dancing masters had of staging the same dance again.

The first attempts at giving verbal expression to this visual and fleeting art form proved obscure. But despite the obscurity of certain words and descriptions used by Guglielmo and Cornazano we can get a rather clear image of the court dances of the fifteenth century. A hundred years later Arbeau's *Orchésographie* not only effectively records all the dances of the Renaissance, but, for the first time, adds historic comparisons and an evaluation of the dances from aesthetic and moral viewpoints.

The importance of these first books on the dance is best illustrated by John Playford's *The English Dancing Master: or, Plaine and Easie Rules for the*

*Dancing of Country Dances* (1651), covering one hundred and four of the social dances of his time, mingling description with abbreviations and symbols for recurring steps and formations, and giving the tunes to each dance. His book was for the next two centuries *the* dance anthology for all English-speaking peoples. Several of these dances are done to this very day and some have found their way onto the stage. Choreographers who want to stage a period piece still find it a convenient reference book in spite of its inadequate system of symbols.

The Enlightenment brought forth the first critical appraisals of the dance as an art form. We find astute observations of dance performances in Casanova's *Memoirs* and penetrating views of the dance scene in France between 1753–74 appear in Baron Friedrich Melchior Grimm's *Correspondance littéraire*. But the most important are Noverre's angry *Letters on the Dance*, which are an invaluable introduction to criticism of the theater dance. His letters have not only created a solid foundation for the development of the ballet, but also have set down aesthetic

principles that have only been modified by later writers and choreographers, such as Carlo Blasis and Michel Fokine.

The best and most vivid views of the ballet of the nineteenth century come from two French writers, Stendhal, who wrote about Viganó's work in exalted terms, and Théophile Gautier who wrote daily reviews for *La Presse*. Both were masters of recording their impressions. Stendhal wrote only occasionally on the dance but always as an enthusiastic observer who realized that the dance, more than any other art form, demands from its audience a participation involving all the senses.

Gautier was far more concerned with the dance than Stendhal. He reviewed it for thirty-five years and incorporated his opinions in brilliant, if strangely biased, criticism. He shared the romantic ideal of *l'art pour l'art* and believed that whatever happened on stage had to create an illusion. "The characters, like the decorations, are painted," he wrote, "and from this collection of harmonious lies emerges relative truth which is the truth of art." His critical

reports are the soundest guide to Romantic ballet, and made a place for dance criticism in aesthetics.

Great writers on the dance have been as rare as truly great dancers, but the twentieth century has been far more articulate about the dance scene than any previous period. Dance literature abounds in monographs, biographies and autobiographies. Every form and phase of dancing has been recorded on the printed page.

Two outstanding Russian ballet critics, who later settled in France, were Valerian Svetlov and André Levinson. Svetlov wrote innumerable articles on the ballet and a monumental volume, *Le Ballet Contemporain* (1911). Levinson, one of the major historians of the nineteenth-century ballet, was a conservative critic who fought Diaghilev and Fokine for sacrificing the pure dance to story ballets and theatrical effects. He defended Gautier's credo of dance for the sake of dancing and all his life remained an adherent of the old classical dance. In England, Cyril W. Beaumont was also primarily interested in classic ballet and is a most prolific

*Two choreographer-teachers. Left: Jerome Robbins. Above: George Balanchine. (Both, Martha Swope)*

writer, with more than forty volumes to his credit. These remain a rich source for dance students.

There is hardly a nation that has not produced a few able writers on the dance. The Germans Curt Sachs and Max von Böhne have given us some very erudite studies. The philosopher Friedrich Nietzsche was obsessed with the idea of the dance as a means of escaping the dullness of life, and the poet Heinrich von Kleist wrote a penetrating essay on movement in his *On the Marionette Theater.* A surprisingly large number of French men of letters have written on aspects of the dance, with the most interesting contributions, mostly on a metaphysical level, coming from Stéphane Mallarmé, Jules Lemaître, Charles Baudelaire and Paul Valéry. Writers like Paul Claudel and Jean Cocteau have written dance scenarios. In Denmark, Hans Christian Andersen loved ballet and often wrote about it in his travel books; and in the United States the short-story writer William Saroyan was responsible for the scenario of the ballet *The Great American Goof,* choreographed by Eugene Loring (1940).

With notation and film preserving more and more objectively the choreography and quality of a presentation, the future historian and student of the art will no longer need to rely solely on the words of the critics. But notation and film can never take the place of the critic's special function. Only he can evaluate dancers and choreographers in the light of history, or the relationships between the dancing, the music, the costumes, and the décor. Only he can help us see the total effect of a performance and distinguish between the effects created by the dancers, choreographers and the dance story. Also, a critic may sometimes have a unique opportunity to become the champion of a new movement, as did John Martin, whose writings in *The New York Times* did much to help the modern dance assert itself in America in the early 1930's.

It will continue to remain the critic's task to provide us with a deeper understanding of the dance and to heighten our appreciation of it. The best among them will help us feel its movement-woven wonder.

# Selected Reading Guide

Amberg, George. *Ballet*. Mentor Books: New American Library, 1949.
  *Ballet in America*. New York: Duell, 1949.
Ambrose, Kay. *Classical Dances and Costumes of India*. London: Black, 1950.
Balanchine, George. *Complete Stories of Great Ballets*. Garden City: Doubleday, 1954.
Benedict, Ruth. *Patterns of Culture*. Boston: Houghton Mifflin, 1934.
Boaz, Franziska. *The Function of Dance in Human Society*. New York: The Boaz School, 1944.
Bowers, Faubion. *The Dance of India*. New York: Columbia University Press, 1953.
  *Theatre in the East*. New York: Nelson, 1956.
Chujoy, Anatole and Manchester, P.W. *Dance Encyclopedia*. New York: Barnes, 1949. New edition: Simon and Schuster, 1966.
Duncan, Isadora. *Art of the Dance*. New York: Theatre Arts, 1928.
  *My Life*. New York: Liveright, 1927.
Ellis, Havelock. *Dance of Life*. Boston: Houghton Mifflin, 1923.
Ernst, Earle. *The Kabuki Theatre*. New York: Oxford University Press, 1956.
Gopal, Ram. *Indian Dancing*. London: Phoenix House, 1951.

Fokine, Vitale. *Fokine. Memoirs of a Ballet Master*. Boston: Little, Brown and Company, 1961.
Fraser, Sir John. *The Golden Bough*. New York: Macmillan Co., 1947.
Haskell, Arnold. *Ballet*. Pelican Books, 1949.
  *Diaghileff*. London: Victor Gollancz Ltd., 1935.
H'Doubler, Margaret. *Dance—A Creative Experience*. New York: Crofts, 1940.
Hering, Doris, ed. *Twenty-Five Years of American Dance*. New York: Orthwine, 1951.
Horst, Louis. *Pre-Classic Dance Forms*. New York: Kamin Dance Publishers, 1953.
  *Modern Dance Forms*. San Francisco: Impulse Publications, 1961.
Humphrey, Doris. *The Art of Making Dances*. New York: Holt, Rinehart and Winston, 1959.
Hutchinson, Ann. *Labanotation*. New York: New Directions, 1954.
Kirstein, Lincoln. *Dance*. New York: G.P.Putnam's Sons, 1935.
Laban, Rudolf. *The Mastery of Movement*. London: MacDonald and Evans, 1950.
Langer, Susanne. *Feeling and Form*. New York: Scribner's, 1953.
Lloyd, Margaret. *The Borzoi Book of Modern Dance*. New York: Knopf, 1949.
Love, Paul. *Modern Dance Terminology*. New York: Kamin, 1953.
Magriel, Paul David. *Chronicles of the American Dance*. New York: Henry Holt, 1948.
Martin, John. *The Modern Dance*. Brooklyn: Dance Horizons, 1965 (original edition, A.S.Barnes, 1933).
  *Introduction to the Dance*. Brooklyn: Dance Horizons, 1965 (original edition, W.W.Norton & Co., 1939).
Moore, Lillian. *Artists of the Dance*. New York: Crowell, 1938.
Nettl, Paul. *The Story of Dance Music*. New York: Philosophical Library, 1947.
Nicoll, Allardyce. *The Development of the Theatre*. New York: Harcourt, Brace, 1957.
Noverre, Jean Georges. *Letters on Dancing and Ballet*. London: Beaumont, 1951.
Palmer, Winthrop. *Theatrical Dancing in America*. New York: Ackerman, 1945.
Sachs, Kurt. *World History of the Dance*. New York: W.W.Norton, 1937.
St.Denis, Ruth. *My Unfinished Life*. New York: Harper, 1939.
Shawn, Ted. *Every Little Movement*. New York: Ted Shawn, 1954.
Sorell, Walter. *The Dance Has Many Faces*. New York: Columbia University Press, 1966.
Tabourot, Jehan. *Orchesography*. London: Beaumont, 1925. New edition: Brooklyn: Dance Horizons, 1965.
Terry, Walter. *The Dance in America*. New York: Harper, 1956.
Valery, Paul. *Dance and the Soul*. London: J.Lehmann, 1951.
  In *Selected Writings*, New York: New Directions, 1950.
Wigman, Mary. *The Language of Dance*. Translated by Walter Sorell. Connecticut: Wesleyan University Press, 1966.

# A Cultural Chronology

| | DANCE | MUSIC—OPERA | THEATER |
|---|---|---|---|
| 1400–50 | Age of the Basse Danse; gradual development of court dance | Ars Nova (polyphony); troubadours and minnesingers | Mystery play cycles |
| 1450–1500 | Dancing masters at Italian courts; Ebreo | Meistersinger | Medieval farces; morality play Ariosto |
| 1500–50 | Ballet de cour; masques and mummeries | Madrigal; Palestrina | Commedia dell'arte; Serlio; Aretino; Hans Sachs |
| 1550–1600 | *Ballet comique de la reine;* Arbeau's *Orchésographie* | Camerata; Jacopo Peri | Marlowe; Shakespeare; Lope de Vega; Cervantes |
| 1600–50 | Ballet à entrée; ballet mélodramatique; masques and anti-masques; Inigo Jones | Monteverdi; Cavalli | Ben Jonson; Calderon; Corneille; Racine |
| 1650–1700 | Foundation of Académie Royale de la Musique et de la Danse; Beauchamp; La Fontaine | Lully; Purcell; Scarlatti; Corelli; Buxtehude | Molière; Dryden; Congreve |
| 1700–50 | Age of Danse Haute; Imperial Dance Academy in St. Petersburg; Sallé; Camargo; Dupré | Age of the Minuet; Bach; Rameau | Bourgeois drama; John Gay's *Beggar's Opera* |
| 1750–1800 | Ballet d'action; Auguste Vestris; Noverre | Gluck; Mozart; Beethoven | Lessing; Goethe; Schiller |
| 1800–50 | Beginning of toe dance; Viganó; Taglioni; Bournonville; Blasis; Perrot | Age of the Waltz; Brahms; Chopin; Wagner; Verdi | The well-made play; Hugo; Dumas Père and Fils; Büchner Gogol |
| 1850–1900 | Rise and decline of the classic ballet; Petipa | Tchaikovsky; Puccini; Bruckner; Mahler; Schönberg; Richard Strauss | Strindberg; Ibsen; Chekhov; Hauptmann; Shaw |
| 1900–1950 | Fokine; Diaghilev; Pavlova; Nijinsky; Balanchine; Robbins; Duncan; Wigman; Graham; Humphrey | Stravinsky; Debussy; Ravel; Satie; Copland; Hindemith | Stanislavsky; Brecht; Ionesco; Beckett; O'Neill; Miller |

| FINE ARTS | LITERATURE PHILOSOPHY | SCIENCE | POLITICS |
|---|---|---|---|
| ate German Gothic; arly Italian Renaissance | Humanism | Invention of gun powder; Gutenberg Bible printed | Feudalism declines; early Protestantism; Huss; Joan of Arc |
| igh Renaissance; Botticelli; eonardo; Michelangelo | Pastoral; Erasmus; Villon | Leonardo; Copernicus; Columbus | The Tudors; Lorenzo de' Medici; Machiavelli |
| ürer; Holbein; iovanni da Bologna | Rabelais; Ariosto; Tasso | Magellan; Vasco da Gama; Paracelsus | Luther; Henry VIII |
| ubens; Palladio | Montaigne; Spenser | Kepler | St. Bartholomew's Massacre; defeat of Spanish Armada |
| nigo Jones; Callot | Descartes; Pascal; Boileau | Tycho Brahe; Galilei | Louis XIII and Richelieu; Cromwell |
| embrandt; Murillo; Hals; analetto; Fischer v. Erlach | Milton; La Fontaine; Congreve | Halley; Newton; Kircher *(Laterna Magica)* | Louis XIV and Mazarin; Charles II |
| ogarth; Boucher; Watteau | Montesquieu; Swift; Addison; Wieland | Newton; Franklin; Linné; Leibniz | Peter the Great; Frederick the Great |
| ainsborough; David; Goya | Voltaire; Rousseau; Diderot; Kant; Hegel | Watt; Lavoisier; Laplace | Seven Years' War; French Revolution; Amer. Independence |
| elacroix; Romney; Canova; aumier; Corot | Stendhal; Byron; Gautier; Heine; Schopenhauer; Kierkegaard | Industrial Revolution; Darwin; Morse; Faraday; Humboldt | Napoleon; Metternich |
| ézanne; Manet; Gauguin; an Gogh; Toulouse-Lautrec; egas; Rodin | Tolstoi; Baudelaire; Dickens; Dostoevski; Zola; Flaubert; Marx | Curie; Roentgen; Pavlov; Einstein; Freud; Edison; Ford; Daimler | American Civil War; Lincoln; Queen Victoria; Bismarck |
| icasso; Kandinsky; Matisse; hagall | James Joyce; Cocteau; Kafka; Gide; Hemingway | Wright Brothers; Marconi; de Forest; Planck; Fermi | World War I; Russian Revolution; World War II; Hitler; Stalin; Churchill; Roosevelt |

# Index

Mexico, 28, 84
Middle Ages, 39–42, *44*, 45, *46*, 90
minnesingers, 41, 42, 47
minstrels, 41, 45, 47, 277
*minuet*, 74, 122
*Miracle in the Gorbals*, 203
*Missa Brevis*, 212
Mitchell, Arthur, 214
modern dance, 72, 158, 163, 164, 170–173, 177–213, 275–283, 296
Moiseyev, Igor, 84–87
Moiseyev Dance Company, *72, 86, 87*
Molière, Jean Baptiste, 118–120
Montez, Lola, *141*
*Moor's Pavane, The,* 209–210
Mordkin, Mikhail, 163, 215, 216
morris dance *(morisco)*, 42, 72, *89*, 90–91, 101
Moulin Rouge, 150, 152, 153
*Moulin Rouge, 264–265*
mummery, *see* pantomime
Munich Opera Ballet, 171
musicals, 266–268
*My Fair Lady,* 263, 267, 268

Nagrin, Daniel, *198*, 213
*Natya Shastra*, 52
Nederlands Dans Theater, 240
Negri, Cesare, 104, *119*, 286
Negro (in dance), 275–283
*Negro Spirituals*, 200
*New Dance*, 198
New York City Ballet, 219, 221
*Nightchanter, 159*
*Night Journey, 192–193*
Nijinska, Bronislava, 171, 172
Nijinsky, Vaslav, 137, 145, *160* 163, 164, 166, 167–170, 173
Nikolais, Alwin, 184, 213, 251–253, *254–255*
*No, Dance from the,* 68, 70
*Noah and the Flood, 260, 271, 273*
*Noces, Les,* 172, 218
Noverre, Jean Georges, 115, 120, 125–131, 138, 143, 163, 288, 294
*Nuove Inventioni di Balli,* 286
Nureyev, Rudolf, *144,* 231, 272
*Nutcracker, The,* 146, 235

*Oklahoma!,* 263, 266, 268
opéra-ballet, 122
Opéra Comique, 126–127
*Opus Jazz, 218,* 221
*Orchésographie,* 284–285, 294
oriental dance, 49–71
*Othello* (Viganó), 134, 136

*padam, 54–55*
Page, Ruth, 215, 216
pageants *(Trionfi, Carri),* 92
pantomime (mimicry, mummery), 26, 31, 33, 35, 38, 44, 45, 53, 56, 64, 68, 73, 90, 106, 107, 125, 131, 134, 143, 220
*Parade, 157,* 158, 170, 172
Paris Opéra, 123–124, 128, 129, 171, 236
*Party Mix, 250,* 251
*pas de deux,* 146, 148–149
*pas de quatre,* 147–148
*passepied,* 101
*Pastorale, 232*
pastorals, 90, 114, 122, 124
*Patineurs, Les,* 230
*pataka,* 51
*pavan,* 73, 101
*Pavillon d'Armide, 160*
Pavlova, Anna, 137, 144, 145, *160,* 163, 164, 165, 173–175, 215, *292, 293*
Pécourt, Louis, 122, 286–287
Peking Opera, 66, *67*
*Penitente, El, 190*
*Péri, La, 140*
Perrot, Jules, 138, *139,* 140, 141, 143
Petipa, Lucien, *140,* 143
Petipa, Marius, 72, 143–149, 164
Petit, Roland, 235, 236, *237*
*Petrouchka, 163,* 165, 166, *167*
Philippines, 64
*piatosa, 95, 98*
Picasso, Pablo, *163,* 170, 171
*Pillar of Fire,* 225
*pirouettes,* 120, 143
*piva, 95*
Playford, John, 294
Pleasant, Richard, 216
*Poem, 204*
*pointes,* 137
Poland, 84
*Polish Mime, 241*
*Pre-Classic Dance Forms,* 74
primitive dance, 9–17, 24, 25, 28, 75–76, 134
Primus, Pearl, *277,* 279–283
*Prince of the Pagodas,* 232
*Prodigal Son, The, 173*
*Prospect Before Us, The,* 230
psychology (in the dance), 72, 218, 225; *see also* modern dance
puppets, 62–63
Puritanism, 110–111, 113, 195, 216
Pylades of Cicilia, 35
pyrrhic dance, 28

quadrille, 74
*réaliste,* 152

Rabel, Daniel, *115,* 117
Rainer, Yvonne, 253, *257,* 259
*Rake's Progress, The,* 230
Rambert, Marie (Miriam Rambach), 169, 226, 230, *232*
Rambert Ballet, 225, 230
Rameau, Jean-Philippe, 122–126, 163, 166
Rameau, Pierre, 287–288
*Rashomon,* 71
Rauschenberg, Robert, 247, *249*
Renaissance, 89–113
*Return of Springtime, The, 148*
Rhodes, Lawrence, *226*
*Rite of Spring, The,* (Béjart) 237, (Horton) 199, (Massine) 172, (Nijinski) 166, 169
ritual (religious), 75, 275
    in the Bible, 18–21, 25
    Christian, 36–47, 50
    Eastern, 49–66
    Egyptian, 21–22, 26–27
    Greco-Roman, 22–24, 31, 38, 45
    medieval, 36–38, 45
    primitive, 10–17, 64
Robbins, Jerome, 72, 115, 148, 205, 218–219, 263, 268, *296*
Robinson, Bill, 263, *274,* 279
*Rodeo,* 216
*Roman de la Rose,* 44
Roman Empire, 22–24, 31–32, 35
Romano, Giulio, *92,* 93
Romanticism, 132–149
*Romeo and Juliet,* 231, 245, 263
*Rooms,* 205
Rosen, Heinz, 171, 235
Ross, Bertram, *192–193*
Ross, Herbert, 218
round dances (circle), 17, 19, 22, 24, 25, 28, 33, 40, 44, 108
Royal Ballet (England), 230–232
Royal Ballet Demonstration group, *148*
Royal Danish Ballet, 231, 237–238
Rubinstein, Ida, 163
Ruiz, Brunilda, *227*
Russia, 84, 143–149, 242–245

Sachs, Curt, 78, 95, 296
Saddler, Donald, 268
Sadler's Wells Ballet, 230
St. Denis, Ruth, 179–181
Saint-Léon, Arthur, 145, 289
Saint-Méry, Moreau de, 288

303

ENGRAVED AND PRINTED BY CONZETT & HUBER OF ZURICH — DESIGNED BY ULRICH RUCHTI